THE CARTEL

Also by Graham Johnson

Powder Wars
Druglord
Football and Gangsters
The Devil
Gang War (originally published as *Soljas*)
Darkness Descending
Hack

THE CARTEL

THE INSIDE STORY OF BRITAIN'S BIGGEST DRUGS GANG

GRAHAM JOHNSON

MAINSTREAM
PUBLISHING
EDINBURGH AND LONDON

This edition, 2013

First published in Great Britain in 2012 by
MAINSTREAM PUBLISHING COMPANY
(EDINBURGH) LTD
7 Albany Street
Edinburgh EH1 3UG

ISBN 9781780576152

A catalogue record for this book is available
from the British Library

Printed in Great Britain by
Clays Ltd, St Ives plc

7 9 10 8 6

To Lenny and Norma, Emma, Sonny, Raya, Connie and Clara

ACKNOWLEDGEMENTS

A big thanks to Jon Elek at AP Watt, and to Bill Campbell and all at Mainstream Publishing.

I would also like to thank all of the interviewees for the information they have provided, particularly the policeman known as the Analyst. I would also like to thank the sources known as Poncho and Hector.

I sourced information mainly from interviews and research. However, to get what I felt to be the truth of a lot of things, I reviewed four of Peter Stockley's books: *The Little Man Who Always Had a Busy Day*, *The Reluctant Vigilante*, *Extenuating Circumstances* and *The Rat They Called a Dog*. I would like to thank Peter Stockley for helping me co-write several chapters of this book. I feel that Mr Stockley has, in his own words, 'helped draw back the blinds on an otherwise obscure period and its happenings'. Sections of *The Rat They Called a Dog* have been copied with Mr Stockley's permission. Mr Stockley refused to name anyone in connection with these events and their identifications have been made by the author from his own research.

I also read *The Belly of the Beast* by Dylan Porter. Dylan Porter refused to identify or name anyone connected with his crimes and this information was pieced together by the author from newspaper cuttings and additional research. Shaun Smith also refused to identify anyone connected to him, particularly those who were involved in attacks on premises he was connected to, and their identities were made by the author and not Shaun Smith.

I have used information published in the *Liverpool Echo*.

CONTENTS

CHAPTER 1

THE BIG BANG

1973

ON A COLD winter's morning in 1974, the richest crime group Britain has ever known was founded in a rain-lashed lorry depot by a man named Fred. The story began with a heavily loaded BMC flatbed truck turning sharply into a disused cargo bay. The freight, stacked unusually high, swayed gently as the wheels creaked over the potholes, but luckily the crates didn't topple. Just like the men who were waiting for it, the rigid-base 7.5-tonner had wide sideboards.

The smell of hot rubber and diesel fumes hung thick in the air. Droplets of damp sizzled off the hot engine, adding to the sense of urgency that animated a small group of tough-looking men huddled in the gloom. One donkey-jacketed warehouseman got busy closing the main gates, to screen off unwanted onlookers. Two others went off to keep 'dixie' on the reed-lined approach roads, making sure that the 'transport' hadn't been followed. A fourth man warmed his hands near the spitting radiator grill before telling the terrified driver to 'fuck off to the pub for an hour'.

'No problem, boss,' the haulier replied, mindful not to ask questions and glad to be out of the dark storm rolling in off the Atlantic.

The cab hadn't even had time to cool down before the owner was busy scrambling onto the trailer behind, impatient to recover his riches. Fred lifted back the green tarpaulin, sending rivulets of rainwater carelessly splashing back onto sacks of foodstuff. But he placed little value on the lorry's legitimate load. Fred pulled away more sacks to reveal a 'parcel' that had been hidden among the wagon's cargo of coffee and tinned fruit.

The heavy wooden cases were pushed off the side clumsily – there was no forklift and no time – then dragged across the loose coal that littered the yard's weed-cracked concrete. The adjacent warehouse, constructed of great flaps of asbestos tiles, had a leaking roof and a pigeon problem. Rays of winter sunlight streamed through the holes and cracks in the tiles; they were the only source of illumination. Decrepit though it was, the structure at least offered some shelter from the elements, and from prying eyes, too, if only for a few minutes, while the graft was carried out. Since the decline of Liverpool's Empire-linked sea trade, this outpost of the distribution yard had been little used. But the area was still well known to the corrupt dockers and their relatives who smuggled stolen goods out of the port regularly. Isolated by surrounding waste ground, the facility was ideal for transferring the contraband that would later revolutionise the fortunes of their dying city.

Fred was incongruously well dressed for the task, sporting high-waisted dark-red flares and brown, spoon-shaped shoes. But he ignored the splashes of mud and oil on his threads, manhandling the cargo roughly until he'd reached the shadowy innards of the covered area. Brainwashed by and high on avarice, Fred was experiencing the adrenalin rush of seeing a parcel 'land', or 'get home' as the process later became known. It was a feeling that would become familiar to the many who followed in his trail, a buzz so addictive, it was claimed, that men would risk long sentences just to be in on it: even more addictive, some boasted, than the stock-in-trade itself.

Feverishly, Fred jemmied open the lids of the crates with a crowbar, revealing a sickly sweet-smelling dark mush wrapped in stained muslin bags and layered crudely in crinkly coloured plastic. Heroin – three kilos' worth.

A celebration was in order – this was the first consignment of Class A drugs that Fred had successfully smuggled through Liverpool docks. Fred headed for one of the nightclubs he owned in the city centre, took off his dripping sheepskin coat and drank to the future of his new venture. Thirty years later, the Cartel that he had inadvertently founded in a grimy post-industrial goods yard had a turnover of billions, employed thousands of people across the world and boasted of a hierarchical structure similar to that of a global corporation.

But the success was no accident on Fred's part. His character was ideally suited to his new job. By day, he was a commercial burglar turned wholesale fence, buying and selling stolen lorryloads of consumer items. By night, he was a pioneering drugs trafficker. On the one side, he was a meat-and-two-veg gangster known on the street for 'fucking' his underworld rivals – betraying them on transactions and bumping them for money. His double-dealing had even earned him the moniker 'Fred the Rat'.

'Because at the end of the day,' a contemporary called Paul Burly revealed, 'he was a rat.

'Around that time, I was sent to jail, and when I was inside, Fred kind of took over a nightclub of mine and he stripped all the equipment from it – the kitchen, the big steel ovens and work surfaces, the fridge etc. When I got out, I went to see him and "took" £27,000 back off him, as compensation. I just walked into his place and took however much was there, in cash.

'Fred couldn't see what he had done wrong. He couldn't fight me either, so there was nothing he could do. But at the same time, he wasn't that bothered. £27,000 was a lot of money back then, but it wasn't a lot of money to him.'

On the other hand, Fred was a shrewd and forward-looking villain. In his new profession, Fred wasn't interested in being a Mr Nice. Pleasantries were for your Oxbridge international playboys. Fred poured scorn on the privateers, flakes and hippies that had hitherto dominated Britain's fledgling drug economy. Fred's ambition was to rationalise the piecemeal drugs trade. On the supply side, he hoped to smuggle in loads of tens, and, if possible, hundreds, of kilos in regular, controllable patterns as opposed to the small amounts of variable quality muled in by opportunists. On the demand side, Fred wanted to take drugs out of the cult scene and into the mainstream market – the housing estates and new towns that made up Merseyside's bomb-cratered post-war topography.

Unlike many of his contemporaries, and most drug lords that would follow him, Fred was not afraid of getting his hands dirty.

His underlings and rivals were always surprised. Fred insisted on being present when a consignment of drugs was being unloaded: unusual behaviour, in hindsight. By the 1990s, the Cartel bosses had learned to remain in the background, strictly hands-off. Trails were covered, connections severed. Deals would often be done months in advance in third-party countries that had few obvious links to the point of departure and the final destination, or at least in places like Amsterdam, Istanbul and the Caribbean. In international hubs there was less chance of being caught.

At the coalface, the criminality was conducted by a small army of couriers, middlemen and distributors, many on wages and retainers. The system ensured that the Mr Bigs rarely came into contact with the product. But for the founding fathers like Fred, things were simple and straightforward. As greedy former petty criminals, they were overly possessive. Like many self-made men, they obsessively refused outside interference in their empires and treated the drugs business like any other organised crime: they had to be kings of their patch, constantly on the plot, having to be seen and heard at all times. They wanted to protect their own assets. They discussed deals in person. They made the decisions, more often than not, in face-to-face meetings. For Fred, the risks were low. The authorities had not yet started handing down big sentences for drugs. Heroin had not yet been demonised for driving up prostitution, burglary, mental illness and family breakdown. For now, at least, there was no reason why he shouldn't handle his own tackle.

But like any entrepreneur, Fred had been careful not to gamble too much, too quickly on his start-up. Three years earlier he had begun small. In an effort to learn his trade, he had first experimented by importing cannabis. He'd soon struck gold, peddling his wares to the city's melting pot of post-Beatles bohemia. The grant-fuelled student population was ballooning and the post-liberal *Abigail's Party* crowd were dabbling in soft drugs. Fred also made contacts in Liverpool's thriving West Indian community, links that would later become crucial to the future of the Cartel.

However, Paul Burly proffered another theory that explained Fred's early successes. 'Fred the Rat was also lucky,' he said. 'It was 1971 when he'd started with the pot: the year of decimalisation and devaluing, and the authorities were distracted by all these things going on in the wider country. While they were looking the other way, Fred started bringing in weed – in truth, I don't think Customs and the police cared that much. It was a very confusing time and people were stressed out – cannabis took people's mind off things.'

Meanwhile, in other parts of the country, a generation of young criminals were making their bones in different ways. In Glasgow's tough Easterhouse district, 11-year-old Ian McAteer was dipping purses and robbing handbags. Dirt poor and effectively orphaned, McAteer was only doing it to buy food for his two brothers and two sisters. His mother and father had split up three years earlier. The family had been taken into care and were now back living with their dad. McAteer would grow up to be one of a huge number of contract criminals that would be drafted into the Cartel from all corners of Europe. By the time he was an adult, all traces of human empathy had gone: he had become a dead-eyed contract killer ideally suited to working for the Cartel as an enforcer, solving internal disputes and being paid in heroin. His services became so notorious that one day McAteer would even be suspected by the police of shooting TV star Jill Dando.

CHAPTER 2

CANNABIS

1975

SHORTLY AFTERWARDS, AROUND 1972/73, Fred approached two notorious armed robbers known as the Twins. He persuaded them to invest some of the money they had stolen from bouncing the counters at main post offices into a string of nightclubs. The Twins agreed, but Fred secretly siphoned off some of their capital to underwrite his planned upgrade into heroin trafficking. He rented, or possibly bought, some lorries and paid off contacts. When the armed robbers found out, they protested on quasi-moral grounds. But Fred didn't share their old-school view that heroin was a dirty business. He carried on moving towards his goal regardless.

By 1974, a wave of economic shock therapy had paralysed the nation. Inflation soared to a 34-year high, power cuts led to a three-day week and conflict in the Middle East had sparked an oil crisis. Two general elections and a miners' strike added to a general malaise and a sense, at the worst of times, that collapse was imminent. If the worsening economy wasn't enough, a fresh campaign of IRA terrorism spread fear across the mainland, leading to a backlash of emergency laws that were rushed through parliament.

Fred saw his opportunity and acted. He sensed that he could make money amid the turbulence. The bonus was that the risk was low: the authorities were distracted. He put his heroin plan into action. Fortuitously, the Cartel had unintentionally discovered its growth model. Success went hand in hand with the phenomenon we now know as disaster capitalism, to use the phrase coined by Naomi Klein in 2007, whereby companies profit from others' misfortune.

His one-time associate Paul Burly explained: 'Fred had looked into the future. He realised that being a gangster wasn't about guns and robbing banks. Fred had realised that power came from money. It wasn't a coincidence that he did well when the economy was going down. They [Fred, his gang and a few other pioneer drug dealers who were operating on the fringes] were just like speculators.'

The other crucial factor in the drugs business was contacts. In the city's Toxteth area, Fred had got to know an officious Afro-Caribbean engineer who wore a collar and tie under his navy-blue overalls. By day, the young family man was a contract fitter, working at the port and in the surrounding industrial units. By night, he secretly unloaded cannabis from docking ships and smuggled the loads out in his van. He then distributed the cannabis to West Indian communities in Manchester, Birmingham and London. His young son Poncho sometimes went with him.

'Most of the West Indians in the different cities knew each other because they had come over on *Windrush* or on the later ships,' Poncho remembered. 'And a lot of them were up for it. Like my dad, they'd come over as tradesmen. But, unlike him, many of them could only get shit jobs, so they needed to make a bit of money on the side. So it was a ready-made distribution network and it was a natural thing.

'It just meant that my dad made a few extra quid. We were comfortable anyway – my dad had come over with a business, and made a good living. But selling weed gave us a middle-class lifestyle in a place where most people had nothing.'

Despite his bourgeois pretensions, Poncho would go on to build on his father's black-market success. Poncho became part of the second-generation Cartel. His gang would later claim the dubious title of being the first to smuggle a 1,000-kilo consignment of cocaine into the UK.

Less than a mile away from where Fred's and Poncho's nascent Cartel was starting up, another organisation was taking root. In 1974, three local constabularies were amalgamated to form Merseyside Police. To the outside world, the force had a tough but modern image. The TV cop series *Z-Cars* had been based around Liverpool Police's new panda patrols. With shiny cop cars linked by high-tech radio sets and set in a crime-ridden new estate, the BBC drama became a huge hit, combining kitchen-sink realism with police propaganda. The message from the top brass was that the old guard was using progressive technology to continue to maintain order. But behind the scenes, Merseyside's new constabulary was slow to change. For many officers, the criminal world was still a simple landscape divided into cops and robbers.

Crime-fighting technology, such as DNA tracing, didn't exist. Fingerprints couldn't be searched electronically. Burglar alarms were rare. Cocky watchmen were the first line of defence against a post-war tidal wave of property crime, a trend that led to 1964 being the worst year for crime in over a century, with more than a quarter of a million indictable offences in the UK. Police interviews weren't taped. Courts took officers at their word, with few challenges to the prosecution. Conviction rates were comfortingly high. Organised crime was low-priority, in the view of chief constables, and could be dealt with by the newly formed Regional Crime Squads: elite units that had been specifically set up to bring down the soaring crime stats.

A new, trendy profession echoed the views of the old coppers. In the lingo of the sociologists, crime in the 1970s was still largely 'relational': based on family ties and close-knit communities. The average villain was still spurred on by traditional 'motivators', such as fiddling the system and earning a bit on the side. Dockers robbed the ships and commercial burglars plundered the warehouses. It had been going on for centuries, and the fact that it had been growing rapidly since the war was just a blip.

But one new recruit into the new Merseyside force had already seen the writing on the wall. Crime was changing rapidly. The inner-city slum dwellers had been shipped out of their prefabs and *Corrie*-style terraces and starburst into a constellation of new towns that circled the Second Port of Empire like a fortress. High-rises dominated the skyline around the newly erected estates in places like Speke, Kirkby and Cantril Farm. In Croxteth and Norris Green, acres of factory-built units formed a new no-man's-land between the suburbs and the countryside. A minority of newcomers had migrated their crime with them but applied it to new opportunities, the most obvious one being the fresh network of motorways that connected them to a whole new market of victims and criminals in other cities. Rather than looking inward at crowded central areas, they were looking outward to counties such as Lancashire, Cheshire and Cumbria, which offered easier pickings. The IRA had blown up the M62, killing 12, in the same year Merseyside Police had formed. The thinking was, 'If the terrorists can exploit the new system, so can we.'

The new generation of gangsters no longer looked at the port as something that would sustain a subsistence living; the eight miles of quayside were now seen as a gateway to the world and all its vices. The young police recruit intuitively understood how 'opportunities of transport', as the police would later describe the process, were revolutionising crime. He noticed that the young Scousers were effective at migrating crime to wherever they went in the country: for example, to Torquay, Bournemouth and Eastbourne, where they took up summer jobs, or to Glasgow, where heroin flowed through links established by religion and football. But the police force, still run along military lines, was static and slow to catch up. The senior and middling ranks were filled with ex-army types, veterans from the Second World War, Korea and Malaysia. Every morning the young recruit had to line up on a parade ground. The shine on his boots was checked for reflections. His whistle was tested to make sure that it still worked.

But the constable wasn't put off. Quietly, behind the scenes, he was determined to make changes. Later, he would become known as the Analyst: partly because of his systematic way of approaching crime and partly because he loved to read law books.

Thirty years later, he would go on to be Merseyside Police's number-one asset in the fight against the Cartel and Britain's top spy in the War on Drugs.

CHAPTER 3

THE RAT

1978

MUCH OF THE old-school gangland missed out on the emerging drugs scene because they looked down on it. Most of them were armed robbers who valued their status in the old underworld hierarchy. According to Paul Burly, the self-styled elite were known as the 'dream-doers', because 'other men could only dream about how they lived and never had the bottle to take the risks themselves'.

He continued, 'They were the men of business who had never held a gun to anyone or worn a ski mask for anything other than its true purpose. They were men who knew what was going on because they were alert and kept their fingers on the pulse of things, especially things which buzzed around the city, like bees do in a hive of honey.

'This is not about the plastic gangsters who frequently got caught but the more subtle ones who managed to stay one step ahead of those elite cops who find detective work so hard that they have to rely on words from the right places.'

He added, 'In those days, drugs were mainly frowned upon by those who flouted the law by hijacking wagons or robbing banks and post office stations – the dream-doers. Those dream-doers frowned on the creeping introduction of drugs, which were being sold by the more affluent yobs, even though they were down the hierarchy. The street yobs who sold drugs regularly rubbed shoulders with the dream-doers as they flashed their hard-earned but highly illegal bundles of money. Those thieves, who so often boasted that they did what lots only dreamed of, were entrenched villains. They would do almost anything to make money but somewhat frowned on the emerging drugs scene.'

Fred did not share the dream-doers' qualms. As far as he was concerned, if other villains didn't want to sell drugs, it just left more for him to make money off. Fewer than five years after starting in the drugs business, Fred the Rat was a millionaire several times over. He'd come a long way. A decade earlier, in the late '60s, he had been little more than an overweight hustler who lived day to day on the stolen goods that he could buy and sell. Before that, he'd been a penniless petty thief who, according to those who knew him, went to church in order to take money off the donation plate.

But in the late '60s he'd struck lucky. A Jewish businessman he knew gave him a loan to start up a used-car lot. From the off, Fred had no intention of flogging low-margin bangers to the working families who lived on the local estate. He had a knack for identifying gaps in the market. He would target the only people he knew who had cash to burn: the gangsters, the serial armed robbers – the dream-doers.

The strategy paid off. Fred's bangers started to move off the forecourt. He charged his criminal clientele over the odds for souped-up Jaguars and top-of-the-range Triumphs, and they lined up to take them off him. Fred had more success selling cars to the underworld than he did to members of the public.

Fred was hungry, but he knew that timing was everything in sales. Instead of pounding the tarmac on the forecourt, Fred went out into the nightclubs and made his pitches over the bar. He made his patter sound casual, as though he wasn't trying to sell anything at all. The main reason it worked was that the punters were drunk and off-guard. The gangsters liked the approach. Soon, Fred was offloading overpriced saloons and junky sports cars to armed robbers. The deals were shaken on over a bottle of whisky that they were paying for in an after-hours drinking den in the early hours of the morning. By doing the rounds in the nightclubs, Fred made contacts in both drug circles and with the armed robbers. The armed robbers were at the top of the criminal tree. Others looked up to them because they took risks. But by the early 1970s, Fred also began to make friends with the small number of cannabis importers and sellers that hung around the fringes of the underworld.

Paul Burly said, 'Fred was a somewhat slovenly car salesman and he mixed a lot with the affluent yobs, and he saw the tsunami of drugs approaching. He could see that in the future society would have more leisure time, and this displayed the need for something else besides alcohol to be introduced.'

Fred was a shrewd salesman. He knew exactly which gangsters he could rip off and which ones he had to be straight with. It was this cunning that would serve him well when he became a drug dealer.

According to Paul Burly, 'He wasn't a particularly successful car salesman, but he made enough to wriggle his way through the expensive club nights, which he had become accustomed to, due to the need to sell his cars to people. The kinds of punters he sold them to exchanged the cars regularly and paid good money to do so – they were the dream-doers.

'Being the conniver Fred was, he could see those who made cash regularly, then he judged them on how they splashed their money about. They all liked to spend big, but some only spent cautiously, just buying drinks for their friends – not the hangers on – drawing the line at over-tipping and checking their bills instead of just paying them. He knew these ones had to be dealt with fairly or he would lose their custom.

'But most of all he loved those who bought drinks for everyone and over tipped – they were the ones who he could sell the rips [bangers] to, and blag them whenever a breakdown would occur. When his cars packed up, Fred lent them a run-around but charged them for it.'

In the early '70s, as he moved between the armed robbers and the drug dealers, Fred had an idea. They were worlds apart, but what if he could combine the two? Use the criminal nous of the dream-doers, and their cash and their back-up to monopolise the drugs market that his other contacts knew about. A wholesale takeover, if you like. There was only one problem – most of the dream-doers wanted nothing to do with the drugs scene.

Fred had a solution – if he couldn't find a willing dream-doer to do his dirty work for him, he would find one by other means. Fred bided his time until he could find the right partners – ones that he could deceive into thinking that they were investing in nightclubs and businesses when they were really ploughing money into cannabis and heroin deals.

The triplets became known as 'the Twins' after one of them was electrocuted on a railway line when they were kids. The Twins moved and thought as one. They were always noticed and stood well out from the crowds. They soon became the biggest dream-doers of all. Fred liked them because they were drivers of big cars.

It wasn't long before Fred latched onto them. Fred was convinced that he could manipulate the Twins in the short term by selling them overpriced cars. But he was also convinced that he could reel them unwittingly into a drug conspiracy. Crime author Peter Stockley has revealed the full story in his book *The Rat They Called a Dog*, parts of which have been reproduced here.

Paul Burly said, 'Fred didn't think the Twins were easy touches, nor did he tag them as shrewd. He thought that he could manipulate them, after he had dealt them a few deals with cars and noticed their weaknesses.

'Like most gangsters, the Twins liked to think of themselves as shrewd, and he certainly buttered that part of their toast, which satisfied their egos.

'Fred played them – he even refrained from trumping them a few times in order to put them more at ease in his company and make them feel superior to him. And it worked: the Twins began to feel that they had become his mentor and – most important of all – they began to trust him.'

The Twins made their living by robbing post offices. The police noted that they were both prolific and choosey – they only targeted high-value post offices. Fred was too overweight to even be their getaway driver, but now and again he provided them with fast cars, and most importantly he offered to 'mind' their cash once the heist had been carried out. He told the Twins that he could 'hide' it among his car-sales bookwork. The Twins jumped at the offer because their booty was becoming too noticeable to manage. By the mid '70s, the Twins had a million pounds in cash, a sum worth several times that amount in today's values.

According to Paul Burly, 'Now they felt more at ease, as they had a fat puppet to mind their money . . . Fred felt on top of the world. He had judged them correctly and wormed his way into their trust. At the same time, the road to the drugs world was getting wider. Now, there was the next stage – he had to find a way to take control of that money, not just be its minder.'

CHAPTER 4

RECESSION

1980

WITHIN A FEW years, the embryonic Cartel benefited from an unexpected boost. In 1980, the economy of Liverpool, then Britain's second-biggest port, collapsed as though struck by an industrial tsunami. For most, the consequences were devastating. For some, it was a gold rush.

Merseyside had been hit by a double whammy. First, there was an underlying structural economic problem. For the previous 25 years, physical trade into the port of Liverpool had been drying up. Economists blamed the malaise on three changes – shipping containerisation, air travel and Britain's integration into the European Community. The port of Liverpool had been slow to invest in equipment to handle containers, compared to competitors such as Tilbury, Felixstowe, Rotterdam and Hamburg. Air freight took business away from ships. Experts also said that Liverpool was on the wrong side of the country to benefit from the increased trade with Europe that had been a boon to the North Sea and south coast ports. But the truth was much starker. The port's decline could not be explained by these three reasons alone. The main problem was historical. Liverpool had been built for Empire and was now dying with Empire. By the 1970s, half of Liverpool's dwindling volume of exports was still bound for Africa and Asia. Desperate shipping agents had failed to draw in new markets such as Europe, China and the US. As a consequence, Liverpool slipped to being the UK's fifth-ranked port.

Unemployment rates in the city's waterfront districts shot up to 30 per cent. According to historian Nicholas White of Liverpool John Moores University, Liverpool had become 'ossified as a marooned imperial seaport in a post-colonial age'. Academic John MacKenzie described a similar process in Glasgow being down to 'specialisation in imperial markets'.

The second blow was the wider recession that had hit the UK. A fifth of the country's manufacturing base had suddenly been wiped out. To boost growth, the then prime minister Margaret Thatcher introduced a near-suicidal course of extreme monetarist policies. The theories had been developed by a school of academics in Chicago who believed in free markets and the power of myths derived from a Wild West TV show. Enforced 'structural reforms', such as privatisation, deregulation and trade union dissembling, had only ever been tried in Third World dictatorships with the help of CIA and shadowy World Bank functionaries, known as Economic Hit-men. The experiment in Britain was the first to take place in a democracy.

In Liverpool, the policies were a resounding failure. Over the next six years, unemployment rocketed until, at its peak, one quarter of the population was out of work. Like economic refugees, an average of 12,000 people each year began to leave the city in search of jobs. Families would be split up across the north–south sociopolitical divide for generations to come. Young people abandoned their Youth Training Schemes for low-paid seasonal work on the south coast. To support their struggling families, redundant construction workers headed for weekday digs in London and far beyond.

Large areas of Liverpool's landscape, parts of which later became a UNESCO World Heritage site, were literally reduced to smoking rubble by demolition works – 15 per cent of the land became vacant or derelict. From a busy population high of 700,000 in the 1960s, when the city rocked the world with the Beatles, Liverpool shrank to around 400,000 and the population continued falling. In the media, a once-proud powerhouse was being viewed as an embarrassing disaster zone. Scouse humour was about Liverpudlians being mocked by outsiders. The 'pool of life', as Carl Jung once described the city, became known as the 'Bermuda Triangle of British capitalism'.

Today, if history repeated itself, the misfortune would no

doubt be swarmed upon by the new elite of globalised disaster capitalists: the corporations and consultants that circle the planet, preying on victims of man-made and natural calamities, the catastrophe specialists that load up people with debt and profit from poverty and misery, 'restructuring' economies into sweat shops and social no-go areas. However, back in the pre-yuppified days of the early '80s, the informal cartel of hedge funds, global corporations, think tanks and casino banks was in no position to administer economic shock therapy to a failing city.

But one emerging sector was looking on, surveying the ruined landscape with desire. Fortunately for them – and thanks to the foundations laid down by Fred, Poncho's dad and their associates – they were also poised to take full advantage of the situation. That sector was organised crime.

Amid the abandoned nineteenth-century warehouses and armies of shuffling, under-confident youths, the criminal underworld immediately saw opportunities where others only saw deprivation and fear. Fred and his supporters had a somewhat warped vision: to rebuild a new economy in their own image. One that they would control. One that would make them very, very rich.

Now, at last, it was their turn. For once, it would be them, the uneducated outsiders, who would take all of the winnings: not the businessmen, or the establishment, or the elite. In effect, the Merseyside Crime Groups, as they became known to the police, thought they could replace the legitimate economy that had just been taken away, filling the black hole with a brand-new system, albeit a black economy fuelled by graft and dirty cash. However, it was one that would generate jobs and wealth for anyone who wished to get involved. A loose alliance of gangsters, contraband smugglers, well-dressed football fans and armed robbers would attempt to remodel themselves as the first disaster capitalists: more right wing than Milton Friedman, more free market than Mrs Thatcher.

At the centre of their vision was an enduring and extremely profitable product: drugs. Still, it was a risky venture – no city in the UK had yet fully opened itself up to the international drugs markets. Never had a regional crime grouping gambled so much on a single venture. The rest of the country's criminals were still largely interested in heists and protection rackets.

From the ashes of the recession-hit economy grew the Cartel: a global business that, ironically, would grow to rival any of the corporations that the new capitalism was throwing up, the extreme form of corporatocracy that was sweeping the world from Chile to London, from Buenos Aires to Java.

At a car park near London's Heathrow airport, an acquaintance of Fred the Rat was waiting by a phone box. Thomas 'Tacker' Comerford was a middle-aged ex-docker with a pockmarked face so rough you could strike matches on it. In between phone calls, Comerford walked slowly back to his silver Ford Granada and smoked.

Comerford had got to know Fred through the nightclub scene, where he'd worked as a bouncer. He'd watched Fred grow rich. Fred had recruited Comerford into the Cartel. Comerford wore £70-a-throw Fila tennis tops that stretched over his beer gut, £100-a-pop Pringle jumpers draped Jimmy Tarbuck-style over his hulking shoulders, and tinted Carrera sunglasses.

Comerford had taken up the baton from Fred but was now outrunning him. He was doing bigger heroin deals, pushing the boundaries of the Cartel a little bit further.

A daring former safe-blower, Comerford understood the need to take risks. While carrying out heists, he had pioneered the use of precision planning and new technology to steal a competitive advantage on his victims and rivals. He was the first bank-robber to use oxyacetylene burners to tunnel into an underground vault. The booty from robberies was then put up as capital to invest in drug smuggling.

Business models that he had developed as a professional bank-robber were imported into the drugs business. A ready supply of money was always on hand to fund the rapid expansion of the Cartel. A docker turned greengrocer known as 'the Banker' took on the role of informal financier. His job was to loan out vast amounts of cash, in different currencies, to underwrite drug transactions in the UK and on the continent. Ten years later, the Banker would be described by Interpol as Europe's biggest narcotics profiteer and its most successful money launderer.

In addition, Comerford found new methods of smuggling that complemented the Cartel's traditional expertise in running drugs overland and through ports. So far, it had enjoyed excellent contacts within the Mersey Docks and Harbour Board, and through family members and corrupt officials. But now heroin and cocaine were being muled in through Heathrow airport in multiples of half kilos. Unlike the good burghers of Liverpool, the drug runners understood that the port's prominence was fading. Air travel and the Common Market were the future.

The route quickly became profitable: so much so that on many occasions, the gang had more heroin than mannitol, the cheap baby laxative that was used to cut the powder prior to distribution. Couriers were often flown to Amsterdam first class to clear chemist-shops' shelves of mannitol, which was more freely available in Holland than it was in the UK. Comerford and his gang began to spend more time in the Dutch capital, which became known as 'the Flat Place'. For the first time, the Dutch courts found that British criminals were appearing regularly before them.

Just like on a robbery, Comerford handpicked his team on the Heathrow connection – buyers, mules, runners and hard men to secure the merchandise once it had 'got home'. Ostensibly, they lived in council houses on windswept estates and drove bangers to mundane jobs or to the dole office to sign on. But behind the scenes they cruised the world on the *QE2*, used posh hotel suites as their offices and partied with some of the biggest bands of the time. Ironically, Comerford refused Mrs Thatcher's offer to buy the council house that he lived in. The portly smuggler and his wife still pretended to reside in a two-up, two-down terrace while really living in a six-bedroom mansion on a millionaire's row in an upmarket district. His neighbours included Liverpool football stars and the founder of the Army and Navy Stores.

But for all his nous, Comerford was a bigmouth. Several members of the Cartel suspected that he was an informant. Drug dealing had brought with it a new phenomenon – large numbers of police snouts who were prepared to trade information with the authorities in return for privileges. This led to heightened levels of paranoia. The ancient codes of silence that had bonded old-school villains together were rapidly disappearing in this harsher world. But one source, a rich businessman who'd grown up with several Cartel bosses, wasn't so sure. The businessman said, 'Some people were saying: "Tacker's a grass."'

'I said: "Well, if he's a grass, he must have grassed himself up, because he's spent half of his life in prison."'

Comerford may not have been an informant, but his loose lips and extravagant lifestyle had brought him to the attention of Customs and Excise investigators. A secret operation had been launched to put the flamboyant street criminal under surveillance. Now officers were plotted up yards from his parked Granada near Heathrow, observing him making calls from a phone box in a car park. Later, they photographed him meeting a man who had been followed by a second team of Customs officers from the airport's arrival lounge. It was the rendezvous they had been waiting for. Comerford and his mule were then followed back to Liverpool.

In a rare moment of insight, the senior Customs and Excise officers were able to reflect on the bigger picture, to put what they were seeing into context. Instead of concentrating on the specific deals, Customs suspected Comerford was part of a much larger operation, one so far not seen on these shores. One shrewd investigator correctly identified Comerford as being part of Britain's first and only drugs cartel, as defined by them.

In a series of reports, the officers described the gang as a small but tight-knit group of middle-aged men from a run-down regional city who specialised in importing heroin and cannabis resin. The members of the cartel, they said, were a mixture of ex-dockers, corrupt hauliers and career armed robbers, and if they weren't stopped now, they had the potential to grow into something much more sinister and hard to control.

CHAPTER 5

DISASTER CAPITALISM

1981

IN THE SUMMER of 1981, the Cartel benefited from yet another unforeseen boost: riots erupted in the Toxteth neighbourhood, close to the Liverpool docks. Many within the predominantly black area called the nine-day disturbance an 'uprising'. For the first time in the UK, outside Northern Ireland, tear gas was used by police against civilians.

For the Cartel, there were several advantages. Since the mid '70s, many black youths had become politicised, partly influenced by the Black Power movement in the States and partly as reaction to the rise of the far right in England. The riots galvanised an anti-establishment view of mainstream white society, an attitude that had been simmering covertly for years. But without a political outlet, the radicalism lost impetus. Much of the anger was channelled into different areas. Villains started to justify their crimes by saying that they were part of an attack on the economy that deliberately excluded them.

In the same year, the Tate & Lyle sugar works, previously a big player in the city's manufacturing economy, shut down. Many black working-class people, with no links to the criminal world, began to think radically. If the system couldn't provide them with a job, then the underworld economy would. Needs must.

Poncho said, 'Up until the Toxteth riots, my family had options. My dad was both a tradesman and a cannabis dealer. The dealing was very much a sideline: a little bit on the side to give my dad a head start. We could have gone either way. But after the riots it was like, "There's no choice – we can only go one way." Even straight-going families started to think like that. The battle lines had been drawn.'

Meanwhile, the Analyst was a young beat copper patrolling south Liverpool. Allerton was a leafy suburb made up of pre-war semi-detached houses. The neighbouring district of Woolton was longer established. One evening the Analyst stopped to talk to a group of rowdy teenagers outside a shop. The area was middle class and there was little violence or thuggery: just high jinks and scallies sporting their latest pair of expensive trainers. Some of the kids were acting up and showing off as usual. It was the Analyst's job to calm them down and get to know them, to build up a picture of the local area, to identify any future troublemakers and pick up some local intel. But one lad in particular stepped into the background and did nothing. He wouldn't engage the Analyst in any conversation. His name was Colin Smith. Smith wasn't a tough guy – he'd lost several fights in school. But he was very streetwise. He would later become known as 'King Cocaine'.

On his beat, the Analyst tried making some contacts on the street. Later, as he moved up the ladder, he tried to turn some of these sources into informants. This grassroots experience would become invaluable. The registered informant would, in the future, become the police's single most effective weapon against the Cartel, at least for a period. Those officers who were good at handling covert sources, as well as those who, crucially, were smart enough to know what intelligence was good, what was bad and when they were being manipulated, went on to become the successful ones. The Analyst made it his business to become an expert at handling intelligence.

Meanwhile, on the other side of the equation, Paul Burly and his criminal associates were becoming aware that more informants were being groomed. In the late 1970s, Paul Burly was jailed for violence and firearm offences. For the first time, he became aware that many criminals were being groomed to become Cartel lieutenants.

Paul Burly said, 'This could mean many things: for example, people who would hire yo-yos in order to give one to the police to allow more laden-down carriers to pass by with what they had.' Otherwise known as 'plants', yo-yos were drug mules who were deliberately sacrificed to the police and Customs by their controllers to distract them from other mules who were usually carrying the bigger consignments on the same flight or ship or who were at the same port.

Paul added, 'Or there were those who would willingly give a kid a gun and prompt them to use it in such a way that it would benefit the outfit they worked for, disregarding the danger they would be putting the youngster into by getting the kid lifed-up or even killed.'

The Cartel also made job offers to members of rival drug gangs, enticing criminals to switch sides in return for cash rewards. In some cases, the Cartel paid the gang members for information that would help the Cartel kill their rivals. Or sometimes they would pay for commercially sensitive information, such as the names of suppliers and buyers, so that they destroy their rivals in an economic way by undercutting prices or limiting supplies.

Paul Burly said, 'A person would turn against his lifelong peers for the rewards offered by the now rich Cartel – greed to kill the seed, or at least its DNA!'

Burly said, 'I met one such candidate for that rat's lifestyle in jail. On the outside he had been a no-mark pimp, but now he was acting like he had been reborn, as if he knew he was heading for a better and more prosperous life with the heavy tag of "murderer" to back up any shout he was to make. His existence behind bars was so cushy and full of favours that we – his fellow inmates – felt he was being looked after by people on the outside, such as the fast-growing Cartel. To test this theory, we tried to discredit him with a plant of his own stuff . . . only to find out that we could not, because although the screws had been advised of the plant, they did nothing about it! Then we watched later as he glided his way with ease through the remainder of his ever-so-short life sentence and was released.

'Upon his release, that man was allowed to work on, and run, nightclub doors with impunity even though the conditions of his licence forbade it. His trial defence of "stress-related syndromes" just did not add up. After all, what could be more stress-related than working on nightclub doors and dealing with troublemaking drunks? Whatever door he ran always had the same distributor coming and going, but they never spoke. Everyone thought it uncanny that these two, who were known associates through previous work, never spoke and yet they passed by one another every day.

'Then, as if that were not most unusual and bad enough, he was allowed to open a security firm, which became engulfed in stories of protectionism. *Panorama* even did a documentary about it, but the police took no action to stop his heavy-handed practices.' Once again, Burly was convinced that the Cartel was using their influence to get the police to turn a blind eye.

During the years before drugs and the Cartel, the likes of Tacker Comerford used to set up yo-yos to drive stolen wagons that would be ambushed by the police while the stolen wagon they really wanted a safe passage for sailed past and on to a successful journey. Burly had seen all this and knew from talking to the yo-yos who had been in prison with him that the Cartel was adopting those very policies. He had his suspicions that Fred the Rat was the one feeding information to the police in exchange for the freedom to carry on his operations. The Twins had been arrested with a third accomplice while robbing a main sorting office. The police had been tipped off and armed officers were lying in wait when the gang stormed into the mailroom to steal tens of thousands of pounds in cash. The Twins had been blindfolded, cuffed and rolled onto the floor, while an officer wearing flared trousers pointed a gun at one of their heads. They were jailed for a very long time.

Paul Burly said, 'I started making some enquiries. The Twins had been my mates and I had respected them. The third guy was called the Patchwork Quilt, so named due to the cuttings he had received and the holes that bullets had left.

'I even got hold of a photograph from the crime scene that shows them lying on the floor at gunpoint. I could never understand why they'd walked into a trap so unawares. It was so unlike them. They had to have been set up. They'd been nicked at around the time Fred the Rat had started setting up his big drugs deals, deals that would net him millions.

'The Twins had given him a million quid to mind by hiding it safely within a straight trading company. Fred had wanted to invest it into his imminent drugs deals, which involved tanks of beer. They hadn't approved. Those twins – like most of the old-school robbers – could genuinely say: "We don't touch drugs."

'Fred had finally got what he wanted when the Twins got put away. He was already minding their money; now he had full control of it. I, along with most of my friends, was 100 per cent sure Fred had grassed on them to get them out of the way, so he could invest their money into his ideas.'

The Twins sent a message out from their high-security cells: 'Don't touch the Rat: if he dies, our money disappears!'

Meanwhile, Fred moved on, untroubled by his conscience and the underworld scuttlebutt. The Rat recruited a new member onto his team. The Banker had already established himself as an independent drug financier. Fred offered him a deal. Crucially, Fred would supply the contacts and some of the money to underwrite drug purchases abroad. The Banker would also put up some of the funds, but he would help with the import and distribution. Fred's drugs racket had increased exponentially and he was desperate to share the load. For the Banker, it was a golden opportunity. It would give him access to the phone numbers of the Cartel's main suppliers of cannabis, heroin and cocaine.

CHAPTER 6

IMPORT

1982

BY THE EARLY 1980s, Fred the Rat was looking to scale up his business once again. He had a good partner in the Banker. Now he needed a method of mass importation that was regular, consistent and secure. One of his contacts told him about a shipping line in the north-east that had a contract with a brewing company. Their job was to export giant metal vats of beer to Africa and then ship the empty containers back to the north-east for refilling, so that the process could be repeated. Fred's contact described the empty vessels to him. They were like giant, cylindrical cans – only three at a time could be fitted onto a lorry trailer. They were spacious and cleaned before they left the port in Africa, meaning that they could be easily filled with contraband. They were sealed with lids and, once they were prepared for transport, difficult to search. But the beauty of the system was simple – the import–export link was so common and had been going on for so long that the authorities on both sides of the ocean paid little attention to the barrels. The contact said that they had been searched by Customs and Excise on only one or two occasions.

Fred was over the moon. This would be an ideal way to smuggle drugs, he concluded. Fred had contacts in Africa who could supply cannabis in huge amounts. In addition, there was the possibility of buying heroin and doubling up.

Fred's gangs got to work. By this time, he was becoming

more cautious. He didn't want to go near the drugs himself. Instead, he put his brother in charge of handling the day-to-day operations. Soon the system was up and running.

The beer scam worked like a dream. Fred had so much capacity and drugs were so cheap in Africa that he could smuggle any amount of drugs that he wished, at any time. Each consignment could hold a maximum of three tonnes. Hundreds of kilos of cannabis were being landed every month, as well as huge bales of heroin. Over the year, it added up to tonnes.

Fred had so much contraband that it was becoming difficult to keep the route a secret. It became common knowledge in the underworld. Associates like Paul Burly were amazed that the news hadn't reached the police. But Fred wasn't bothered. If anything went wrong, it was his brother who'd cop for it. Fred was by now strictly hands-off.

Paul Burly said, 'When the Rat did begin his importing, it was done so openly that I was convinced that he had a bent copper from the top of the pile, or someone higher, which meant an awful lot of people were going to go to prison, because with all such deals there have to be bodies. Suddenly there were drugs everywhere. The city was flooded with cannabis, heroin and everything else. When bodies were called for, the Rat threw in his uncle and brother during two separate operations. In his mind, nobody would suspect that he had thrown in his own family . . . they had been the starters.

'One night, I went to visit a woman I know, and I found a large holdall in her house. Inside it, there were a couple of shopping bags full of cannabis oil tightly wrapped and bound in plastic, and packs of white powder, which I assumed was coke. To add to that lot, there were lots and lots of two-pound bundles of tightly wrapped grass.

'I immediately knew whose bag it was; the woman's daughter had a boyfriend who worked for the Rat. I phoned Fred and said: "Come and get your fucking shite right now." At first, he denied it was his. But I knew I was right so I told him that he had put me in danger. "You prick!" I shouted down the phone. "You know that if the police were to find that stuff in that house my feet would not touch! Tell you what, wanker, seeing as I would have done the time, I'll keep the stuff and sell it to one of your competitors. How much is it worth: fifty, a hundred grand?" At this point I heard him gulp, so I smiled and put down the phone. Then waited. Fred immediately changed his tune; he was stuttering when I picked up the quickly returned call. "Sorry, Paul, really sorry. Can I have the stuff back, please?"'

He sent round a man on a motorbike to collect it. Paul took a small package containing £10,000 off the courier before pointing out where the large holdall was: underneath a mobile betting office on the car park of the Bow and Arrow pub. Crime author Peter Stockley revealed the full story in his book *The Rat They Called a Dog*.

Fred started to invest in property and businesses to wash his drugs money. He employed an accountant to manage his portfolio. Soon the accountant became a powerhouse within Fred's empire and was involved in key decisions, becoming the kingpin of his laundering operation. It was nothing for the accountant to have £1 million plus in dirty cash in the loft, not to mention the rusty old cement mixer in the corner of the garden, which often housed the weekly rake-in from the accountant's businesses, usually totalling some hundred thousand pounds.

The accountant ran the managers whom the Rat hired, men of pristine character who had also run doors, so they had the experience of both sides of life. However, there were many altercations between them, and one of the doormen, the Brum, began to dig into the accountant's past. He came up with evidence of the accountant's dishonesty and showed it to the Rat, who replied, 'What do I want an honest bookkeeper for?'

One day, the Rat upset Paul Burly again. They fell out over a debt of £15,000 that Paul said Fred owed him due to some building work. Fred refused to pay. Paul couldn't find Fred to exact payment. Weeks passed with Paul looking and Fred dodging – then a terrible misfortune struck Fred. Both his house and the accountant's, in Knowsley and Ormskirk respectively, were burned down by arsonists. Luckily, however, the cement mixer had not been tipped up. Paul smiled as he denied involvement. Fred was furious: the £1 million in dirty cash reputedly stored in the accountant's loft had also gone up in flames but not even a crispy bit had been found by the firemen!

Fred wore many hats; none, however, had 'roughneck' written on the rim. As usual, he stood back while the police gave Paul a terrible time, but they could not pin anything on him. The Rat continued to import drugs. Paul couldn't believe how openly he did it without being targeted by their special squad, due to the damage the drugs were doing to society.

Paul Burly said, 'During my life some things have glared out at me as being abnormally sinister. I first noticed such things as a drug cartel being formed, almost publicly and with nothing being done about it, until the hold it had on our society became much too strong to break and those hooked on drugs were too far gone to be withdrawn from it. The rot had set in before any really big arrests were made; then it was only the underlings.'

Paul found himself in an inexplicable pickle soon after that and ended up in prison for six years for manslaughter; he had been forced into defending himself against a yo-yo who had a gun. Paul took the gun off the young man, but during the ensuing struggle the gun went off and Paul was left standing over a lifeless body. Had the Rat been involved? Paul had no idea and swears that the trouble-causing young man had forced the fight. From minute one, he suspected the Rat strongly, but as his sentence passed he found himself promising only to extract the type of revenge that was called for if pushed hard when he got out.

CHAPTER 7

CONSPIRACY

1983

AS WELL AS the ideological changes to crime, there was also practical help on hand for the Cartel. The community in Toxteth began to see itself as a no-go area for police. Street dealing began to flourish. The interface with the outside world – a street on the district's border – became known as 'the front line'. A main thoroughfare called Granby Street became a free-for-all drugs hub, attracting punters from all over the north of England.

Conspiracy theories began to flourish in the ghetto, fuelled by a sense of isolation and powerlessness. Community leaders warned drug dealers and punters that they were playing into the hands of the ruling white elite.

Carl John, the brother of a world karate champion and club doorman who was later shot dead, said, 'Suddenly people – local people – were dealing drugs on Granby Street without fear of the police. There was a big surge in cannabis and heroin. The theory was that the politicians were turning a blind eye to drugs, to calm the population, similar to the tacit agreement that occurs in prisons, when the screws allow drugs onto the wings.' Carl John went on to become an award-winning documentary maker: his film *Crackhouse* (2003) showed the terrible effects Class A drugs were having on his community.

In the white areas, the conspiracy theory was less sinister but equally shocking. It was claimed that the city had been abandoned by the rest of the country. Depopulation was not an accident, according to locals, politicians and community leaders: it was the result of a political decision made somewhere, even though they could not quite put their finger on it. The government's lack of enthusiasm to prop up the port and industries were cited as evidence of a secret deal to slowly kill off the city.

Thirty years later, some of the theories were proved to have at least some basis in truth. Newly released government documents revealed that Mrs Thatcher's then chancellor Geoffrey Howe suggested 'the option of managed decline' towards the city, warning her of the dangers of over-committing 'scarce resources to Liverpool' in a futile attempt to save the city's economy. Such a policy, he thought, would be akin to throwing good money after bad. Howe argued that Liverpool was almost beyond help, in terms of economic stimulation.

'I fear that Merseyside is going to be much the hardest nut to crack,' Howe said. 'I cannot help feeling that the option of managed decline is one which we should not forget altogether. We must not expend all our limited resources in trying to make water flow uphill.'

Of course, such a policy would have to be kept secret: the discussions, and the documents that described them, were confidential. Howe acknowledged that the suggestion that the city could be left to decline was potentially explosive.

'This is not a term for use, even privately,' he warned Mrs Thatcher. 'It would be even more regrettable if some of the brighter ideas for renewing economic activity were to be sown only on relatively stony ground on the banks of the Mersey.'

There was no evidence that 'managed decline' involved a conspiracy to subdue the population with heroin. But at the time, many believed that the rumours were true. The Cartel lost no time in playing on the story to further its aims. Lord Howe later denied that he was 'in any sense advocating managed decline'.

In 1983, a twenty-year-old mixed-race doorman called Curtis Warren was jailed for five years for armed robbery. Like most young bucks from Granby Street, he was trying to enrich himself to hoist his standing off the floor, where surviving is to live and you live to survive. He kept trying various things to make wads instead of settling for wage packets. In Frankland Prison in County Durham, he bumped into a fellow Scouser: hard man Paul Burly, who had been jailed for manslaughter.

'When I met him inside, Warren was wondering just what he had to do to get the start to build on,' said Burly. 'He was one of those swinging-spider robbers who kept doing lots of petty things without really learning from them; something like a brickie wanting to start laying his bricks from the eves down. On the out I had helped a few such kids: they had ended up shitting on my doorstep, but that didn't change my attitude to helping if I could, especially as they had literally nothing going for them. You could tell they'd be in and out of jail for the rest of their lives because those lads had no idea how to avoid it in their attempts to get on. No others in their area seemed to care, because they wanted out themselves. They reminded me of coal miners who didn't want their kids to be coal miners but taught them the job anyway.

'I sat him down in my cell and said: "You've got to stop being a dickhead. You've got to stop being a fucking robber, because you'll never make any money and you'll keep getting nicked. Stop acting on impulse and plan the rest of your life now, while you've got the time to think." I told him that if he wanted to be a villain, so be it. "But use your fucking brain," I said.'

Paul Burly had a friend who was known as the Banker. He told Warren to contact the Banker once he got out. The Banker could set him straight by lighting up the pathways.

At around the same time, an 18-year-old school leaver went for a job interview as a salesman. Dylan Porter was gangly and wore glasses. Nervous energy made him appear twitchy and agitated. But he was no geek. People warmed to Dylan because he was open, funny and unthreatening. But his easy-going nature masked cunning and street wisdom beyond his years.

Dylan said, 'At the job interview, the man goes, "You're born to do this job. You're a natural salesman." But it was the usual story – he turned round at the end of it and said: "Sorry – you're not qualified enough."'

Dylan was from the wrong side of the tracks. His mother was a violent alcoholic who was known for glassing people in the face.

Dylan said, 'I learned from an early age that alcohol was the worst drug in the world. I didn't want to waste my life – I was ambitious.'

The aspiring salesman did what government minister Norman

Tebbit had urged the unemployed to do. He got on his bike and searched for work. Tebbit, the then Trade and Industry Secretary, had refused to believe that rioting had been a natural reaction to unemployment. He urged the jobless to be more resourceful – and more mobile. Dylan found that Tebbit's words were out of touch with reality. He went to Jersey but struggled to find work. Returning to Liverpool depressed, he ended up on a Youth Opportunities Programme for six months.

'It was at that point that I said, "Fuck it." It was then that I started to see things differently. Instead of being optimistic, I started to view life a bit darker. That's what happens when you're young and you can't get a job. For instance, I began to look at the government as being the biggest criminal, as though I had been betrayed by it: not only in a jobs sense, but in other ways as well. For instance, I thought the authorities' view on alcohol was hypocritical. They promoted it, but I saw the bad effects of it in my family. There was a lot of anger around, blaming politicians for this and that.

'I started selling a bit of weed if I couldn't get a job, then it was justified in my mind. I was buying an ounce of rocky and selling it to my mates. Harming nobody, I thought.'

Throughout 1982, smaller riots erupted across the UK and into the following year as the monetarist vice tightened. In Liverpool, street-fighting gave way to political battles. The hard-left Militant tendency, led by a well-groomed, fast-talking ex-fireman called Derek Hatton, took control of Liverpool City Council. The city was the only one in the UK to offer resistance to Mrs Thatcher and the Labour Party, which many socialists believed had lost its bottle. On a ticket of jobs and services, Hatton began building council houses and extending social care. But the cost of struggle was high. The city sank further into debt, and 49 councillors were eventually removed from office by the unelected District Auditor for refusing to sanction redundancies.

Meanwhile, another trafficker was bringing in heroin using the Heathrow connection. Unlike the rough-looking Thomas Comerford, Paul Dye cut a James Bond figure on the international smuggling scene. He was friends with diplomats, sported a black tie at official functions and loved technology. Dye was the first known villain to use a hand-held computer to record drug transactions, according to Customs and Excise – a habit that would eventually lead to his downfall. Though he was London based, some of Dye's heroin was sold on into the Cartel and Dye would later become friends with several of the organisation's main players. Within a year, he became fabulously wealthy – suspiciously so. Even Dye thought so himself. It seemed too easy. He kept hundreds of thousands of pounds lying around his house. Dye was at a loss to explain why it was so easy to smuggle heroin into Britain all of a sudden. Then he claimed he'd found out the reason why. Dye boasted that he had been given safe passage to smuggle heroin into Britain. He was telling members of the Cartel that the British government was tacitly allowing heroin into the country to suppress the youth.

'They're scared of a revolution,' he said. 'The gates were opened after the riots. There were smaller riots in 1982 and 1983, and the government panicked and turned a blind eye while heroin was brought in. It was only a short-term measure to distract the youth.'

Meanwhile, on the other side of the fence, the Analyst was busy making his way as a beat bobby. The Analyst didn't buy into conspiracy theories, but the young PC did believe in one criminal conspiracy. He was of the opinion that the new generation of heroin dealers were, for the first time, deliberately and methodically carrying out market research on the drugs market. The Analyst was convinced that the men at the top of organised crime had identified several specific subgroups. In simple terms, at one end of the scale they had identified a large body of low-level, passive drug users who mainly smoked cannabis. Pot was largely seen as harmless and sociable. At the other extreme, there were very powerful hallucinogens, such as LSD, that were taken by a minority of more daring and experienced drug users. Their numbers were small, but the niche was profitable: so much so that peddlers were setting up their own labs to meet demand.

'Then in the early '80s,' the Analyst noticed, 'the drug dealers did the market research and realised that there was a gap in the market. There was a place in the middle for an alternative drug. And that's where heroin suddenly came in. At that time, it was very much seen as one of the next generation of drugs. The key thing was that it wasn't viewed as being a nasty drug.

Heroin was an ideal fit – seemingly both suited to consumers and the dealers. At that time, users didn't know that it was addictive and destructive – they were just interested in the high.'

At around the same time, the Analyst discovered that the Cartel was consolidating existing transport opportunities with new ones. First, the Cartel exploited the boom in package holidays. 'Who owned the coaches? Would Customs bother searching a whole coachload of families coming back from Spain?'

Second, the Cartel began relying on air travel that had opened up as a result of the founding of the European Community. The haulage industry boomed.

Then, finally, they stumbled across an unexpected helping hand – Liverpool Football Club. 'On a simple level, it had to do with football and the UEFA,' explained the Analyst. 'When Liverpool FC began playing abroad, it became the gateway to Europe for a lot of criminals. What resulted was the phenomenon of the "travelling Scouser", these lads who would first go pillaging and then settle for periods of time in towns and cities and make connections.

'The bottom line was that Customs didn't see it coming, especially what happened in 1983 with heroin.'

By 1983 all of these various factors converged. The conditions for the Cartel were right. The result was a heroin burst across Merseyside. The epidemic started on council estates in Croxteth. Deprivation and unemployment were high and the local villains had an 'in' with the Cartel. Croxteth was quickly dubbed 'Smack City'. Other hotspots appeared on the Wirral and in Birkenhead.

The Analyst said, 'Suddenly, there was a definite contrast in the city. I remember going on police training courses and telling people that I'd arrested people for possession of cannabis. But they started telling me about heroin and a lively distribution network.'

From his own research, he noticed that the Gorbals in Glasgow and towns in the north of Scotland were mirroring Croxteth's problems. The 'travelling Scouser' was spreading his vices. In Scotland, Liverpool criminals had befriended career criminal Ian McAteer. By now, the ex-petty thief had graduated to the major league of Glasgow's underworld. He was always in and out of court. The jury saw him as a smart-suited, well-groomed and courteous defendant. But the real McAteer was a different character altogether. He had become a 'ruthless, evil, savage street fighter' according to one Strathclyde detective. Like many criminals who would later enter the drugs business, McAteer had a curious but beneficial characteristic: he seemingly felt nothing for other people. He didn't even feel anything about himself. The detective noted that McAteer was also a 'highly dangerous organised criminal who appears immune to human feeling'.

CHAPTER 8

HEROIN

1984

'ARE YOUSE ON the smack yet?' the punter asked.

'What d'you mean?' Dylan Porter replied. Dylan handed the lad his usual purchase – a black finger of oily cannabis, wrapped in cling film. He was doing his rounds, selling weed to jobless youths in Bootle pubs.

But the lad persisted, blocking his way a bit. 'Have you tried the smack yet?' he asked again, a touch cockier this time. Making sure everyone could see, that he was in the know about the latest buzz, even when his own dealer was clearly out of the loop.

'No,' Dylan said, pushing further inside the smoky bar to order a pint and serve up some more of his £5 slivers of resin. 'But I'll find out about it, OK.'

Dylan first heard about heroin in 1984. All of a sudden, the drug had become as fashionable as Reebok trainers and Ellesse sportswear.

'After the lad had asked me about heroin in the pub, I started asking around about it, but no one knew what it was,' Dylan said. 'Except an older feller at the bar in one of the other pubs that I served up in, who I respected. He warned me not to get involved. "Stay away from that shit, lad," he told me, "or you'll end up in the gutter or in jail."'

But for the time being there was nothing to worry about for a young, ambitious drug dealer. In the early days, heroin was marketed by the Cartel as a harmless high: not exactly fun-seeking

THE CARTEL

but a deeper alternative to pot that dealers claimed was cheaper in the long-run. 'More buzz for your buck' was the catchphrase.

To make it seem more inclusive, sellers didn't target the underclass: the main market was among the solidly working-class punters that frequented the pubs and the clubs, including women and 20-something men. To observers, they didn't seem like the kinds of people who wanted to throw their lives away: these people wanted to enjoy themselves; they had hopes and ambitions. Ironically, they were the same strata of C1 and C2 voters that in the south of England had formed the backbone of Mrs Thatcher's support, the same core of voters that had been targeted by the Murdoch press to sweep the conservatives into power: 'It's *The Sun* Wot Won It'.

However, up north the story was different. Coma-inducing opiates started to become popular with doleites desperate to make eight hours of boredom pass in two, without spending a fortnight's worth of giro at the bar. Users even celebrated the arrival of heroin on the streets.

'It was all "laughing" at first,' recalls Simon Murphy, who later became addicted for 11 years. 'It was something to smile about, share with your mates – there was nothing seedy about it. Really sound people were taking it, lads who you respected or girls who you fancied.'

People started smoking heroin on foil openly in pubs and in parks, as though it was normal. In each bar, Dylan encountered groups of 'shiny, happy people' chasing the dragon and listening to Pink Floyd's *The Wall* on the jukebox.

He recalled: 'The old fellers at the bar were joking to the younger ones sat around the tables: "Are you on the heavy gear today?" Then they'd roll about laughing, as though it was all one big joke. It wasn't at all taboo. So I was watching this, thinking: "There's loads on it and I've got to start selling it instead of cannabis."'

Within weeks, Dylan switched to openly knocking out heroin on a quiet close in Bootle. Within a week, he and his partner were trading an ounce of heroin per day. Each ounce cost Dylan £1,100 but generated £2,800 in sales, leaving £1,700 profit.

Dylan said: 'I sold around 560 bags at £5 each every day – each one is 50 mg. Sometimes the lot would go in about two hours. It was like selling socks on a market stall. I was dressed in a Fred Perry T-shirt and a pair of Adidas shorts. I was making so much money I was giving the notes away – I didn't know what to do with it.'

A wholesale supplier of heroin hadn't been hard to find. Dylan's cannabis dealer had quickly linked him up with a low-ranking member of the Cartel. Fred the Rat and Comerford were still bringing it in – and a lively network of middlemen had set up as distributors on the key estates. One distributor was a local hard man called Tommy Gilday. After scoring his ounce in the early evening, Dylan would 'work' through the night, cutting the brown powder into £5 bags.

However, the changes were not only on a personal level. The explosion of Class A drugs began to change the criminal landscape as a whole. Even villains who refused to get involved had to prepare for a future where the old codes didn't matter. Shaun Smith hailed from a traditional crime family that valued fist-fighting and looked down on drug dealers. As a young 17-year-old buck, Shaun became a bouncer to learn the ropes.

Drugs had made the underworld more cut-throat. Shaun was given a criminal apprenticeship that his elders told him would stand him in good stead for a dog-eat-dog life. A known hard man called Dom schooled him in the art of debt collecting. One day Shaun was shown how male rape could be used as a weapon.

Shaun said, 'We went to collect a £20,000 debt from a house in Bedford. As soon as the punter opened the door, I hit him with a little scaffold bar and he stumbled back into the hall. He was a big fat cunt, 18 or 19 stone, with baggy trousers on and grey hair. He wouldn't pay, so I started looking around the house for cash.

'Then I heard Dom saying, "Go on, go on," coming from downstairs, and when I walked into the kitchen, he was getting stuck up the big fat feller from behind. Dom was also taking pictures.

'Afterwards, we just left a number for the punter to ring. It was blackmail: "You don't pay up and we send the pictures out." I got £50 for that. Six months later the fat feller hanged himself out of shame.

'I thought: "This must be just the way life is."'

The political situation in Liverpool became extreme. Gangsters and politicians formed alliances. The Liverpool 8 Defence

Committee was set up by local people and community leaders after the Toxteth riots to protect black people from the rise of the far right. Many members' motives were genuine, but two drug-dealing brothers called Delroy and Michael Showers became influential. Michael Showers rallied community support to mask his illegal activities. In the guise of a community leader, he even appeared on BBC's *Question Time* programme.

In 1984, the BNP staged a national rally on St George's Day at the Adelphi Hotel in Liverpool city centre. The Liverpool 8 Defence Committee attacked the far right. Ironically, some of the neo-Nazis that they fought included enforcers used by the Cartel. In Toxteth, the Militant party that controlled the city's council attempted to pay off another gangster and future Cartel enforcer called Stephen French in a clumsy attempt to gain influence. He ripped up their £500 bribe in front of them. Many young Cartel members began to train in martial arts and Thai boxing.

Meanwhile, at street level, Poncho was trying to impress an uncle known as Scarface. Scarface's partner was known as Kaiser – they were inseparable. Despite being relatively young, Kaiser and Scarface had moved up the criminal ladder quickly. Poncho was still on the bottom rung: selling weed on the front line and on Granby Street. But he was keen to catch the eye of Kaiser and Scarface, with a view to getting some proper graft under his belt.

Kaiser and Scarface cut a dashing pair on the crime scene. They were both keen sportsmen and were charismatic, striking figures. Poncho was mostly skint. He liked smoking weed and dropping acid but was keen to learn.

Scarface made his money as a 'facilitator' for older criminals. The dealers in Toxteth were resisting the pressure to sell heroin. On the front line, a message had been daubed on the wall: 'Newsflash! This is Toxteth not Croxteth. Strictly ganja.' There were stories of vigilantes attacking heroin dealers and self-appointed 'taxmen' stealing their money. Kaiser took a dislike to heroin after his home was burgled by smackheads. One day, Poncho, who liked taking LSD, had mentioned that he was going to experiment with heroin. Scarface hit him and said, 'Don't ever go on that smack.'

A few miles away, Colin Smith was being brought up in a

council flat in the Allerton area, near the childhood home of John Lennon. The local beat bobby was the Analyst. Colin's dad John had been a boxer, but he preferred talking to violence. He'd started selling cannabis while a pupil at New Heys Comprehensive school. By the age of 17, Colin was a middle-ranking distributor, handling drugs smuggled in from Amsterdam and Morocco through Liverpool docks. An old school pal said that he'd bought a new top-of-the-range VW Golf for cash. The same day one of his mates wrote it off, but that night Smith went out and bought another. 'That's when you started to realise just how much money he was making,' said the friend.

The second generation was up and running.

CHAPTER 9

PAVED WITH GOLD

1985

ACROSS THE CITY in the North End of Liverpool, Dylan Porter was now rich enough to pay for all of his mates to go on holiday. It was 1985, and Dylan had been in the heroin business for just one year. He bought a string of fast cars. Grafters returning from Europe with holdalls full of stolen designer clothes came straight to him, because he bought the lot with cash.

Business was booming because there were few risks. Guns were rare and the worst thing that happened was that someone would bump him for £5. The police posed little threat. There were no mobile phones so interceptions didn't happen.

Dylan said, 'The police could see you openly selling but not catch you with the gear on you. Even if I had a bundle of 40 bags, if I saw a busie, I'd throw them in my mouth and swallow them. Be sick five minutes later. One day, I got nicked with money in all my pockets, but they had to let me go. Today, you just get nicked for having cash.'

As a new market, the business was still relatively straight – only a minority of dealers 'bashed' the gear up with additives. A £5 bag could last an average user two days, according to Dylan, because the heroin was high purity. Some dealers were proud of the fact that they sold heroin, as though they were doing themselves and the community a service.

'If people asked me how I was doing,' recalled Dylan, 'I would reply cheerfully: "I'm selling the brown on Jersey Close."'

'And they'd say, "Is right, are you making a few quid?" as though they were talking to a joiner or a car mechanic or something like that. It was good news at a time when there was no good news.'

But by the end of the year, the tide had begun to turn. The attitude had changed. The first signs of heroin's ravages started to surface. Young girls started selling their bodies in suburban streets. Previously well-behaved young men suddenly turned into serial burglars, robbing their neighbours' houses. Stick-thin addicts known as 'creatures' began to roam the estates like zombies. Mothers had to lock their kids in their bedrooms until they had gone through cold turkey.

Dylan said, 'It started to go dark and I was like, "Fucking hell, is that what heroin does to you? Surely not . . ." But it was – it was like a fucking bomb had gone off out of the blue. It was a genuine shock.

'I didn't know – people started saying that I was selling poison. Vigilantes started forming, and people began snarling at me. The same people who'd politely enquired about business six months before would shout across the bar, "Are you still involved in that shit?"

'And I'd go, "Fuck off. No way, mate – I've sacked all that now," out of embarrassment, and I'd drink up and get off quick. But it was a lie. I was panicking and ashamed.'

In July 1985, jet-setting heroin dealer Paul Dye was caught smuggling heroin through Heathrow. He was eventually convicted of trafficking £100 million's worth, after Customs officers retrieved details of payments to Pakistani suppliers on his Psion HC 100 personal organiser. Dye was bitter, claiming that he'd had tacit immunity from the government. He argued that the establishment no longer feared a rebellion from Britain's jobless youth. The government had defeated the striking miners. The police had developed a new public order policy to deal with disturbances. He said that they were now confident they could withstand any revolutionary tendency. The miners had been roundly defeated. Therefore the authorities had, according to Dye, reversed its short-term policy of allowing drugs into the UK.

Meanwhile, bouncer Shaun Smith's underworld apprenticeship took a sinister turn. One day Shaun and his friend nearly killed a man while testing out terror tactics.

Shaun said, 'One night, I was sitting in my nan's having a cup of tea with my mate and we went out because we were bored. We found this feller crying after the pubs had let out, saying that he was going to kill himself. We pretended to be good Samaritans, but it quickly turned nasty.

'We took him back to my nan's. My mate broke his fingers and he was saying to him: "I'm going to shag you," just to see what effect it had on him.

'Later we walked him out dead quiet – he was sobbing, and then we knocked him out and ran away.

'The next day he was found right outside the police station with serious head injuries – we guessed that the police had put it down to falling over when he was drunk or something. They didn't get on to his fingers or head wounds. He was on a life support machine for three weeks.'

Paul Dye might not have been right about a heroin conspiracy theory, but he was right about the police being more prepared for public disorder. In October 1985, low-level riots kicked off in Toxteth once again. The disturbance was a potential nightmare scenario for Merseyside Police. A reveller from London had been stabbed at the annual Toxteth carnival, which led to the arrest of a local youth. The suspect's family and friends said that the police had got the wrong man. Within hours, hundreds of angry people laid siege to Admiral Street police station demanding his release. The police station was bricked and bottled.

Rumours abounded that the local gangs were planning to ambush a police patrol and start a full-scale riot. But this time the top brass had a plan. They referred to their recently published, but secret, public order manuals on how to proceed. To provide context for the course, a raft of reports had been commissioned by the Home Office to explain why citizens suddenly rose up. In one called 'Policing Problems on Housing Estates', the Home Office Police Research Group said that the 'common themes' behind disturbances were high levels of unemployment, deprivation and poor policing relations. The public order manuals outlined how officers should respond to riot situations. The tactics had been quietly developed behind the scenes since the first wave of riots in 1981, and many senior officers had been through the programme.

The technology used on the training courses was crude: a

curious mixture of early computer modelling and lo-fi 'situation room' maps that looked more like board games. The scaled buildings were made up of miniature wooden tower blocks and toy cars that represented police vans. A set of ring binders contained the instructions, a step-by-step guide on how to deal with riots.

At the core of the manual was a fictional British town called Sandford in a county called Sandfordshire. The poor part of town was called the Carruthers Estate. It was here that the best and brightest from constabularies all over the country were invited to pit themselves against an unfolding public order situation. The aim was to make decision-making more effective, and to standardise riot control across the country. The course taught officers to look for 'tension indicators'.

The result of the new research and the policing policies that grew out of it was two-fold. First, the 1985 riots were quashed because riot training improved police effectiveness and understanding. Second, Merseyside Police were no longer prepared to pussyfoot around sensitive issues. Officers became bolder and took more risks. It gave Merseyside Police the confidence to go back into Toxteth and take back the no-go areas. A new officer class of thinking-men's coppers were drafted in. It wasn't long before one particular officer was headhunted to take up the challenge. The Analyst had been recruited to a new section called the Toxteth Team, a designated policing unit that had been formed in 1982 but was only now coming into its own.

But it was like fighting fires: as one was put out, another one flared up. On the street, police tactics were working, but on a strategic level, the Cartel was stealing a march.

In late 1985, Scarface and Kaiser dropped their resistance to selling heroin. They wanted money and they were no longer scared of the backlash from the local community. In addition, other dealers started selling heroin and they saw no point in not doing the same. One of the Cartel's newly prosperous dealers, a gangster called Tommy Gilday, was looking to expand his patch. He had flooded the mainly white North End of the city with drugs and was now keen to strike up an alliance with the black gangs in Toxteth. Granby Street and the front line offered great potential. Punters came from as far away as Hull, Leeds and

Cumbria to score, because Liverpool wasn't as policed as their own areas. But until now they had only been able to buy cannabis.

Gilday's opportunity to enter the market was an unlikely one. One day, one of his gang stole a car belonging to a friend of Scarface. Scarface tracked down Gilday and bashed him up. But bizarrely, as is common in the underworld, they struck up a mutual respect, which grew into a kind of friendship based on how useful they could be to each other.

Gilday started selling cut-price heroin to Scarface to distribute in Toxteth. Poncho started selling the cut-up wraps on Granby Street. The alliance set a precedent. The predominantly white, middle-aged members of the Cartel began forming partnerships with younger black villains from Toxteth. A former bag snatcher turned armed robber called Curtis Warren became friendly with the Banker, an emerging boss in the Cartel, who was set to take over from the likes of Fred the Rat and Comerford when their time was up. The Banker took to Warren immediately. Warren had come with some good references. Warren told the Banker that Paul Burly had advised him to make contact. In addition, Warren had been 'grafting' with a convicted armed robber and drugs importer called Stan Carnall. They had done some drug deals together in Amsterdam. Carnall was on the Banker's firm. There was also a connection through one of Warren's girlfriends. All in all, Warren was well connected and ripe to be groomed for a top slot. The timing was also fortuitous. Fred the Rat had opened up his contacts book to the Banker. The Banker now had the power to buy cocaine direct from the Colombians and heroin direct from the Turks. In time, he would pass some of these numbers to Curtis Warren. Curtis would be working for him and Fred the Rat.

Another example was a taxman called Stephen French, who struck up a relationship with the network of nightclub owners, bouncers and cocaine traffickers that fast-tracked him into the business.

A black gang called the Solid Gold Posse, mainly involved in heists, also began doing business with the Cartel. It wasn't long before the main black players were absorbed into the Cartel, forming influential factions in their own right.

Meanwhile, Fred the Rat was still the king of the Cartel. The underworld and Paul Burly, who now walked the twilight zone, estimated that of all the drugs in the UK, Fred had brought in 60 per cent. Yet despite Fred's enormous wealth and power, the old-school gangsters weren't afraid to beat him up. Fred had ripped off so many people that he became used to being accosted and punched at almost every party he attended. But he had thick skin. He let it wash over him by claiming that at the time of whatever deceit he was being accused of he had been playing a certain role that had been suited to the circumstances of that particular deal. Paul Burly said, 'He let things go by blaming the hat he had been wearing on the occasion of the aforesaid trespass. For him, the most important thing was making money.

'Make your own mind up as to why he was never killed, as he opened the biggest chain of nightclubs in Liverpool and shit on people from that great height . . . Lord knows, I came near to doing it myself once or twice, and the Twins stabbed him when they got out. Lots and lots of people have hit him but left him prostrate on the floor rather than taking him away and burying him. He's had the luck of the Irish as far as his life is concerned, because he just loves to fuck his friends and belittle them. He can't throw away his car-salesman hat, that's his trouble.

'As for his dealing in the drugs world, he was very successful . . . Maybe that was his saving grace. Those who relied on his imports didn't mind him being hurt, but they didn't want him killed. Who knows?'

CHAPTER 10

TRANSPORT

1986

1986 WAS A critical year for the Cartel and the police. Both sides got more sophisticated in their struggle for dominance. The starburst of heroin across the city turned into an epidemic.

The Analyst said, 'It was simple – the change mostly came down to transport again. One kilo of compressed heroin, unadulterated and uncut, was much easier to ship than one kilo of cannabis – and much more profitable.

'Established crime groups started setting up in Toxteth. They became more visible and Granby Street became a supermarket for drugs.'

The boom was underpinned by more complex methods of sale. Dylan Porter set up the first dial-a-dealer service, partly out of shame. By putting the handover at arm's length, no longer would he have to come face to face with his punters or the public. He employed several runners to ferry drugs anonymously from a mini call centre. The only rule was that punters had to have a verifiable land-line number. The huge profits were attracting investors keen to get a slice of the action. A property developer from London offered Dylan a partnership. As the dial-a-dealer service expanded, the partner sourced secure houses and flats.

Dylan said, 'I was doing good business, so people were lining up to back me. I had enough money to self-finance, but taking on another partner was about much more than that. It was about going up a level. I was a salesman. I was successful. But I was just selling the wrong product.'

In Toxteth, a young armed robber and blackmailer called Colin Borrows found a sachet of cocaine that had been hidden near the Toxteth's front line. He took it to a yardie he knew, who washed up the base into crack cocaine. Colin Borrows went on to officially become Britain's first crack dealer. He was the first peddler to be arrested for manufacture of the drug.

The public were rapidly losing trust in the police's ability to hold back the tide. Increasingly, they were turning to vigilantes to stop the drugs. Enter Shaun Smith, a rising star in the world of doormen and freelance enforcers.

On one assignment, a rich scrap dealer paid Shaun £3,000 to cut the ear off a drug dealer who had beaten up his son.

'Me and my partner booted the door off the dealer's house,' said Shaun, 'and there were four of them sitting there having a weed. When someone is that frightened you can't knock them out. But I cut the top of his ear off, wrapped it in a bit of wallpaper and showed it to the scrap dealer.

'Suddenly, in my world, you had to be a bullying, backstabbing twat, just to get through the weekend. But I refused to go down that route – although I was violent, I refused to be a backstabber. I was always totally upfront about what I did.

'People would ask me to plug people for debts. If it was justified, it would be strongly considered or passed on if it wasn't. Life's too short – there's too many wolves in sheep's clothing.

'That's the effect drugs was having on everything.'

In Toxteth, the heroin epidemic had created a gold-rush atmosphere. Young villains were desperate to raise the money to invest in heroin. Like pyramid salesmen, the older members of the Cartel egged them on.

Poncho said, 'It was a case of, "If you can raise the money to buy a kilo, you're in. And if you get in now, you're in at the ground floor and we're going right to the top." People were panicking; they realised that there was a once-in-a-lifetime chance for ordinary villains to join a big firm and make it big. No one wanted to miss out.'

It was a cute move by the Cartel: a way of recruiting general criminals into their ranks quickly.

As a young PC in the Toxteth section, the Analyst noticed

a young tearaway known as Cagey running around in a stolen car. A few weeks later he understood why – in the latter half of 1986, ram raiding took off.

The Analyst said, 'If you could fundraise to buy a kilo of heroin then you were up and running. You couldn't go to the Prince's Trust to get a loan. Consequently, there was a real push on opportunist crime. Smash and grabs at jewellers' shops became very lucrative. Then ram raiding became the crime of choice in 1986 and 1987.'

On the streets, there was a run on high-powered stolen cars. The stakes were high, so the ram-raiders morphed into sophisticated criminals. The cars used back-to-back radios and decoys to fool police during high-speed chases. While a raid was taking place, raiders used 'second cars' to ram police vehicles, to cause a distraction. Venues that sold desirable consumables were targeted with precision: ski shops (particularly those selling the Berghaus brand), leather goods, sportswear and high-quality clothing shops of every description.

The Analyst said, 'They'd load it into the car and hit the city with a decoy to take the chase. On one level, it literally changed the fashion. But the main purpose was making money to get on the ladder. Ram raiding suddenly became the economic driver for the drugs industry.' The clothes the ram raiders stole became fashionable because either they were designer labels that were generally out of the reach of normal people or they had a certain novelty value. For instance, on one occasion the raiders stole hundreds of high-end ski suits, which became an instant style hit on the streets. Soon the stolen clothes achieved must-have cult status. People wanted them because they had a certain kudos.

The successful candidates – gangsters like Johnny Phillips, Curtis Warren, Stephen French and Cagey – ploughed the money they'd made from robberies into drug dealing and became fully paid-up members of the Cartel. However, though they were sophisticated on the street, they hadn't yet figured out how to get to the next level, how to secure themselves within the Cartel, to make national and international contacts and to wash their money. The wealth they were generating was very much seen as short term and for showing off.

These problems had largely been solved by those at the very top. The most senior members of the Cartel, several of who were now millionaires, were taking their first tentative steps into money laundering. Several opportunities had just presented themselves. First was the Big Bang on the London Stock Exchange and banking deregulation. This allowed the Cartel to invest in stocks and shares, especially in the newly privatised utility industries. In addition, they were able to wire bank deposits around the globe with few questions asked.

Changes in the property market also helped. Gangsters were now snapping up ex-council houses under Mrs Thatcher's right-to-buy scheme. In addition, the housing boom outside of Liverpool offered golden opportunities for investments. The rise of package holidays and closer links with the EU had led to proliferation of currency-exchange shops. This DIY money-laundering service became the method of choice for the higher echelons of the Cartel.

But on the street, entry-level Cartel members continued to spend their money on cars, clothes and women. The culture of ram raiding turned high-powered cars into status symbols. Drug dealers would hire cars for months on end.

The Analyst said, 'When the new Orion Ghia came out, I spoke to the manager at Avis on Mulberry Street in Toxteth. He told me that there was a queue out of the door and that they had three loaders stacked with Orion Ghias all on order.'

Once they had made more money, the dealers started buying the cars outright for cash. An up-and-coming gangster called Johnny Phillips – who would later team up with Curtis Warren – bought an RS Turbo Cosworth with a private plate.

The Analyst said, 'It was a superficial image that represented superficial wealth.'

The Analyst began to study the structure of the gangs. At the bottom of the hierarchy, there were street runners who earned £100 a day. Their responsibilities included moving the stashes of drugs around to the middlemen and keeping the street dealers supplied. Predominantly young, the runners were disillusioned foot soldiers who'd been tempted to pack in their YTS schemes and take up a 'cultural education' under the wings of the Cartel.

The Analyst said, 'If you weren't educated officially, this was a real opportunity. They'd started out robbing cars, then doing burglaries, and now they were running drugs. Even being a runner was a gargantuan leap into the big money; the spoils were far greater than kicking in a door and stealing a telly.'

CHAPTER 11

SURVEILLANCE

1987

THE BORDERS OF Toxteth melted into a gently sloping neighbourhood called Dingle, a predominantly white dockside area. An influential crime family with Filipino heritage dominated the area's crime scene and quickly became affiliate members of the Cartel. Their HQ was a run-down pub, affectionately known as Black George's, on a *Coronation Street*-style estate built in Victorian times to house dockers and Irish immigrants. Two brothers, the de facto leaders of the family, often spent their days drinking in another nearby pub called the Pineapple. At lunchtime, the bar was busy with straight-goers pouring in from the docks and nearby shops sneaking in for a quick pint. The brothers would hold court at the bar, sipping champagne and snorting cocaine. Dom Pérignon was a bestseller in the pub, a surprise hit in a traditional boozer with little to celebrate other than a good Sunday League team. But the brothers were generous, often standing rounds of drinks for the ordinary punters 'because they were working'. The anecdotes spoke volumes to the Analyst. For all his insight, he refused to buy into the liberal idea that poverty caused crime.

According to the Analyst, 'People drive crime. Even in poor areas, people can choose whether they want to commit crime or not.'

However, he did believe that two changes in lifestyles had helped persuade increasing numbers of young people to join the

Cartel. The first was the growth of consumer society and the second was a culture of expectation about social security benefits.

The Analyst said, 'It's about personal values: how you're wired up and whether those morals are in there. But there was suddenly a lot of pressure on ordinary people in society to have the trappings of wealth. They began to see extreme luxuries being advertised on the TV and they didn't think: "I don't need that." Instead, they thought: "How can I afford that?" In the adverts on telly, you didn't see anyone in a little kitchen any more. People saw this, so they aspired to having the big kitchen. That led to a world of debt, which pushed people towards crime. That was one of the factors that was weaving its way through the population then. Society was changing.'

In Toxteth, Scarface and Kaiser were able to afford American-style kitchens with fitted Hygena units, the latest Formica tops and a state-of-the-art ice-water dispenser in the fridge. Thanks to them, the drugs supermarket on Granby Street was now selling a new line – heroin.

Colin Borrows was offering crack cocaine alongside them. One time, he got stopped with a bootful of cash by the police. 'Where did you get this?' the coppers asked.

'I'm a drug dealer,' Borrows said, knowing that they couldn't do anything because he didn't have any crack on him. Those were the Wild West days. Cash had not yet been demonised: criminalised, some would say later. Some police officers didn't quite know where they stood or how to react to the changing criminality. There was still trepidation around the concept of a no-go area.

The dealers didn't want to lose the support of the local community, which provided them with cover in the form of the no-go area. So they kept the Class A drugs quiet, propagating the myth that the trade was a harmless outlet for Rastafarianism, ganja being the main supply.

The police realised that if they could break the myth then that would be half the battle. Officers had tried several tactics to take back the streets of Toxteth. First, they tried direct intervention: arresting suspects in small patrols along traditional lines. But the gangs deliberately blocked off the main thoroughfare at Granby Street. High-powered cars were double-parked back to back, so that police support teams couldn't get to their colleagues if things went wrong. This was a deliberate ploy to make a no-go area more tangible specifically in an area known as the 'Toxteth Triangle' so that drug dealers and punters felt even safer. The impromptu blockades were also partly done to disrupt the police's new public order tactics.

The Analyst said, 'So what happened was that the dealers just stopped outside a popular haunt called the International Cafe. They just double-parked and started talking and traffic couldn't flow: deliberate disruption to meet their intention of creating a no-go area. It meant that they could close it down at will, and if we went in there to police it, they could lock us down.

'It made it very dangerous. One day we went in there to make an arrest. We pulled up outside the cafe to get the suspect. The plan was to grab this feller who was wanted by us in connection with a previous crime. But it all went quickly wrong. We were literally surrounded, and a car backed in behind us so we couldn't move.

'The reinforcements they tried to send in to get to us couldn't get into Granby. And we ended up literally getting kicked up and down the street. There were eight of us and the gangs probably put two hundred onto the street. They were on the roof. It was a case of literally dragging everybody that was in the team back into the van at the same time as they were getting punched and kicked.'

Unable to move by car, the era of the Z-cars was over, at least in Toxteth. The patrols got back to basics and began walking around on foot. But the gangs' spotters always seemed one step ahead and saw them coming. To get round this, the police installed a secret surveillance camera in a wall on the front line. But the dealers quickly discovered the ruse and signposted the lens with graffiti – 'Police camera found here'.

Finally, after many setbacks, the police decided on a revolutionary tactic aimed at taking the fight into the heart of the dealers' lair. A massive undercover surveillance operation was launched to film the dealers in action 24 hours a day. The police took advantage of the fact that much of Granby Street was still being revamped following the riots. Building sites littered the area. They hired a Portakabin and set up a dummy construction area right in the middle of Granby Street. Three surveillance officers were hidden inside the cabin at all times and could only come and go in the dead of night, when the coast was clear.

'We thought, "Can we do this?"' the Analyst recalled.

'And we decided, "Yes, let's give it a go."'

'Then we found a couple of nutcases mad enough to do it. We soon gathered a whole load of evidence of street dealing. Then, after each buy, we tracked the punters as they walked off or drove away so that when they left the area, we picked them off – to prove that they had been sold drugs.

'That was the first big operation to reclaim the streets for the public, because most people wanted something done about it. It finally broke the ganja myth, because we recovered heroin as well.

'People tried to break into the cabin, but it was all locked up and secure. The lads were in there three days at a shout, and to minimise the risk of compromise, they came out in the middle of the night, and another shift went in. We had to be really careful round our times: different days, different hours of the night.

'The dealers never suspected for one minute, because they were standing right outside the thing, sometimes deliberately hiding behind the cabin because they couldn't be seen from the street – and all the time it was camera'd up.

'Before the strike came, we moved the container out so that the street got back to normal.

'Then at six in the morning, everybody's doors go off the hinges. The next thing, all of the dealers were sitting in an interview and we were saying, "That's you, isn't it?" pointing at the telly, replaying the videos.'

Operation Eagle was a major blow for the Cartel and street distribution was turned on its head. The Cartel needed time to regroup and reorganise. But the hiatus gave the police time to take more ground. The Analyst spent the next two years walking the streets and winning back the support of the ordinary people. The Somali community were willing to engage, but some young black people literally stood in his way.

The Analyst said, 'As a young officer, you couldn't back down. You just had to stand your ground. The person may have been twice my size, so I wasn't going to roll around the floor fighting. You've got to learn to talk your way out of it. Don't rise to the bait, but don't give in either. I just kept saying: "I'm going to walk down here, Granby Steet – it's something I've got to do.'"

The police success signalled the end of the two-year heroin boom. But the effect was counter-productive. A large number of addicts, disparagingly known as creatures, suddenly appeared on the streets like zombies come back from the dead.

Dylan Porter said, 'That's when I started seeing smackheads for the first time – no one had ever heard of the term before, because when supplies of drugs were plentiful, they stayed indoors. Now they were in groups of 30 and 40, stood on the street, looking for gear. That's when they started booting in doors and robbing videos in desperation. They were withdrawing because there wasn't enough heroin to go around. That's when I knew to get out of it. It had become shameful.

'But for that window of eighteen months to two years, between 1985 and 1987, it had been good business. It was still a lucrative business, mind you, but now it had become a dirty business. Before that no one had known the consequences – prostitution, crime, lives wrecked.'

Meanwhile, halfway across the world, in Colombia, the National Police were having similar success but on a grander scale. After years of trying, they smashed the country's most powerful cocaine exporters, known as the Medallín Cartel. This would result in the single biggest strategic break that the Cartel would ever get – just at the point when the Liverpool ring was at its weakest and on the verge of disintegrating, because of the heroin drought. A rival group called the Cali Cartel took over in Colombia, and it was looking for partners in Europe.

CHAPTER 12

CRACK

1988

JUST AS THE police thought they were getting on top of heroin, the Cartel moved the goal posts. Crack cocaine became the new product. Within two years, Colin Borrows set up three crack houses in Toxteth, generating £40,000 a day at their height. When the market became saturated, he sent his salesmen far and wide to all corners of the UK in a bid to find virgin territory. Boasting that in total he was responsible for getting 100,000 people hooked on crack, Borrows claimed that his proliferation press-ganged numerous girls into prostitution and caused a crime wave. Not caring whether his victims lived or died, Borrows rationalised his destruction by arguing that he was simply taking capitalism to its rightful extreme.

'I just did what Mrs Thatcher told me to do,' he explained. 'I got on my bike and built up a business from nothing. I did it to feed my family.' Borrows described himself as the Richard Branson of the drugs world.

However, pride came before a fall. Later that year, he was arrested for running Britain's first fully functional, industrial-scale crack factory.

Borrows was not the only Cartel member feeling the heat. Dylan Porter was also getting stressed out by the heroin business: too much stigma, too much attention from the busies; it was all becoming too much.

'I got off to Sweden for a while for a break from it all.

Obviously, I wasn't dealing over there, but still, I couldn't resist grafting. We ended up pillaging the place, all that "Scousers abroad" caper – cashies going left, right and centre, wage snatches, doors of shops going in etc. But it was good just to get away from the brown: robbing wasn't tangled up with all the politics and mind games that come from selling heroin.

'Eventually I came back to get involved with the business again. But by this time, my partner, the person I'd brought in from London, had got greedy. He'd taken over my round. He didn't want to split the money. He set me up with a shotgun. He asked me to go and pick up a gun hidden on a railway line. I did – but I got SWATTED by the specialist firearms team straight away. All those guns pointing at my head – the first time a SWAT team had been used in Liverpool, according to the front pages the next day.'

Looking on from the sidelines, Kaiser and Scarface could see the bigger picture. Too many people were getting nicked, hindering the growth of the Cartel. If they were going to expand, they'd have to relocate away from the firing line. For the first time, the Cartel was learning about what police would later refer to as 'displacement'.

Scarface and Kaiser started to go to Amsterdam to buy their Class A's at a discount. The visits inspired global ambitions. Why not set up shop in the Dam full-time? Why limit themselves to sending the gear back to Liverpool? Why not start shipping drugs direct to London, Manchester and Scotland? Then to other countries – Ireland, Germany, Russia? 'The World Is Yours' was their motto. Props, of course, to Tony Montana.

The grand plan was to create a mobile global commodities outfit that could buy drugs at the source in South America and Jamaica. Then they would smuggle them to wherever the best prices could be achieved. The model was later identified by experts, revolving around Kaiser and Scarface's roles as 'independent brokers' and 'global citizens'. The research was done by criminologists in Amsterdam, and Kaiser and Scarface's operation was one of the first examples of the new phenomenon.

To put the plan into action, Kaiser and Scarface left Liverpool and based themselves in Holland. Scarface had no option: he had the decision made for him. One day he got arrested and charged by police in Liverpool for a slew of serious offences. But he escaped from a police station after being momentarily left alone in a room. He put a chair through a window and jumped from the first or second floor onto the street below. He went on the run abroad before meeting up with Kaiser in 'the flat place'.

The first objective was to raise the capital to buy into a big drugs deal. Amsterdam was wide open. Only one other serious Cartel member had been based there: a founding father of the Cartel and convicted heroin smuggler called Delroy Showers, who'd been popular in post-riot Toxteth street politics. A handful of Scouse potheads ran 'bits and bobs' around the city and back to the UK on the Hook of Holland ferry. But other than that, the competition was low.

Scarface and Kaiser needed money because business in Liverpool had cooled off. The police were continuing to disrupt supplies of heroin, and the crack boom had levelled off as the local market became saturated. Kaiser and Scarface had ridden the first wave, but in the new dog-eat-dog environment they were being written off by the underworld because they were skint. Behind the scenes, they had been one of the first of the mid-level Cartel dealers to invest their money in properties and businesses. However, they refused to cash it in to fund the Amsterdam venture; the 'kidnap money', as it was known, was for a rainy day.

Through a corrupt Asian businessman, Kaiser and Scarface had bought a block of flats with a retail development underneath in Dollis Hill, north London. In addition, they had shares in two big Chinese restaurants in Newport and London. Poncho was given the job of looking in on the businesses while they traded in Amsterdam.

'Money laundering is not about getting a return on your legit investment,' Poncho explained. 'It's just about keeping your money safe in the long term but at the same time gettable at short notice. You're not looking to get dividends from it, because if you get bogged down in the details of a business then it makes you vulnerable. All they wanted to do was bounce round the world doing drug deals, not wait in for the man to come and fix the washing machine. That's one of the great misunderstandings about the relationship between drug dealers and their money, and this whole mysterious world of money laundering.'

THE CARTEL

The deal in the Chinese restaurants that Kaiser and Scarface had bought was simple: they didn't want a share of the £3,000-a-week profits, just an assurance from the Asian owner that they could get quick access to their principal, and other assets if required, at a moment's notice.

Kaiser and Scarface began buying weed, cocaine and heroin to send back to Liverpool. To send out a message to the other gangs in Amsterdam, they played bullish. When a Moroccan dealer tried to rip them off, they threw him into a canal – which was quite unknown in the hippyish culture of the Jewish quarter and the squats that grew up around the drugs scene. But it wasn't only their no-nonsense approach that made them stand out: Kaiser and Scarface had eclectic taste in clothes. Their trademark look included cowboy shirts and Texan-style buckle ties. On business, they wore Moss Bros suits and called themselves 'the Management'.

'They finished each other's sentences,' said Poncho. 'They could read each other's mind when it came to business.'

In 1988, Kaiser and Scarface began planning to smuggle a 1,000-kilo load of cocaine into Britain: the first time anyone had attempted such a quantity. First, they headed for Jamaica to tap up some old pals: they wanted an introduction to the Cali Cartel, based in Colombia. They were spotted drinking champagne on a yacht with known criminals. In an upmarket Jamaican resort, they met a gay South American aristocrat. The fixer gave them a 'who's who' of Bogotá's underworld and promised to link them up with a few contacts.

Scarface and Kaiser immediately flew to the former Spanish colony. In Colombia, they thrived on the heavy situation. Using the aristocrat's contacts, they set up a few test deals, sending several kilos back to Amsterdam. They lived like kings off the proceeds. Even the cleaners of their luxurious apartment looked like models, according to Poncho, who visited later. The housemaids often spent more time in between the Egyptian cotton sheets, getting 'sorted in the morning', than cleaning the bathroom.

Fun times aside, Bogotá was a dangerous place. Kaiser and Scarface witnessed a bar being blown up. Gunshots were common. The local news was full of judges and cops being assassinated for going up against the drug barons.

Instead of being put off, Kaiser and Scarface were ambitious to move on to the next level. Rather than a few kilos here and there, they wanted to purchase a metric tonne. But so far, their Colombian contacts had been reluctant. Either they were too small fish or they wanted huge deposits, way out of the reach of a couple of opportunists.

However, a chance meeting in a Bogotá bar would change their fate – and that of the Cartel – for ever, giving them a shot at the big time while simultaneously offering the Cartel an opportunity to go from a ragtag collection of petty criminals and mid-level dealers into an international drug-trafficking gang that would be capable of swamping Europe with drugs for years to come.

For several weeks, Scarface and Kaiser had been monitoring what they called a 'big bad crew' that occasionally turned up in a bar that they frequented. Scarface told Poncho he could spot them a mile off, telling him, 'They wore suits, they turned up in Mercs and 4 x 4s and they always had big lads hanging around them.'

Time and funds were running low, and soon Kaiser and Scarface would have to return to Europe empty-handed. According to Poncho, one night, a frustrated Kaiser decided to try his luck with the curious barflies who looked like gangsters straight from central casting.

'Hi, I'm Kaiser,' he beamed to the boss, hand out in peace. 'I know who you are and I want to do business with you.'

At first, the gang seemed friendly, but an hour later Kaiser found himself in the back of a car being driven into the mountains. Scarface had become separated from the group as the bar had got busier. One of the gang cocked a gun to Kaiser's head. 'I think we should kill him; he's DEA.'

On the inside, Kaiser was sweating, but in his mind he was thinking: 'There's no way I'm gonna let my nerves get me killed.' He did what he'd been brought up to do when faced with a stressful situation: he made a joke of it. He began 'arsing about', as Poncho put it, disarming the Cali bosses with his mischievous charm.

Instead of killing Kaiser, the gangster gave him the benefit of the doubt. Instead of being buried in a shallow grave, astonishingly he was invited to stay at the family's ranch for a few weeks. A driver was sent back to the bar to pick up Scarface.

According to Poncho, the pair spent a month galloping around the plantations on horseback. More like a holiday than a drugs deal, they posed for pictures wearing panama hats, bandoliers and two handguns in side holsters. The Scousers found that the Colombians were on their level.

The plantation was run by a high-level Colombian cocaine salesman called Lucio and his younger brother. The brothers were part of a powerful mafia which was connected to and ultimately headed by first cousins Raul Grajales Lemos and Luis Grajales Posso. The notorious Urdinola Grajales family publicly portrayed themselves as legitimate businessmen, but most of their companies were fronts for their drug and money-laundering operations. Bribery, corruption and violence had allowed them to build a huge cocaine empire. A fleet of aircraft and sea vessels transported tons of cocaine to Western Europe. Their trademark method involved concealing cocaine inside containerised shipments of fruit. At the time, the Grajales organisation was becoming active in Western Europe. Later they established new routes into Eastern Europe and the former Soviet Union. They needed salesmen in Amsterdam; hence their sudden friendship with Kaiser and Scarface.

Kaiser and Scarface weren't fazed. The irony was that Scarface and Kaiser didn't really believe the hype of the underworld. Instinctively, they understood that most gangsterism was an act. In real life, the Colombian overlords looked like family men. The phoney image applied to themselves also: Scarface and Kaiser understood that they had no real power. They traded on the fact that people were conditioned to react to gangsters in a certain way. In Liverpool and Amsterdam especially, they manipulated that fear and winged it to their advantage.

'The reason they got on with South Americans,' Poncho said sentimentally, 'is that they were friendly and family orientated – much like the people back home.'

After a few weeks, Kaiser and Scarface put their proposition to South Americans, spelling it out that they wanted to export a superload of cocaine from Colombia to Holland. It had never been done before. Curtis Warren and Colin Smith, the future Cartel bosses who made 1,000-kilo imports standard, were still relatively small-time dealers back in Liverpool. The Colombians liked Kaiser and Scarface so much that they agreed to waive a big up-front payment. They would supply the load 'on tick' on the condition that the Scousers provided the transport from Venezuela to Europe. Kaiser and Scarface would only have to pay a small deposit to cover local transport and storage costs.

Poncho said, 'One of the Colombian brothers called Lucio had grown very fond of Kaiser and Scarface. He described them as "humorous" and "warm-hearted". He offered them a deal. In the end, they would only have to pay a £25,000 deposit to cover the cost of wrapping up the cocaine in sealed plastic and transporting it from Colombia to the coast in Venezuela. That's a dream deal.

'Kaiser and Scarface had been saving up a kitty for a while, thinking that they were going to have to pay hundreds of grand, which they didn't have. So financially, it wasn't a risk for them.'

The basic plan was to smuggle 1,000 kilos from Venezuela to the Caribbean and then to Holland. Kaiser and Scarface decided to keep the operation as simple and low-cost as possible. They would buy a small yacht and sail it themselves on the 5,000-mile (8,000-km) trip, the model that's known in the trade as 'crashing the port'.

Kaiser and Scarface immediately returned to Holland via Jamaica to put all the pieces in place. In Amsterdam, they recruited a red-haired, mustachioed Dutch aristocrat who had fallen on hard times. The posh smuggler needed fast money to save his family's property portfolio from being repossessed. Every week, Kaiser and Scarface met up with him and his wife at the upmarket Harry's American Bar in Amsterdam. The joint was a popular haunt for visiting Hollywood stars, but the group could often be seen sitting in the corner animatedly planning the venture, which they dubbed Operation Swagger.

A smuggling operation is a complicated business requiring hundreds of decisions to be made. The team decided to hire a couple of experts to share the load. Two German businessmen, who later made a fortune manufacturing Ecstasy tablets, were recruited to take care of logistics, which included buying a suitable boat, testing the boat, renting a safehouse, buying a van, taking care of paperwork and planning the route. A fourth man, a South American who had experience of working in the Caribbean, was hired as a translator and general all-rounder.

From the start, Scarface decided that he was going to do the important bits himself. He would sail the boat, despite having no experience of yachting or navigation. That would cut out middlemen and reduce costs. Kaiser would stay in Amsterdam to drum up interest in potential buyers. Scarface chose his crew – the Dutch aristocrat and the South American – leaving the Germans on land to help Kaiser.

Poncho said, 'Scarface was good at everything, one of those competent all-rounder types who do well in life. He had a can-do, kinda DIY attitude that is common among those Scouse drug-dealer types: "I'll do it my way, it can't be that hard." It was a kind of arrogance, but part bluff and part youth as well. He was jammy. His attitude was, "If you take the risk, you get the rewards." He was right. And if you're looking after the coke, you've got control, and ultimately you decide who gets a share of the profits.'

Back in Liverpool, the police had no idea what was going on. The crack boom had been taking place on and off for two years, but officers on the beat were just becoming aware of it. The last thing they were expecting was a second wave of cheap cocaine to come flooding in.

The Analyst said, 'The first time I came across crack was in 1988. We were bringing a stolen car back into the station at around three o'clock in the morning. We were in uniform and a taxi driver flagged us down and told us that there was a woman being raped by the side of the road. So I got out, ran over and the suspect stopped what he was doing and got on his toes down an entry. I ran after him. He waited at the end of the alleyway and it turned into a fight and a free-for-all. I hit him as hard as I could with my truncheon, but he shook it off, like something in a cartoon. It didn't make a blind bit of difference.

'My mate came looking for me, and eventually we got him back to the station. In his pocket there were 40 or 50 wraps of crack cocaine. The next day he had no idea of his behaviour or what had gone on. That was crack.'

But the effects weren't just physical. Crack reset the relationship between police and criminal. The dealers became increasingly hostile. In court, one criminal threatened to steal the officer's new car.

The Analyst said, 'It's not just a myth. Before drugs, criminals almost had a respect for the police. They saw us more of an occupational hazard rather than something to be hated and resisted at all costs.

'I remember I was in a restaurant with my family having a meal, and a guy who I'd nicked for a commercial burglary came over. There's always that moment, a bit of tension when you think, "What's going to happen here?"'

'But he said: "Can I buy everybody a drink?"'

'It was a relief. Of course, I said no, but his attitude wasn't hostile. That started to change – the dealers started to threaten us when we were giving evidence in court.'

CHAPTER 13

VOYAGE

1989

THE STILL SEAWATER glistened like a plane of apatite crystal. The crew were dozing below, gaining momentary relief from the laser-like, searing, bedazzling heat that gave no quarter during daylight. The silence was isolation-tank quiet, broken only by the gentle kiss of the water on the hull and the occasional toll from the gong-like sea bell that Scarface had bought from a tourist shop in Guadeloupe.

'Action stations,' he suddenly shouted. 'Fucking hell – action stations!' The blast of his voice triggered an explosion of kinetic frenzy, as the crew jumped from their bunks and got into the zone. Scarface never slept, preferring to scour the horizon with his military-surplus binoculars that he'd bought at a yacht chandler's in Cape Verde a few months previously. His vigilance had paid off. A US Coast Guard cutter was skimming towards him fast, seeming almost vertical in its haste, like a dolphin doing a trick. Suddenly, Scarface's UHF radio crackled to life with the USCG call sign, ordering them to stop and prepare for boarding. Ominously the voice said: 'We will not shoot unless fired upon.'

The stealthy black boat slowed down only to bank slightly one kilometre off Scarface's stern, seamlessly launching two small inflatables into the sea. One took position 100 yards off Scarface's starboard bow, the other equidistant but to port. Upon announcing their presence, the American commander enquired about Scarface's destination, last port of call, number of firearms aboard and number of passengers.

The cutter came alongside, the forward gunner sweeping Scarface's deck. Though it was daylight, a fiercely powerful spotlight, so hot that it made the water bubble with steam, was brought to bear to dazzle and intimidate the target.

'US Coast Guard. This is a routine safety inspection,' the loudhailer boomed. But Scarface noticed that two or three of the heavily body-armoured sea warriors standing on the deck of the cutter sported Drug Enforcement Agency insignia.

Poncho leaned back, grinning. 'Scarface told me he'd thought, "Fuck. There goes my 1,000 kilos. There goes the rest of my life."'

Meanwhile, 4,000 miles away in Liverpool, the Cartel was maturing nicely. It was 1989. A number. Another summer. The Cartel had scraped through the heroin drought and a London-based gang known as the Turkish Connection began to re-establish supplies. Crack use had levelled off, but then unaccountably its growth began to rocket again. It seemed that heroin and cocaine use, somehow, worked in tandem.

The Analyst noticed three changes. First, there was an explosion of 'poly-users' – addicts who took heroin and cocaine together. The other two changes were on the business side: money laundering mushroomed and independent dealers began to operate alongside the Cartel.

The Analyst said, 'By this time the heroin users had chaotic lifestyles. Crack was introduced and it was a form of mixed medication. The drug dealers started to make serious money. They'd been around for a few years, but crack brings with it a windfall.'

The superficial wealth turned into proper financial wealth. Firmly back on its feet, the Cartel invested heavily in the fabric of Merseyside, snapping up bars and property at breakneck speed. The late 1980s property boom became a vehicle for legitimising their money.

At the same time, a new group of independent drug dealers began to operate outside of the Cartel and under the radar of the police. The buoyant black economy could now support various sizes and shapes of organisations. The independents didn't want to be gangsters or hugely wealthy, shunning heroin and crack in favour of low-key 100-kilo-a-time cannabis deals. Unlike the hot-headed and vengeful Cartel members, the independents were stoical, never getting involved in disputes and always writing off debts to preserve stability. They regularly kept £100,000 cash in their houses but rarely got taxed because few people knew the full extent of their business.

The Analyst began studying the independents: 'If he's selling to you, you'll agree on £100,000 worth of cannabis and that's what you'll get. You will get the gear. He will get his money. Simple economics, no credit, no pressure.

'They saw that there was the aggressive environment in Toxteth, where there was also violence between rivals. They saw a gap in the market, which was based on brains not brawn.'

Everyday working people formed small syndicates to cash in. A psychiatric nurse joined up with a personal trainer. A group of taxi drivers formed a kitty to trade cannabis in much the same way as a share club. The independents were seen as liberal, but conversely their business ethics were puritan. Credit was always refused. Reason, not trust, was the stock-in-trade, because if deals went wrong independents had no way to rectify problems.

The Analyst said, 'It's your typical feller who lives in a normal house. The only difference is that he may have lions on the stone pillars outside his house in north Liverpool somewhere. He might have a couple of businesses, shop fronts, sunbed shops: businesses that provide a service for cash, so that money can be laundered.

'They are quite intelligent. They set themselves a threshold of criminality that they are not prepared to cross.'

The independents targeted specific communities. One wholesaler only supplied cannabis to dealers who in turn only distributed in sixth-form colleges. Sixth formers didn't want to go knocking on doors in a bad part of town. The social nature became more acceptable. Another only supplied workmates and people connected to a Sunday League. Wannabes and show-offs didn't last long in the smaller, stabler markets.

The Analyst said, 'I remember we raided a hall of residence and we seized a shoebox full of cannabis. The student went to prison. His career was ruined and his parents were asking why.'

By 1989, even the street-level crime groups within the Cartel became more sophisticated. The more intelligent approach of the independent combined with the organisational skills of the higher Cartel members began to rub off on the lower orders. Gone was the Klondike, fill-your-boots-while-it-lasts approach. Dealers started applying business principles to the drugs industry. Many started buying investment properties to rent out to the expanding student population.

Often they stayed within their own comfort zone, as regards money laundering, such as the pub and club sector and door security. As a consequence, a plethora of security companies suddenly opened up that would become the building blocks of organised crime across the country. In turn, the security companies left the Cartel ideally poised to exploit the source of the next windfall – the dance era.

Meanwhile, ex-heroin dealer and shotgun merchant Dylan Porter was beginning a four-year sentence, having been convicted of possession of a firearm.

But things were looking up for Kaiser and Scarface. According to Poncho, in late spring 1989, Scarface had moved into the next stage of Operation Swagger, the plan to smuggle 1,000 kilos of heroin from South America. Just three months before his boat was stopped by US Coast Guards, the planning was still being carried out. First, Scarface had taken the small yacht that had been purchased especially on a test trip. Along with a couple of girlfriends and several team members, Scarface had sailed to Cape Verde, a collection of ten islands in the North Atlantic 570 km off the coast of West Africa. The Cape was a popular stopover for the yachting set. Scarface was cash rich. Though overpriced, he bought lots of equipment from a chandler's on the island, including military-standard binoculars and a powerful UHF radio.

The dummy run went like a dream. Scarface discovered that he was a natural sailor and felt confident enough to go live for real. In June 1989, Scarface set off from Amsterdam on the three-month round trip to South America. Rammed tight with supplies, conditions were cramped: only two people could sleep in the cabin and one on deck under the stars. The South American was let go when they reached the Caribbean after he got on Scarface's nerves. He was replaced by a second Dutchman.

The pick-up in Venezuela was smooth. The 1,000-kilo consignment was loaded and sealed within secret compartments in the wooden hull. However, the first leg of the return journey proved fretful. From Curaçao, at first they made a beeline north-east, setting a diagonal course straight for Europe. The plan was to avoid American-owned Puerto Rico like the plague and crash through the natural barrier that formed the Lesser Antilles, at the centre of the archipelago around Montserrat. But they received some last-minute intel that the British were stepping up patrols around colonies such as the Virgin Islands and Anguilla. Dutch Marines had also been spotted at Sint Eustatius and Saba.

Instinctively, as though he was chasing through the backstreets of Toxteth, Scarface swung a right and headed deep into the southernmost parts of the Caribbean Sea. St Lucia and St Vincent were usually blind spots for the drug-sniffing authorities, but to his disappointment Scarface found the waters heading towards Barbados swamped with DEA gunboats and US Coast Guard interceptors. Since the invasion of Grenada six years earlier, the US was now treating the island as its own real estate. Coastal security had nearly reached mainland levels of paranoia. But by now Scarface had no choice. He'd have to take the chase and take his chances.

Skilfully, Scarface avoided several run-ins by sailing off chart and swinging in between islands – literally dots of palm-fringed sands where they'd sit in a cove, waiting for the fast boats and choppers to pass. But one day a US government ship got them in their sights.

'Action stations,' Scarface shouted. 'Get out of bed now. We're getting a tug off the Americans.' Thinking on his feet, he ordered the two Dutchmen, half-asleep after being woken, to change into their tight-fitting, brightly coloured trunks. 'When they get alongside, act gay. Camp it up. I want the soldiers to think we're homosexuals. I don't want them hanging around.'

Fortunately, the aristocrat, whom they'd nicknamed 'the Baron', looked the part. He had longish hair, a YMCA moustache and a sinewy, sun-kissed body. Scarface was also thin and deeply tanned. Quickly, he covered his chest in oil. Within seconds, the US cutter was alongside. Scarface invited the armed US agents to come aboard – in his best Lily Savage gay Scouse voice.

With the barrel of a high-calibre belt-fed machine gun sweeping the deck, Scarface kept his cool. The boarding party consisted of three USCG members and two DEA officers. The first cop pointed a handgun at Scarface. Two others threatened the Dutchmen with shotguns. Immediately the USCG commanding officer went below for a 'safety inspection', to check the bilge pump and general seaworthiness of the vessel. He counted the flares, fire extinguishers and deck throwables, such as life jackets, rubber rings and inflatable buoys. At one point when he inspected various tanks, he got painfully close to the cocaine. But Scarface knew his job was maritime law – it was the DEA's job to rummage for drugs.

Meanwhile, the DEA interrogated Scarface on the fly bridge. Scarface blagged his way around the false IDs. When asked the purpose of his visit, he told the officer that they were some of the many gay hedonists returning from the debauched party season in the Caribbean.

Poncho said, 'He played on the stereotypes of the gay Westerners on holiday and the homoerotic US soldiers who are too macho for their own good. One of them was pointing an assault rifle at the Dutchmen, who were sweating. It was cheesy, but it worked.'

Scarface began to flirt with the DEA officers and invited them to check down below in the cabin, where the 1,000 kilos were hidden behind a few millimetres of varnished marine ply. The DEA officers declined, making just a few cursory checks of the wheelhouse. They glanced at the paperwork and declined the offer of a more intimate search.

Poncho said, 'Scarface was a clever bastard. He knew that the searches and inspections often took more than an hour. But he knew they wouldn't want to spend an hour with three semi-naked gay men in a confined space. The DEA gave them a walkover. After that it was plain sailing all the way back to Europe.'

Scarface loved it: he was blown away when one day a family of whales started following the boat, shooting up water out of their blowholes and jumping high into the air and crashing down. He went all hippyish, loving the freedom, just wearing shorts all day on the deck. His body got tanned more deeply and he went sinewy and strong.

Back in Liverpool, Scarface's gang were working at the less adventurous end of the chain. Poncho was in charge of selling crack cocaine on the street. He was in partnership with one of the Cartel's more unusual franchises – an African church.

The church had been smuggling heroin into the UK for eight years following the riots. The minister used his position as a cover and his flock as runners.

Poncho said, 'Then we started the crack off and then the powder, selling shots in little bags, things like that. The local lads were natural drug dealers, and with the black connection as well, it made it very strong. I had a crew of my own – there were six of us. Two went to jail. Two are dead. The other one: his head's gone through all this. I got stabbed – they gave me an hour to live. Everyone was fighting for position.'

Frequently, there was in-fighting along racial divides, but the Cartel always stopped for money.

CHAPTER 14

RELOADED

1989

OPERATION SWAGGER WAS entering its final phase. Scarface's yacht had cleared the West Indies and was belting across the Atlantic, full speed ahead. So far they had been at sea on the return journey for a month. Since being stopped by the DEA, they had had two weeks of plain sailing across the Mid-Atlantic. Now there was a little over ten days left till home, and they found themselves snaking around the west coast of Africa and into the home straight. Scarface began doing press-ups on the deck, shaking off the hippy cobwebs. From now on, there'd be no more pot smoking to while away the hours. He needed to stay straight, prepare himself for life back in the big, bad city. Back to business.

The drop-off in Europe was the riskiest part of the mission. According to Poncho, instead of beaching the load along an isolated stretch of coast in Spain or Portugal, Scarface decided to go for broke and crash the port.

'Fuck it,' he told the crew, 'I'm going to sail her right into the Dam.' The Dutch aristocrat winced at the prospect: his payday was in sight, but he knew the dangers that lurked behind the liberal facade of his home country. The port of Amsterdam handled 70 million tons of goods annually and was the fourth most important in Europe. But the sea lanes were exceptionally busy and patrolled by some of the heaviest maritime surveillance in the world. If you got caught trafficking, you could expect heavier sentences than in the UK, contrary to popular belief.

The Baron tried to persuade Scarface to head for Tariffa or Cadiz on Spain's windy Atlantic side, where he had contacts who would get the gear on land. But Scarface was worried. What then? How would he get the gear through mainland Spain and France back to the Dam? He hadn't planned for it.

'I can't be arsed messing about with sorting trucks overland,' Scarface argued. 'It's time and money and we've got no security.' He meant they didn't have enforcers to ensure safe passage. The bars in southern Spain were crawling with modern-day pirates – most of them British – who'd love nothing more than to take his gear from him.

'I'm going to crash the port and that's that. I'm berthing her right outside my flat.' The voyage had been a long three months, and Scarface was desperate for land. Desperate to spend a night with a woman. Desperate to start shifting the merchandise. Desperate to get back in the game. He knew the Colombians would immediately start itching for their money: they'd want to start getting it back to Bogotá before Christmas.

One foggy September morning in 1989, the yacht found itself on choppy waters just outside the main terminal at Amsterdam port.

'Head for that light,' ordered Scarface. It was still dark and a lighthouse marked the opening in the harbour wall. The Baron brought the wheel around, on course straight into the main shipping line. The tiny vessel was dwarfed by container carriers 1,000 times its size.

But in the confusion and poor light, suddenly they overshot the port entrance without realising. They ended up bobbing alongside the harbour wall at the far side. It was almost as if the Baron hadn't wanted to steer her in – as though he'd lost his bottle at the last minute. Not since their brush with the DEA in the Caribbean Sea had they been so vulnerable. Any passing Customs patrol boat would surely give them a pull now and inspect the boat. Giant CCTV cameras mounted on thick girders and housed in steel and glass weatherproof casings recorded the sea traffic for miles around. Scarface trained his binoculars on the control tower – surely the harbour master must have been wondering why the blip on the radar had failed to navigate the dangerous shipping lanes and sail into the quayside – a potential flag to the port *politie*. But surprisingly no one came. At one point they came within twenty metres of a gang of dockworkers and builders repairing a stretch of barrier on land. But instead of reporting them, the workers simply waved, their cigarettes glowing in the twilight.

The Dutchman desperately tried to steer the yacht back out to sea. But they were trapped. Scarface was ratty, but he remained calm enough to gauge the situation. He ordered them to go with the flow, keeping tight to the harbour wall to keep their profile as low as possible.

Astonishingly, they had a million-to-one stroke of good fortune. The wall seemed to go on forever, and at any moment they were expecting a Customs boat to roar up from the rear. But unexpectedly they came to a sharp break that they assumed was a corner but turned out to be the end of the wall. Astonishingly, they'd reached an opening: a small lock that had been left unsealed. Even the Baron was shocked. They manoeuvred the boat through it quickly, disappearing from view behind a bend, and amazingly they ended up on the still waters of an urban canal, heading into central Amsterdam.

'How the fuck did that happen?' exclaimed Scarface, as they floated past a bonded warehouse and then into an upmarket residential area. After several hours of finding their way through the spiderweb of canals, they berthed right outside the prearranged safehouse that had been rented by Scarface's German partners. They'd made it home with a load potentially worth around £300 million at street value.

To top it all, they had got in a day earlier than scheduled. A few days earlier, Scarface had sent a UHF signal to a ham-radio enthusiast who was being used as an intermediary and was on the payroll. The message was simple: the time of arrival. But Scarface had overestimated the amount of time it was going to take. He had banked on the entry into the official port taking longer and having to hang around for the day, taking care of permissions, paperwork and passports. Having bypassed the harbour, this timetable had become irrelevant. Consequently, when they did arrive a day early, Kaiser wasn't at home – he'd gone to collect two mid-ranking drug dealers who represented notorious Liverpool crime families and senior Cartel members. They'd just flown into Schiphol, invited by Kaiser to have 'first dibs on the gear'.

The Cartel overlords would have first refusal on the load, getting in on the ground floor to pre-order however much they wanted. Kaiser knew that they had the money to pay for the amounts that were being negotiated. Crucially, in addition, their brothers-in-arms within the Cartel had the manpower and skills to get the consignment back to the UK and the muscle to distribute it once it was on the street. The pressure was on: soon the Colombians would be arriving, cash bags at the ready.

Poncho said, 'What you have got to realise is that to be invited to share in the load is a big privilege. That's the beauty about being in the firm. You've got to be very lucky to have a contact who can get gear in. And basically, if you are chosen to take some of it to sell, it's like being blessed: you are getting handed the chance to become very rich, very quickly. It's kind of like winning a contract, but you don't have to tender. You just have to be part of the bigger picture, someone who's got a track record.'

Kaiser also needed workers. The following day, Scarface called Poncho back home in Liverpool saying, 'Send a couple of our lads over. There's a bit of graft there for you – we need a hand.'

Poncho and his cousin called Ronnie decided to go. But like so many aspects of organised crime, the reality was less Mafia and more Mickey Mouse. The Scousers could be unreliable and immature.

Poncho said, 'We were told not to fly, as that would make a fuss, bearing in mind that crime families were flying into the Dam to get served up their parcels. We were less important, so we headed south to catch the ferry. We stopped off in Aldershot to visit our mate in the army. We were surprised how mad and violent it was – we didn't know army towns were that rough. Even for us, fresh off the front line, the whole place was like the O.K. Corral. There were army lads fighting the townies and pub windows going in every five minutes. I got into the madness straight away and bunked into a nightclub, pretending to be a dancer. We got pissed, then went back to the barracks to play cards with the squaddies.

'We missed the boat twice. Finally we got on the crossing. Got pissed again. I shagged a girl in the bogs, who was on holiday with her mum and dad. But we'd got the wrong boat and all that. We ended up in a beach resort miles away from Amsterdam, popular with day-trippers and no one else.'

Poncho called Scarface for a lift, but during the wait the rock 'n' roll continued. Poncho got into a row over a game of pool with a gang of Scottish tourists. In revenge, he spiked one of them with an Army-issue morphine tablet that they'd been given by the squaddies back in Aldershot. Two hours later, a mysterious Dutchwoman turned up dressed in a beret, sunglasses and trench coat. She saved them from a potential hiding – the angry Scots had discovered that they'd been hustled and drugged.

Poncho added, 'The girl who came for us looked like someone out of the French Resistance. But she was beautiful – totally fit. It turned out that she was Scarface's new wife. He'd married her before he'd left for South America and she'd waited for him.

'On the way into Amsterdam in the car, I kept seeing billboards with a girl on them. I was thinking: "I know that face." And it was her: the woman who picked us up, Scarface's new bird, who was in the front passenger seat.

'It was then that I realised that Scarface and Kaiser had hit the big time. They were already living like superstars.'

The driver was a straight-goer employed as the firm's courier. Kaiser had paid for a runaround Ford Fiesta XR2 to be modified to make it faster; it cost £8,000.

Meanwhile, back in Liverpool, doorman Shaun Smith still refused to deal drugs – and still refused to join the Cartel. But he was extremely tough, so few would even think of messing with him. The drug lords respected him, even though he wouldn't allow gear to be sold in any of the venues he protected. The bosses, ironically, saw his influence as helpful. Non-druggie gangsters like Shaun Smith and the old-school hard man Paul Burly acted as a counterbalance, keeping a check on the power of certain unruly wings of the Cartel that were now flaunting their wealth and coming into the firing line. In doing so, they were also alienating themselves from the general flow. If need be, the Cartel felt that Shaun and Paul could be manipulated as enforcers, each backed up with small armies of foot soldiers. However, neither would get involved with drug dealers or fight for them under any circumstances. By now, the Cartel had decided to try and become part of a conservative underworld establishment.

Shaun joined forces with a well-known nightclub-owning family who'd built up a reputation for being good with their fists. Shaun had built up a company providing security to over-35 venues in the leisure industry all over the north-west. He was totally independent and didn't need anyone else's help. But the family asked Shaun to run and oversee their nightclubs because they couldn't handle the headaches in the increasingly violent drug-ridden underworld. Shaun's reputation provided a big boost to their empire. Soon he married into the family and became close to his brothers-in-law. His door-security company began to police lots of new nightspots.

Shaun said, 'I bought a pub in Kirkdale, which is like Beruit. The pub was called the Halfway House. I ended up running that for sixteen years while I built up my door business into one of the biggest around.'

A couple of local kids called Sidious and Kaim used to come in and play on the one-armed bandit. Shaun had known their dad since he was 12. The dad played in his pub's footy team. Shaun was even friendly with their grandmother. Though they looked harmless enough, the lads were third-generation Liverpool scallies who had been brought up in one of the city's toughest areas. Kaim and Sidious's mum and dad had never worked in their lives, preferring petty criminality and shoplifting. Some of Kaim and Sidious's mates had mums and dads who hadn't worked for 20 years either. And their mums and dads hadn't worked before them. This new generation was wild and unsocialised, cut off from much of what mainstream society had to offer. They didn't recognise hierarchies, or reputations, or old-school codes of conducts. They weren't scared of anything. They were fearless and ruthless to the point of inspiring terror.

Little did Shaun know that the mischievous rats who had once sneaked in the saloon bar door to play on the fruit machines and scavenge ciggies were growing into monsters. One day, they would turn on him. One day, they would turn on the Cartel. One day, they would threaten the existence of the biggest and most powerful crime machine that the UK had ever been burdened with. One day, they would even threaten the police with an unprecedented display of shock and awe.

CHAPTER 15

THE PARCEL

1989

WHEN THE GANG linked up, it was straight down to business. When he arrived in the Dam, Poncho hadn't seen Scarface for a couple of years – he looked older and more distinguished. He had a 'sailorish air' about him, according to his nephew.

Poncho said, 'He'd lost his youthful look, even though he was only 29ish, 30ish.

'Outside the safehouse, there was a white van with a window at the back. There was a guy with a ponytail, loading up oversized cardboard boxes containing the gear – each one was about the size of a washing machine box and contained one hundred and twenty kilos of cocaine.

'Kaiser was there with us, overseeing. He was cautious – it was his idea to load the van up. He wanted to keep moving the gear around and had lined up a second safehouse. I don't think he fully trusted the German silent partners. The boxes were heavy and awkward, and that's why it needed me and the ponytail guy to load them up.

'Scarface then drove me and Ronnie to the second safehouse, where security was much tighter. Only us three would know about it – because we were family. He told us to not even tell Kaiser – not out of disrespect. That's just professional – everything is on a need-to-know basis. Everything is compartmentalised, in case someone gets nicked. Kaiser had organised the safehouse, in terms of paying someone and getting a scout etc., but he'd left the final choice of location to Scarface – so that even he wouldn't know where it was.

'When we got there, Scarface told us to put the gear in a loft, which had a pull-down ladder, and then we would meet him in a bar round the corner.'

Before Scarface got off, he opened one of the cardboard parcels and pulled out a 'box' – the trade name for a kilo of cocaine. He threw it to Poncho and said, 'We've made it, kidder – that's yours.'

But Poncho threw it back and said, 'Don't worry about it. You don't have to do that – we're family and I'm not expecting anything. It's your graft.'

Scarface told Poncho to bury the kilo for a rainy day. If he were to get it back to Liverpool, then cut it up and sell it in bits, it would be worth around £100,000. But Poncho knocked it back, feeling embarrassed. He knew he'd make a lot of money in the Dam anyway.

He added, 'But when we got to the bar, he gave me a line anyway. It was 100 per cent pure and mind-blowing. I was stuck to the chair, it was that powerful.'

On his second day in Amsterdam, Poncho was given the job of liaising with the Colombians, who were now in Amsterdam. Gradually, as Scarface and Kaiser arranged shipments back to Liverpool, the money would start flowing back to them. Poncho's job was to ferry repayments back to the Colombians.

But the majority of the revenue was pure profit. A few days later, Kaiser bought a brand-new Ferrari Testarossa for more than one hundred grand in cash. The gang began washing its money through the exchange bureaus near Dam Square in the city centre. Poncho took the money in bags containing tens, sometimes hundreds of thousands, of pounds in cash and changed it into high-denomination guilders.

Poncho said, 'One day I spotted some Moroccan street rats who'd tried to have me off when I'd first arrived in Amsterdam. Scarface jumped out of the Ferrari and put a hammer in the main guy's head – right there, in the middle of Dam Square, in broad daylight. The message was: no one is going to fuck with us. He was fearless.'

Scarface also splashed out on a Volvo 750 Turbo and a Mercedes SLK. In a bid to conceal their illegal income, Kaiser and Scarface invested in front companies. The most successful was a commodities trader that sold computers to Russia. The legitimate businessmen involved soon took a shine to Kaiser and Scarface – and their cash pile – and invited them to invest in other ventures. Ironically, they started to make lots of money legally. It seemed that crime paid, at least for now.

Meanwhile, the profits from the sale of the cocaine began to roll in. On average, each pure, uncut kilo was sold for £20,000. The total turnover was approximately £20 million, out of which Kaiser and Scarface drew a first tranche of 'wages' totalling £3 million each. The Colombians were given £5 million for the cocaine. Poncho didn't know what happened to the other £9 million but strongly believes it went to several 'family' members directly connected to the two principals and high-up members of the Cartel.

Poncho: 'The Dutch aristocrat was given enough to pay off his debts, but the operational costs of the boat and the crew were minimal compared with what the main men got. Basically, between Scarface and Kaiser, and other direct members of the family, their cut was £15 million. That was just from wholesale revenue.

'But one day, Scarface told me that the total amount generated by the inner circle – that included them, plus several family players, plus several Cartel bosses – was nearer £50 million. There was the initial £20 million generated by wholesale transactions alone, which didn't take into account the revenue made by the next layer of distributors, which also formed part of the inner circle. Then a handful of senior Cartel members back in Liverpool, who were the high-ranking middlemen, made £30 million by cutting the 1,000 kilos into, say, 2,000 kilos and then selling them on.'

Following on again, there were huge multiples made by the lower distributors, who cut the drugs with adulterants up to six to eight times, retailed in street weights known as halves, quarters and ounces.

Poncho said, 'In the first tier, wholesale deals, they were very flexible about price. One kilo on its own was £28,000. If you were buying four or five kilos, it was £25,000. They would never go below, say £18,000. If you were buying 20 kilos – it's £19,500. It's not like corporate business – it's informal and a bit mysterious, and it's not uniform. For instance, you can get a good deal if you are mates with us or you have a good reputation in the underworld. If you've got your own transport, a £25,000 kilo will come down to £20,000, just like that.'

Not long after the parcel had landed, the German backers were forced out of the deal. They had expected £25 million of the profits from the first- and second-tier sales. But they were paid off with between one and two million quid's worth of cocaine, according to Poncho, and £100,000 in cash. The Germans were furious, but there was little they could do because they feared the growing power of the wider Cartel. The Germans swallowed the deal after they were placated by other members of the Cartel. If they could supply the Cartel with a new drug called Ecstasy, they would be compensated with a bigger share of the profits. Rationally, they went along with the plan and did not take revenge on Kaiser or Scarface.

In time, Ecstasy proved very profitable and the Germans grew very rich, very quickly. A few months after they had done their first big E deal, the Germans bought a luxury yacht and celebrated their fortune by throwing a party. Partly out of jealousy, Kaiser gatecrashed the event but was snubbed by one of the Germans. Kaiser picked him up and threw him in a bin – literally.

'Don't you dare ever blank me,' Kaiser bawled at the man, who'd been pushed into a container on the deck; 'I don't care how much money you've got.'

The superload firmly established the Cartel in Amsterdam. Other deals started moving Poncho's way. Moving between different apartments and hotels, Poncho began 'freelancing' on the side, supplying two- or three-kilo parcels to small independent smugglers from Liverpool, who in turn distributed to Bradford, Leeds and Birmingham.

The economics were simple. 'I sold them a kilo for £25,000,' said Poncho, 'and on top of that, the buyers paid a mule £3,000 to get it into the UK. So, by the time it got back to Liverpool each kilo cost £28,000. Each was cut into 36 ounces of powdered and crack cocaine. Each ounce was then sold on at £1,250 an ounce in Liverpool and £1,500 to out of town.

'But it was too strong what we had – it was like putty. Suddenly, I was getting pestered by a lot of the Liverpool dealers to serve them up. But you had to be careful because of the politics. If there was a drought then the price went up to £50,000 a kilo.'

Meanwhile, at the top, Scarface began smuggling drugs to Russia.

Poncho said, 'He'd already set up a business selling second-hand computers, cigarettes and machinery parts to ex-Soviet Union contacts. So they just started to stash coke in the containers. Then he started smuggling weed in from Morocco and selling it to the highest bidder in the Dam, no matter where they were from. It was a case of, "We don't need the UK any more." They started to sell drugs all over Europe.'

In the winter of 1989, a mid-ranking dealer from Liverpool called Curtis Warren was hanging around in Amsterdam. Warren would go on to be the richest criminal that has ever been caught in British history.

The authorities could never work out how he got his break into the big time. Warren had got a big leg up from the Banker and Fred the Rat, whom he worked for. They had given him some excellent drug contacts. But Curtis was ambitious. He wanted a separate channel so he could stand on his own two feet. He liked working with the Banker; they'd become close. But he didn't want to be Fred the Rat's bitch all his life. Warren had gone to Amsterdam to make a change.

Poncho revealed how Kaiser and Scarface introduced Curtis to the Colombians, the brothers who had supplied them with the 1,000-kilo load.

Poncho said, 'Curtis was only doing bits on his own. He was doing some reasonably big stuff with the two Mr Bigs he was in with. But he hadn't landed a big parcel as yet.

'He met a doorman in Amsterdam who could get him a few kilos here and there, which he was doing on the side for himself. He was ambitious to do bigger deals but couldn't get an intro to the South Americans we knew. Then one day we took him to a party in Amsterdam and he met Lucio's brother. Lucio was the top man in Colombia who supplied us. Then Curtis started doing stuff with them. They did a couple of little ones and then they tried to do a big one.

'We had a little competition going between Curtis and our kid. To be honest, we thought Curtis was a show-off. He even took Lucio's little brother back to Toxteth, a mad thing to do. Riding up and down Granby with him, showing off.

'Curtis was buying big cars while our kid stayed abroad well out of the way.'

Curtis had missed the point, according to Poncho. Instead of looking inwards and sending cocaine back to Liverpool, the Cartel was now looking outward and exporting to other, ex-party countries. They were the markets of the future, where profits were high and the risk of getting caught was low. Meanwhile, Curtis was focussed on only smuggling drugs back to the UK, where he enjoyed the familiarity of operations and the status afforded to him by the criminal hierarchy there.

Eventually Curtis was given a full-time contact within the Cali Cartel. He was a newly arrived 'salesman' called Mario Halley, who smuggled his money back to South America by exporting new BMW cars there. At around this time, Curtis's pal Colin Smith was no more than a preferred distributor. He was given first dibs on Warren's consignments, taking ten kilos a time for local distribution in south Liverpool. Scarface and Kaiser retained their more senior contacts in the Cali Cartel.

However, Curtis Warren's excesses had not gone unnoticed. The police might have been losing the war on drugs, but one officer was determined to revolutionise the way they fought. In 1989, the Analyst was coming up through the ranks.

The Analyst said, 'Some of the older officers didn't understand what was going on. But drugs was something that interested me. I'd gone into the world of being a detective in 1989 and decided that this was the world I wanted to be in. I enjoyed the different kinds of policing. There was the proactive and the reactive. The reactive was all about working the clues. The proactive was going out to make our own clues and catching the baddies that way. As far as career progression in the police goes, you do your burglaries, and then you do your robberies, and then you're on to the drugs. That's where I was now. Ironically, that progression mirrored the career path of someone like Curtis Warren, who had gone from being a street thief to being an importer.

'I started to lean towards a more progressive approach. Proactive policing is much better. I started to have much more success with a good team of the right people than I would have had with a bigger reactive team that just plodded on.'

CHAPTER 16

LUCIO

1990

PONCHO SOON BECAME a crucial link between the Cartel and the Colombians in Holland, a kind of smugglers' mobile Mr Fixit. One day Lucio introduced Poncho to a low-ranking female Cali trafficker who'd lost track of a container containing 20 kilos of coke in Amsterdam port. Poncho had grown up breaking into containers around Liverpool port – he was considered an expert at retrieving goods.

Poncho said, 'We were established by then. There were 20 firms in the Dam: Triads, Yardies, Russian mafia, Albanians, Moroccans, Turks, you name it. But we were now considered the main boys, because we had all the gear. With that status came other things. We had a little team who knew how to solve problems, and the Colombians respected that.

'We were Scousers. We weren't going to sit around Amsterdam and wait for the work to come to us. We were competing with firms from all over the world, so we wanted to show that we were up for anything, to make sure that everyone came to us. We never stood still. We didn't want the Colombians drifting off to become mates with anyone else. So we treated them well, just like they'd treated Scarface and Kaiser well on their farms.

'For instance, we had a Dutch lad on the firm who was a creeper – an expert burglar. I got him to break into the port, over the wall, but on the first go he couldn't find the container.

'We also knew a lad whose dad worked as a crane driver. We

gave him the tracking number of the container, and a few days later he said that he'd found it. But the bad news was that it wasn't near the outer wall, where we could have broken it – it was being stored in a special compound near the harbour area, deep inside.'

Poncho didn't want to lose face and pull out – it was important that the Colombians respected the Cartel for being game. But he faced two problems. First of all, there was a risk that the whole thing was a police trap. Had the container been moved to a secure area because Customs were suspicious? Were they waiting to pounce when the owners came to collect their merchandise? The second problem was simpler: how could he get into the secure area?

Poncho said, 'I'd been robbing freight out of Liverpool port since I was a kid. We used to call containers "loadies". The big lorries used to park up near Chinatown. We used to cut the bolts and clean them out of stuff. But sometimes they were police set-ups. So you had to be careful.

'There's a simple test to find out whether the container has been opened and rummaged in by Customs or whether there's a policeman waiting inside. Each container has a seal on it – a loop-shaped piece of aluminium. If it's a new seal, then it's obviously shiny and clean and you know someone has broken it the day before. But if it's an old, unbroken seal, you can rub your finger on it and it will taste of sea salt and grime and diesel – because it's been in the hold of a big fuck-off ship for months.

'We sent the creeper back into Amsterdam port to do the test on the container in the secure area and it came back salty – the container was safe. No one had broken the seal. It was safe to go.'

That night Poncho got his extraction team together: several Cartel foot soldiers armed to the teeth and wearing balaclavas. The plan was to covertly extract the cocaine. If they got rumbled, Plan B was to simply blast their way out, SAS-style.

Poncho said, 'We were waiting in the van ready for the go – it was tense. If we got caught, it was 20 years in jail, so we weren't going to get caught – the police were getting shot and we were off if necessary.

'But as we were getting into the zone, suddenly a gang of five or six Colombians came into view. We knew they were

Colombians because they were dressed in white coats and mad shirts, even though it was fucking freezing.

'Alarm bells began to ring: they were walking right up to the gate and looking around and we knew they were going to crash the place – that's how they do it, they don't give a fuck.

'We realised that the woman in charge had double-crossed us and played us off against another gang. So we stood down and fucked the job off.

'But it didn't damage our relationship. That's what you've got to do: you've got to make sure everyone knows that you can do anything and you've got the arse if necessary. That's how it is: it's a rough-and-tumble game and them's the breaks.

'When Lucio found out, he was grateful to us for just showing we were loyal. Lucio kept supplying us with gear.'

The Cartel settled down in Amsterdam to a life of Ancient Roman-style pleasure. Poncho spent his days having sex with high-class hookers on a sun lounger next to a sunken pool underneath an upmarket brothel. The girls cost 3,000 guilders a time. Poncho said, 'They were better than the Page 3 girls in *The Sun*. We were snorting cocaine off their arses and all that.'

Scarface's tastes were more eclectic. He liked Enya, ethnic music and ambient house. Meetings took place against a background of New Age meditation music. Afternoons were spent browsing the galleries in the artisan Jordaan quarter. One day he bought eight New Age paintings for 250,000 guilders. Weekends were spent ice skating and water skiing. Kaiser was a movie buff who liked going to the cinema and listening to Led Zeppelin on his state-of-the-art hi-fi.

Back in Britain, the conditions were right again for market innovation. For the first time in a generation, there was a collision between popular culture and drug use. Drugs went mainstream across the UK. The phenomenon was called rave or dance. Once again, the Cartel was able to lift itself to a higher level by piggybacking on the latest trend.

Helped along by Scarface and Kaiser's Colombian connection, cocaine prevalence in Britain and Liverpool rose sharply. For the first time, cocaine had become socially acceptable within the working classes. The Cartel began investing in dance clubs. New licensing laws allowed clubs to open later.

Economic improvement stimulated demand. With the help of

Tory minister Michael Heseltine's regeneration programme, parts of Liverpool were starting to recover from the early '80s bust. Money flowed in. The Albert Dock complex, a London-style riverside development, was up and running. The Beatles museum opened. Two years earlier, ITV's *This Morning*, hosted by Richard and Judy, began broadcasting from the banks of the Mersey. Wasteland was being turned into something more reasonable.

Punters at raves and dance clubs took 'cocktails' of drugs. No longer did they see themselves as either pot-smokers or Class A users. They were both. Dealers boasted of selling between 100 and 1,000 Ecstasy tablets per night.

The Analyst said, 'So you've got a whole new marketplace that has suddenly been created. The net effect for drug dealers was that you were increasing your number of consumers. Cocaine had pushed the niche market for heroin and cannabis wider. Alongside that, the distribution networks were becoming wider because they could bring cocaine from South America. The relationships are starting to build, as Liverpool criminals become established in Europe. So they're realising it's not just Pakistan and Afghanistan. So you've got another conduit of cocaine going into Amsterdam, where our criminals are becoming established. By their nature, some of our Merseyside criminals were quite forceful in establishing their territory and their position in the hierarchy.

'Your Liverpool criminal has a reputation, going back to the '70s: the low-level jokes about the wheels disappearing off your car. But in reality they were good at moving in on crime and taking it over, even in places abroad.

'So in Liverpool there was a multi level of criminality starting to establish itself, depending on market forces and consumers: the bottom line is that society had the money to pay for it.'

The Analyst noticed that there were groups, such as those behind Operation Swagger, bringing in drugs from everywhere. Ecstasy that wasn't made locally was being trucked in from Holland. Heroin flooded in from North Africa and Turkey. Cannabis was coming across from Spain, cocaine from South Africa and Colombia via the Dam.

For the Analyst it was the first time that the shape and structure of the Cartel became apparent. The more successful members were those with a number of elements to their business. By now, Colin Smith was Warren's deputy. Colin Smith and Curtis Warren evolved into CEO-type figures. But there was room enough for many like them within the Cartel. The Analyst noticed that the newcomers were learning the trade from the people who had set up the networks in the 1970s and '80s.

The Analyst said, 'It's easier to develop an existing supply chain and enhance a going concern than to start a drugs network from scratch. No one started on their own without any historical associates such as Thomas Comerford.

'The Banker is an example. Curtis was in a relationship with his daughter, so is that how he started to build up? I don't know whether the Banker was a hands-on drug dealer. But the police recovered a lot of money from him, so how did he get his hands on that?

'The more established ones like him got into the money laundering and financing. But how do they get to where they are? There had to be that progression.'

The Cartel began to adopt a hierarchy.

The Analyst said, 'It's like the police, which has its own hierarchical structure with ranks and roles. You could break it down into an organisational chart that shows you've got your CEOs at the top. You've got your MDs, who meet with similar MDs from supplier crime groups and talk about the wider implication of drug importation: how do we get the commodities across?

'So we now need a distribution network below them. How do we break that down? How's it going to get from Colombia to the coast in Venezuela? Once it gets to the coast, how's it going to be hidden in the ship? Lead ingots or welded into the superstructure? Or is it going to be a parcel, hidden in the ship itself? We will weld it in to a plated area on the ship, because no one will find it in its own partition.

'So you need managers below the MDs to organise these options. OK. So we decide we will fly the welder out to South America to build the compartment on the ship. Or in some cases, they will have it first built in the UK and fitted here too. So, if they knew, for instance, that a ship they are using is going to be in the UK a few weeks before it's going back to Venezuela, then they would have a compartment built here and fit it while it's here in the UK, then fly the welder out to make sure that it's fitted correctly and it's finished.

'So below the managers you need professionals and tradesmen to do these jobs, and below them the runners and fixers, who are keeping it ticking all over.

'The hierarchy rapidly starts to embrace a lot of people.'

Specialist marine engineers and underwater welders were approached by the Cartel. They were flown out to Colombia and Venezuela to cut secret compartments into the hulls of ships. One specialist contractor even helped build an unmanned submersible unit that could be bolted onto the outside of a ship or towed underwater.

The Analyst said, 'It's incredibly long-term planning. "If that ship comes in every two months, then we will bring 1,000 kilos every two months rather than take more risks when we bring in 200 kilos every week." That's the kinds of decisions they started to make. They realised that greater planning and sophistication leads to larger quantities, which in turn meant you're in a better position to negotiate with the Colombians.'

The Analyst found out that some members of the Cartel were buying for as low as £9,000 a kilo in Colombia and selling in Liverpool at £34,000 a kilo, wholesale. So that would generate a profit of £25,000. However, some dealers were selling it cheaper into the 'general market' – in Amsterdam or to cut-price distributors in Liverpool – at £17,000 a kilo. Even though this was selling at half price, it was done to boost high-volume sales or to reward preferred customers or to undermine rival independent dealers. The Cartel liked to push smaller wholesalers out by undercutting them. The reduced selling price meant lower profits: buying for £9,000 and selling for £17,000 left a profit of £8,000 per kilo, but such was the nature of the drug market.

The Analyst said, 'When it's sold at £34,000 a kilo, that's even before the adulteration process has started. Of course, you have got to pay people along the way. But you are quadrupling your profits without even being involved in distribution.

'In anticipation of the arrival of the cocaine, you will contact the wholesalers – the drugs equivalent of a firm like Costco – and say to them that the commodity is coming in and it will be batched in 200-kilo batches. You ask them: "Do you want to put your name to ten kilos of these?" So people do.

'What did happen was that some wholesalers were given those 200 kilos on tick and then given a month to pay it back. At

£34,000 a kilo you'd have to pay back £7.8 million. That came back in staged payments during the following month, which is easier than someone lumping a big load of cash back.'

The pressure on the wholesaler to pay back the debt was eased by the 'bashing' process, which took place below him in his distribution network. One kilo became three. If they sold the weaker kilos on at £34,000, there was a clear profit of £68,000 on their original kilo. Multiplied 200 times, the inundation of cash allowed Cartel wholesalers to draw down their debt quickly. What started as 80 per cent pure cocaine ended up at 20 per cent by the time it was cut and bagged into ounces.

CHAPTER 17

REPRISE

1990

LIKE ALL CRIMINAL organisations, the Cartel needed an expression of power at street level. No matter how big the godfathers became, they had to be seen to be 'kings of the patch'. Force and violence needed to be projected downwards to maintain the hierarchy to make sure that while they were busy abroad no one took liberties at home. Twenty years later, that power was put in the hands of teenage street gangs. But in the 1990s, when it all began, the job fell to nightclub security. In the long term, the practice turned out to be a lot less beneficial to the godfathers than they had expected.

But for now, their use to the Cartel was not only based on blood-curdling violence: door security firms were also excellent distribution systems. Their tentacles reached deep into the nightclubs in which the new drugs were sold: door security provided hundreds of ready-made point-of-sale outlets that were secure and highly mobile.

For many bouncers, the early days on the doors were a rite of passage into a previously unexplored universe of organised crime. In turn, the experience acted as a bridge between a closed, martial world and the Technicolor decadence of '90s Britain. The trip was all the more crazed because the rise of the foot soldier had collided with the rave phenomenon. Ecstasy culture was in full swing. Millions of ordinary people were getting off their heads. A drug-fuelled tectonic shift in attitudes and lifestyles was underway for an entire generation. Barriers were coming down and prejudices were melting away in the sweaty hedonism of underground clubs springing up all over the country. However, not all faces were smiley ones. In the background of the loved-up generation, sinister criminal forces were manoeuvring into position to take advantage of the shift in the new underworld order.

Almost overnight, the security firms that provided doormen to police the exploding club culture became the building blocks at the foot of the Cartel. Old-style mobs bonded by family ties and heavily involved in relational crime, whose power bases had been built on the gangland manors they ruled, were jostled out of position. The message was clear: 'You might control the importation, but we control the distribution: the Cartel needs us.'

Security firms rushed to fill the vacuum. As discrete concentrations of massive firepower, often consisting of 50 or more steroid-fuelled hard men, they were an unprecedented force to be reckoned with. Though doormen were essentially mercenaries who were hired by the week or month, their loyalty to the firm that employed them often transcended the normal rules of work. A unique, regimental-style group bonding was their secret weapon. The unbreakable relationships were based on comradeship and competition.

Another key factor was 'back-up'. Doormen often felt invincible because they knew they could call on each other to fight as a united front. A doorman would often fight (to the death on some occasions) in a dispute that didn't involve him directly or bring him any tangible gain. The reason was simple: because he knew that one day, he or his family might need to rely on his colleagues to fight for him in return.

The ascension of the security firm was also timed nicely to coincide with society's new gun culture. For the first time in criminal history, a large number of villains had access to cheap firearms flooding in from places like Eastern Europe. Tokarev handguns, AK-47s, MAC-10s and Mini ERO 9-mm sub-machine pistols became near standard-issue weapons on the street, to those in the know. They were often smuggled into the UK by a shady network of Balkan dealers dubbed the Croatian Connection.

Security firms quickly got armed to the teeth, adding to their deadly repertoire with weapons of choice such as machetes, samurai swords and meat cleavers. Opponents were given no quarter.

With the new underworld warriors came new battle rituals and tactics. The most bizarre was the 'call-out'. In response to a threat, usually a dispute with a rival firm, the security boss would 'call out' his bouncers in a massive show of force. Some call-outs were nothing more than pumped-up muscle-flexing on a grand scale, the gangland equivalent of a military parade. The security firm would march through clubland in a convoy of cars and 4 x 4 jeeps, before alighting en masse and snaking like an army through a no-man's-land of pubs and clubs, looking for confrontation. The message was clear: 'My troops are ready for battle if need be.' The Cartel bosses had not banked on such an axis of power, one that they suddenly realised could, if need be, overthrow them, in the underworld equivalent of a military coup. Unnaturally and against the grain, power was moving down the hierarchy from the apex to the base.

Other call-outs were sudden calls to arms, in which a gang of doormen were brought together quickly by pager and mobile phone for a sudden attack using their favourite tactic: overwhelming firepower. The old guard was caught off balance by this new phenomenon. Like special forces on a conventional battlefield, door teams were able to cut swathes through their enemy's ranks with ease.

Their battles for power and influence were bankrolled by drugs profits earned under the motto: 'Whoever controls the door on a club controls what goes into that club and what gets sold inside.' Basically, door teams were the new gatekeepers of the Ecstasy trade. If a dealer wanted to sell pills at a rave, he would more often than not have to give the doormen a piece of the action for the privilege.

This happened especially when confronted by the growing number of powerful black gangs that were emerging from Liverpool's Toxteth ghetto and Manchester's Moss Side. They were mean-looking mobs that were equally determined to extract their tribute from the gold-rush dance floors and would not allow anyone to stand in their way. For the first time, black villains started to form security companies and take doors from predominantly white gangs. The conflict led to racial tensions within the Cartel, the success of which hitherto had been built on an easy-going alliance between middle-aged white villains and young black drug dealers.

Some lower- and middle-ranking members of the Cartel recognised the new power of security firms and were determined to build bridges between the importation arms and distributor doormen. One such face included Stan Carnall, a haulage contractor who sometimes acted as a go-between between the bosses and major-league Colombian suppliers such as Lucio. Carnall was part of a Cartel cell run by Curtis Warren. Carnall had grown rich providing Warren's transport. He was also linked to nightclubs and door firms. The power and money that he made available to his doormen allowed some of them to leapfrog to the top of the league.

The downside was that doormen were hotheads who turned to violence for little or no reason. For instance, they often fought each other to win security contracts, and the violence disrupted drug sales and drew attention from the police. Cartel bosses who worked together – the whole reason for having a Cartel was to form a loose alliance of groups with shared interests and goals – found themselves dragged into disputes over wide-ranging differences because of the doormen they indulged. The murder rate was alarmingly high.

Shaun Smith refused to sell drugs in the nightclubs he worked in, but he started getting dragged into call-outs. He said, 'It was basically a show of force, a display of strength and weapons and how far you were prepared to go. Some people weren't getting paid, but they went along because you worked for a company or you were loyal to your mates. It signalled the start of a new era, and if you could control loads of doormen, then you could get a lot of power.

'Sometimes the call-outs were against gangsters who'd been involved in trouble in a club. But the packs of doormen would have no respect for reputation or position. They'd just dish it out. Up until then, these armed robbers and whatnot had ruled places, but that changed and it was a kind of land-grab and the old fellers lost.'

A nightclub called Quadrant Park in Bootle, one of the first superclubs to open up in Liverpool, became a big market for

Ecstasy tablets. More than 2,000-plus people enjoyed an all-night entertainment licence until 8 a.m. But the atmosphere was sometimes dark: people were robbed, several girls claimed that they were sexually assaulted or raped, and a young lad died there. However, for most, the crowd was a family, elevated to cult status. They went there, swallowed their Es, and forgot all about the real world outside the Quad's four walls.

Punters recalled some girls not being able to remember having sex, let alone who with or with how many men. Young men didn't dance: they ran on the spot and gurned their faces in ecstasy. Some remembered urinating in their pants. Teams of street thieves known as 'have-offs' roamed the dance floor stealing expensive coats. The heat and sweat made wearing breathable Gore-tex Berghaus jackets practical and fashionable: a trend that would stay with Liverpool's street gangs for 20 years. Only the bright colours would change. By 2005, teenagers wore nothing but black. But back in the early 1990s, these were the consumers who would pay for the Cartel's next big expansion. With this in mind, the drug dealers were forced to bring the doormen under the umbrella. They became part of the networks, their entry a shrewd political move to keep control.

CHAPTER 18

DANCE

1991

BY 1991, THE Cartel was raking in hundreds of millions in windfall profits from dance drugs, cocaine and the old staples of heroin and cannabis. The big question was where to invest the money. The answer was staring them in the face: Britain's new and burgeoning underclass.

Despite the pockets of synthetic prosperity in the local economy that were helping to boost the Cartel, the wider picture was bleak. In 1991, the British economy as a whole slumped into recession, having shrunk by nearly 4 per cent in the previous quarter. The early 1990s recession officially became the longest in Britain since the Great Depression some 60 years earlier. Unemployment in Britain rose from 1,600,000 to nearly 3,000,000 between April 1990 and February 1993. The unforeseen consequences were devastating. A second generation found themselves jobless. With the trade unions broken, working-class communities found themselves defenceless, even more vulnerable than they had been a decade earlier. A new underclass was born, cut off from the rest of society. For the first time, law-abiding citizens who would have never thought of dealing drugs got involved. As disaster capitalists, the Cartel saw another opportunity. The Cartel was only too happy to fund and franchise these start-ups in the poorest communities, a kind of underworld *Dragons' Den*. Affiliated drug gangs began to spread out across suburbia and further afield into towns and villages.

THE CARTEL

In 1990, a groundworks firm owned by a wide-boy builder called Frank Smith collapsed during the property slump. Frank lost all of his money and his health declined. In desperation, he decided to go into the drug-dealing business.

At first, Frank started growing skunk cannabis in his house in Thatto Heath, St Helens, with his mates. His punters included lads from the Wirral with loose connections to the Cartel. After a tip-off that his house was about to be raided, Frank joined thousands of jobless grafters and underclass entrepreneurs in the 1990s black economy of choice. He got into smuggling tobacco from the continent.

But the foot crossings to Calais were tedious and often unprofitable. During the long coach rides and night-time ferry crossings, he started to read up on how to make synthetic drugs, such as speed and MDMA. What resulted was a kind of narcotics version of *The Full Monty*. But instead of becoming strippers, the hapless doleites became industrial manufacturers of amphetamines. The venture started off as a kind of amateurish chemistry set, a comedic cottage industry. When the Cartel muscled in, it ended in a nightmare for everyone involved.

Meanwhile in 1991, Kaiser and Scarface landed several big loads and grew richer. Keen to expand further, they returned to Liverpool to check out the burgeoning rave scene, with a view to playing the market.

Poncho said, 'Bars were opening at a fast rate. The criminal element seemed to rise. There was a crossover between the legit business and the drugs side like I'd never seen.

'Scarface and Kaiser came back. They got loved up in the whole acid house thing. They started seeing new birds, building new relationships with other underworld people. In the end, like all the other villains, they bought a nightclub.'

On returning to the UK for a break from Amsterdam, Poncho realised that it was now just as profitable to sell cocaine by the gram in the UK as it was to smuggle it by the kilo across borders. The sheer number of new consumers had flipped the market: well, if you were a middle-ranking 'worker' anyway. Poncho wanted to run his own operation. Rave culture had injected cocaine into consumer culture. His younger brother, a business student called Hector, had set up a discreet 'round' delivering gram wraps to posh girls, footballers and glamour models in the north-west.

Hector said, 'I started off by buying an ounce and giving each of the lads who sold for me seven grams each, which they'd sell on for £100 each. Then it suddenly mushroomed because cocaine went mainstream. Acid house brought drug culture to middle-class people and they wanted Class A's – and they had lots of money.

'The upshot was that I got used to partying and shagging. I was making £3,000 a week in between snorting and fucking the girls I was selling to outside in the car.

'Then we started selling to people all over the country – all we had to do was meet them at service stations in Knutsford, Sandbach and Keele. I remember driving back from Birmingham with 26 ounces of coke in the boot and £30,000 in cash. But I was more interested in getting back to a bar called Kirklands for last orders. When you're grafting, you have a sixth sense that you're not going to get caught: it felt comfortable even though I was doing 130 mph on the motorway.'

The combined effect of dance and the second recession saw the crossover between Class A drugs and a greater number of working-class people who wouldn't have previously been involved with them. The Cartel's organisation got more complex. For the first time, the police encountered crime groups with 100 people involved in distribution alone.

Demarcation between jobs and responsibilities became more defined. The Cartel appointed specific negotiators and transport managers in the UK.

The Analyst said, 'There was an incident where someone flew out to South Africa, so we knew that they were expanding. They developed protocols such as "green copy", which is the paperwork relating to a police raid: that would be an insurance policy to prove that the police had intercepted a load. So if you'd taken a consignment on credit and it got confiscated by police, then if you could show the bosses the "green copy" then you had a good excuse. Business got rationalised.

'They started to learn from mistakes. For instance, if a load went down, there was a steward's inquiry into what happened and what weaknesses there were in the organisation. It was a second criminal's gold rush, in which they were clamouring to make their fortune in a very lucrative market, but at the same time they wanted to manage the risks.'

As the Analyst looked on, he realised that in some ways the police were struggling to catch up. The drugs squad was still insular to the force and had few powers outside Merseyside, never mind abroad. The theory was that the Regional Crime Squad would pick up villains who went outside the city. The traditional methods relied on reactive policing, which was all about 'working the clues'. Officers were stuck in a time warp in which crimes had to have a deposition site with evidence that could be followed through with an evidential investigation.

The Analyst said, 'It was a one-dimensional approach as opposed to the multi-dimensional approach we have today. So we had a situation by the end of the 1980s where officers would have a choice. Do they investigate the armed robbery, the tie-up, the aggravated burglary? Or do they investigate the travelling networks? It was almost "spin a coin" as to which was causing the most harm. Of course they would go after the aggravated burglaries because there was an immediate, tangible threat, but there was this firestorm that the travelling networks were causing.

'The dealers were making associations in obscure places like Whitehaven in Cumbria and then sending drugs up there to sell in towns. They were making hostile takeovers in all different parts of the country. And we were watching this, thinking: "What is going to be our response? We've got to get it right."'

CHAPTER 19

CURTIS

1992

BUT ALL WAS not lost. *BANG!* Door goes in. The dreaded 'Knock' – the term used by Customs and Excise for a raid. In early 1992, the authorities struck the first major blow against the Cartel. Curtis Warren and 27 other members of his outfit were arrested in connection with a 1,000-kilo shipment of cocaine. His de facto deputy and preferred distributor Colin 'King Cocaine' Smith was also captured. For the first time in a decade, the authorities had a chance to destroy the Cartel once and for all.

But all was not won either. By now, the Cartel, if not Warren's own bit of it, was operating a terrorist-style cell system. If one cell got taken out, theoretically the others could keep on going. One member of the Cartel had copied the idea from the IRA. The gangster was effectively Warren's boss – or at least allowed him to operate in Liverpool in return for old-fashioned-style tribute. The secretive villain took a share of the profits in return for strategic protection of Warren's cell within the Cartel. It was known that this man had close links with Dublin gangsters and the IRA.

In Amsterdam, Kaiser and Scarface were living proof that the cell system worked. They had been doing 1,000-kilo loads long before Curtis Warren, and carried on doing them long after. They have never been caught.

Poncho said, 'Curtis would not have got the leap into the big time if it wasn't for those two. When Curtis got nicked in 1992, the police and Customs found photographs of Curtis together with Kaiser and Scarface at a boxing match in Los Angeles. They were always flying off round the world, trying to outdo each other. The police showed Curtis the picture and said to Curtis: "We know these two are European overlords, but we don't know who they are. Tell us." They were trying to get Curtis to grass on Kaiser and Scarface. Of course, he didn't – he was staunch. But the point was that the police and Customs knew there were people even higher than Curtis and they wanted them.

'They knew that the window was only going to open for a few months, that they had a limited amount of time to bust everyone before the barriers went up and everyone outside Curtis's crew laid low.

'They had heard about Scarface and Kaiser and had vague descriptions but had never ID'd them properly. The police actually thought they were from Holland or Spain: they didn't even realise they were British. That's how below-the-radar Kaiser and Scarface had become.'

Kaiser and Scarface had learned three basic lessons to stay ahead of the law.

1. Stay away from the Cartel's HQ in Liverpool.
2. Deal drugs remotely.
3. Do what you say. If you say that you're not going to be hands-on, don't go near the gear. If you say that you're going to stay straight, don't party. If you say that you're not going to show out, do exactly that. Stay low-key.

Curtis Warren's problem was that he hadn't practised what he preached. Curtis told his underlings that he never showed out. But he could be irrational and contradictory, according to Poncho. He refused to party, telling the lads that he was saving his money. He refused to buy new clothes, claiming he was cautious of 'showing out' by being flash. He hung around outside the International Cafe in tracksuits and Lacoste polo shirts. But by the same token, he then kept drawing attention to himself by driving around Toxteth in high-powered cars with visiting drugs dignitaries from various countries.

Poncho said, 'To us, Curtis was an accident waiting to happen.

Scarface and Kaiser even regretted introducing him to Lucio, as Curtis getting nicked brought heat onto the Cali Cartel. Mario Halley got nicked.

'But in fairness to the Colombians, they soon adapted and restructured, and the gear kept coming – and no one else got arrested from their side.'

As Curtis Warren was entering jail on remand, Dylan Porter was coming out after serving three years for the shotgun. A reformed criminal, he vowed to stop dealing drugs. He set up a shed-building company. The hours were long, the graft hard and the general public were finicky about their back gardens. There were green shoots in the economy but not to the extent that planting concrete posts would earn Dylan the £3,000 a day he was used to: his wages from drug dealing before he went inside.

In Holland, Scarface went to Antwerp to buy jewellery. On Savile Row, he bought racks of suits after flying into Biggin Hill private airport for the day. A small fortune was blown on solid platinum watches, rings and bracelets in Paris. At one point he offered £15 million to buy a private jet. But he settled on buying a cheaper share in a used Gulfstream jet.

It was just as well. Alarmed by the arrest of Curtis Warren, in July 1992 Dutch police set up a specialist unit to investigate British criminals. To the Dutch, all English were Brits and they had not yet learned to differentiate between the Scousers and the rest. But within months they had identified 150 British drug dealers, the majority of them linked to the Cartel. The detail was uncannily accurate. A secret report said that the majority operated in the local market and were reasonably professional. Though they couldn't identify Scarface and Kaiser by name, the report stated that they were involved in the large-scale trafficking of cocaine, LSD and E to the UK, Scandinavia and Australia – and even the US. While the Dutch controlled hashish from Cyprus, the Cartel controlled hash to the UK. The Dutch police also identified several currency exchanges that had washed tens of millions of the Cartel's money. Scarface and Kaiser began to feel the heat. Their Spidey senses began to tingle danger.

Poncho: 'It was time to get off – we just knew it. There was something in the air in Amsterdam; you could tell that Curtis getting arrested had changed the game, ever so slightly. And it was no longer in our favour.

'I'd come back to Liverpool to sell cocaine with my brother, so I was a bit insulated in that sense, in that I wasn't on offer in Dam Square. Scarface and Kaiser were a bit higher risk: they had bought a nightclub in Liverpool but were still going back and forth to Amsterdam. But they soon realised it was now time to pull out of the Dam altogether.

'Fortunately, they had started hanging around with celebrities and agreed to act as security. In Holland, they took care of Michael Hutchence from INXS. So they'd made a few contacts in the music business, and in Hollywood, New York, Miami: places like that. So they picked up and then they went to the States – they'd got some good links over there.

'In New York, Scarface was protecting rap stars such as Naughty by Nature and the acts off *Yo! MTV Raps.*'

Poncho added, 'They didn't really need the money. It was just a bit of fun, which fitted into their globetrotting. They knew they'd get nicked like Curtis if they kept going to Holland, so that was that. It kept them out of the Dam until things blew over.

'They were big fellers with loads of cash, so stars took to them. The stars knew they didn't want anything, so they relaxed. Then they worked with Alice Cooper and Danny DeVito. Scarface and Kaiser were clean drugs-wise, but they partied with the rock bands. Scarface used to say to them: "Take my jet." And some of the rock stars would be snorting on his private Gulfstream.'

Back down to earth in Liverpool, the Cartel decided to invest some of its profits in bricks and mortar. Money laundering came into its own. In 1992, Liverpool Polytechnic was transformed into John Moores University by an act of Parliament. Tens of thousands more students flooded into the city. The Cartel put up much of the money to build many more student flats than would be required. Colin Smith was on remand, but later he set up a property company on a suburban street. The assets included several million pounds' worth of student properties.

The Cartel recruited legitimate investment managers who, according to police, 'simply ran a parallel industry'. In turn, the Cartel bosses began to look and act like corporate executives.

One report compared the Cartel to terrorists because they used the same 'techniques in transnational crime'. The senior figures were described as 'rationally economic' men who used extreme violence in pursuit of goals and, of course, secrecy to defy laws. The Cartel employed a dodgy accountant who'd once worked for a big chain of bookmakers. He taught the Cartel to use a money-laundering technique known as 'starbursts'. A deposit of dirty money was put into a bank account using a shell company. Under complicated standing instructions, the bank was told to wire small portions at random into accounts all over the world. Tracking it down over multiple jurisdictions was very hard. While Curtis Warren languished in jail, his lackeys got busy starbursting a portion of the £87 million that he had made on a 1,000-kilo consignment smuggled two years earlier, in 1991. Investigators missed the boat trying to recover the money, and once it was gone, they spent the next 17 years trying to track it down.

But as the profits of the Cartel grew, they could no longer rely on offshore havens, which could only wash money in small amounts. They got into a scheme known as 'smurfing'. This method involved the introduction of small but numerous cash deposits into European economies. The Cartel realised that it was a myth that money launderers used city states and offshore havens. It was too complicated and time-consuming. The most efficient places to hide money were big countries: the US, Italy, Switzerland, Russia and Austria. They were proved right – two-thirds of all money laundering is now concentrated in just 20, mostly First World countries, according to Donato Masciandaro's 2004 book *Global Financial Crime*.

The Analyst was part of a new generation of coppers who understood the drugs market. They'd served their time on the streets when drugs were prevalent. He noticed that criminals were stealing a march on law enforcement. The sheer numbers of drug criminals seemed overwhelming. There was a gold rush and everyone was getting involved because it was lucrative.

But from a policing perspective, the enforcement style wasn't really switched on to the new level of criminality. The numbers of Regional Crime Squads covering the region weren't sufficient. Traditional police officers preferred to target burglars over drug dealers because they saw an imminent threat with the burglars. Meanwhile, the firestorm that had started around drug profits edged closer.

The Analyst said, 'It was a perfect storm: the club scene

combined with providers to a different market. Suddenly drug dealers had numerous opportunities to start distribution. If you were a drug dealer, you had several options. Do you do E's into the clubs? Do you do heroin back to the inner cities? Or do you bring cocaine in and get the average member of the middle class involved: the type of person who's going out into the city centre for an average night out with a line of coke. You can see it anywhere now: people who go into the bars and are using cocaine recreationally to enhance the evening. But that started in the early 1990s. Or do you trade off amphetamines, which became popular around the time of E's as another buzz, another hit.'

In St Helens, unemployed builder and failed drug dealer turned tobacco smuggler Frank Smith saw a gap in the market. Speed was a poor man's Ecstasy, but if it could be made on an industrial scale the potential was enormous. Clubbers in the suburbs were already getting bored with the high cost of designer drugs. 'Stack 'em high, sell 'em cheap' was Frank's motto. He continued his research into chemistry and rooted out contacts who could help him. On the supply side, the Cartel was looking to diversify. They started talking.

The Analyst said, 'You started to see a number of different markets with a number of sophisticated criminals who wanted to be a jack of all trades. They wanted to build relationships with the distribution networks involving different people in different environments who could supply a number of different commodities. In that sense, Liverpool criminals were ahead of the game.

'By the early '90s, our Liverpool criminals had been established for 20 years: the travelling networks abroad and over here had been established back in the 1970s. They were ahead of the game because they had been involved in building working relationships across Europe.

'For instance, prison was important. When they had been caught and gone into prison in Holland or Germany or wherever, they continued their education and built relationships with people in prison in Spain and Holland and right the way across the continent.

'When you get to the '90s, when there was a need to import to meet demand, the Liverpool criminals had already got ahead of the game from what they were doing during the ten or fifteen years of growth, even at a low level. Even before that, people were coming from all over to Liverpool to buy at street level.'

At street level, the heady cocktail of super profits, violence and competition to join the Cartel warped the club scene. The Quad nightclub closed down, but other violence-prone nightspots opened up one after another. One club was a typical example of a venue of its time with links to organised crime. It had had a chequered history. Not long after opening, the club was shut down after serious drug and violence problems. When it reopened in 1992, the level of threat was such that only doormen with serious martial-arts training could cope. They were highly paid. The doormen involved later ran security at the world-famous Cream nightclub.

The market for drugs inside the club was so lucrative that two drug dealers from Toxteth started turning up in BMWs and Porches, trying to intimidate the door staff. The plan was to be deliberately provocative by hitting girls and throwing money around, to draw the door staff into a war.

Like most doormen, the security preferred one-on-one straighteners to settle disputes. They won and considered the matter settled fairly. But the drug dealers claimed they'd been publicly humiliated. A short while later they came back – armed with an Uzi sub-machine gun. They fired it at the doormen at point-blank range. They ran right up to the entrance and peppered the door with bullets. No one was injured, but the use of guns was emblematic: they were becoming common.

The clubs were gold mines for the dealers who sold the tablets inside. At other superclubs, some doormen were making thousands of pounds a week by controlling the supply. There were two ways of operating. One was for the head doormen to buy the tablets themselves in bulk and hire their own dealers on a wage to sell for them inside. The doormen then stopped other rogue dealers from getting inside, thereby creating a monopoly.

The other method involved extracting a tax from existing drug dealers. The head doorman cut a deal with an established 'team' of dealers and runners. The percentage from each tablet they sold varied between 25 and 50 per cent. Dealers who weren't part of the set-up were beaten up if they were caught selling inside the club. Their drugs were often confiscated and then recycled back into the club: handed to the 'authorised' drug dealers to sell. The models were a win–win situation for the doormen. Many grew very rich. One club owner estimated that 'one in ten' of the doormen he employed became millionaires as a result of the E trade.

The traffic was on a massive scale. Almost everyone in certain clubs was on E's or similar drugs. Thousands of tablets were being 'knocked out'. In some places, if disapproving, old-style doormen came on heavy to the punters and dealers, they'd get told off by the owner.

A private detective who was employed by a nightclub chain to spy on corrupt doormen reported that 'law-abiding' nightclub workers were soon 'overwhelmed' by the drugs trade. Only one in ten bags of Ecstasy tablets was confiscated, he reported. Even those that were taken from ravers were resold by corrupt doormen. He told how one punter was caught with seven hundred tablets hidden in a jacket. Instead of calling the police, the head of security passed the drugs on to tame dealers. He described the supply as limitless and said that there was no incentive for doormen not to become complicit with the drug dealers.

The report stated: 'The clients' contractor pays head doormen £500 a week, which all of the lads considered to be a good wage. They can make that in one night at the weekend.'

The illegality led to other serious breaches. At one club, doormen were observed exploiting vulnerable young women. They regularly had sex with women high on drugs inside and outside the premises and then went straight back to work.

Meanwhile, Fred the Rat decided that he was going to relocate to Spain. By now, he was fabulously wealthy. Estimates put his fortune at between £50 and £100 million. But the gang wars, the door squabbles and Curtis Warren's arrest had given him the jitters. He'd never been caught for drugs. Fred had accumulated a string of legitimate enterprises, including several construction-related businesses, several pubs and nightclubs, a huge number of properties and a formidable landbank (an investment used by property speculators in which land is stored up in trusts). It was time to get out while the going was good.

CHAPTER 20

RETURN

1993

SCARFACE AND KAISER continued their rock 'n' roll lifestyle in exile for around a year. When they were convinced that the heat from Curtis Warren's arrest had died down, they slipped back into Amsterdam once again. It was time to get down to business. Another 1,000-kilo load was organised from South America. The deal went off smoothly. But they noticed an undercurrent of violence sweeping through the Dutch capital. It had lost its innocence.

Poncho said, 'The scene had definitely toughened up. There was an edginess in the air now. Gone was the lazy, hazy way of doing things, of getting stoned, sunbathing or nipping into the cat house in the afternoon. The whole Liverpool firm was massive now. It was up and running at full speed now, and it was serious. There was definitely more internal competition.'

The world that Scarface and Kaiser inhabited became increasingly brutal, and though they might not have liked it, they were swept up in the tide of violence. Scarface was linked to the murder of a drug dealer who had been thrown out the window of a block of flats during a party, and he was also rumoured to have been involved in the deaths of three other men, though he was never convicted of any of the crimes.

Unlike many gangsters, Scarface and Kaiser did not crave status through violence, according to Poncho. In the early 1990s, Poncho claimed that many 'plastic criminals' – villains who pretended to be tough but weren't – got involved in the Cartel. He said that 'they were charged off cocaine and steroids'. The rage led to gang wars such as the dispute between a doorman called Stephen Clarke and a rival family.

Poncho said, 'The kind of violence that was going on between doormen back in Liverpool was sporadic and seemed to have no goal in sight, whereas the violence that Scarface and Kaiser got involved in was more often than not planned and the outcome was always to improve business.'

Lucio and Scarface grew closer. They even looked similar and were often mistaken for twins. One time Lucio asked Scarface and his Scousers to collect a debt from a fellow South American who was flying into Holland from the US with 'mad money'. The cash, reputedly several million dollars, had been stolen from Lucio a few months before. The contract was a sign of how close they were – and how powerful the Cartel were in the eyes of the Colombians.

Scarface made a call to Liverpool and recruited a 'team' to carry out the raid. But in the end, the job turned out to be so sensitive that Scarface and Kaiser agreed to go on the raid themselves. They realised that failure could sour their relationship with Lucio. They stormed the South American safehouse wearing balaclavas and sporting assault rifles.

Little did they know that the US Drug Enforcement Administration had followed the shady South American from the US. The DEA had been stepping up operations in Amsterdam to combat Ecstasy. The details of what happened next are unclear. However, later Scarface was arrested. He was released amid claim and counterclaim that the raid had blown an undercover US operation.

By 1993, the senior Cartel strategists realised that supply of drugs was outstripping demand. The growth of Ecstasy had levelled off. For a couple of years, the Cartel's lower-rung salesmen had been pushing out into the countryside, trying to stimulate sales and set up with people like unemployed builder Frank Smith. But the process was painfully slow as it still relied on out-of-town dealers driving to Liverpool once or twice a week to stock up on supplies. Decisions were made: now the Liverpool dealers would take the business to them. The franchise system was set up. Cartel dealers would be sent out to live in Wales,

Hull, Cumbria, Cheshire and Lancashire to settle in communities. Nothing would be left to chance: local dealers wouldn't have to travel to Merseyside. They would be supplied from a local hub – and if they didn't want drugs then they would be forced on them. The Analyst noticed the change.

The Analyst said, 'The Liverpool criminal was thinking: "Do we really need someone coming to Liverpool to buy a couple of ounces? Isn't it easier if we go out and distribute six ounces a day as opposed to waiting for someone to buy one ounce every week?"

'So they were going out to the outlying areas, to places like Cumbria and Yorkshire. You look at Cumbria and think there's no drugs industry there. But the Scousers have been out there and set one up because they've realised people want drugs.

'So, as opposed to someone from Whitehaven coming down on a Friday to stock up on what they wanted to sell over the weekend, the idea was that they would have it there ready to go and they would set up a distribution network that ran itself.

'So they were starting to franchise and to organise. They would settle there and build the relationships. Once they had got it up and running, someone local would take it over because they had the local knowledge of criminals and users, and then our Merseyside criminal can just worry about the distribution network, so they were effectively franchising the local sales out.

'It's like McDonald's. The Merseyside criminal comes in, teaches them their trade and then he goes away to maintain the supply chain.'

The Analyst noticed how the Cartel was adapting ready-made travelling networks to sell drugs. For instance, Dorset police would report that a Liverpool gang were committing burglaries locally. The network remained, but the crimes changed.

The Analyst said, 'It goes back to how the city started. For instance, building a motorway network around Kirkby: you've got the M57, M58, M62 and the M6 on the doorstep of Kirkby. So do the Kirkby criminals come into Liverpool to commit crime in a poor and troubled city? Or just as quickly do they travel out to more lucrative opportunities anywhere in the country?

'They knew that the law enforcement wasn't as switched on. So they could travel to a rural shire district and be involved in burglaries there, where the risk of being caught was minimal and the pickings were better.

'But the shrewder individuals used the money that they made to step up into the drugs trade. But not everyone involved in the chain became a drugs dealer. There were people involved in these travelling networks such as hauliers, transport companies, taxi firms – that type of industry – so people were making the money there.

'In some ways we are blighted by the travelling Scouser.'

As the parochial networks spread out across the UK, their tentacles began to link up with the bigger, international lines coming in from Holland, France and Spain. All the time, the networks were becoming more efficient and less visible, meeting away on farms in Shropshire, trawler boats in Cornwall and roll-on, roll-off ferries in the north-east.

The Analyst said, 'There's almost that acceptance, more historically than currently, that the criminal from Liverpool gets out there because they've got that reputation. If you ask me why a drugs cartel was established here, with an international presence, then it's because we're probably 15 years ahead.

'When the drugs trade started to gather momentum and people started to get involved, the Merseyside criminal could draw on previous experience and say, "We've got the makings of the networks in place already."

'For instance, if they'd have gone out into Holland and robbed a jewellery shop and then got the stuff back over here, then they got it back somehow or other – effectively they had established a distribution network which was then exploited for drugs.

'It needs to become more sophisticated, but the principles are in place already. Being ambitious and up-front as they are in going about their business, they exploited the opportunities and were ahead of their colleagues.

'They then gave the product to their colleagues in other UK cities, so it stopped them from having to gain the knowledge. If you were from Newcastle or Birmingham, it was easier if you took a 200-kilo batch off the Liverpool criminals, because it was easier than setting up a distribution network and an importation network yourself. Why bother when every two weeks you could have the 200 kilos from the Scousers?'

CHAPTER 21

THE SEQUEL

1993

SUDDENLY THE REGIONAL Crime Squads were rallied to stop the process of the Cartel spreading across the UK. On one occasion, the Cartel was sending 200 kilos to Birmingham every month. Sometimes, it was sent as one batch. On other occasions, it was split into batches of between two and twenty kilos, and ferried on a train by a fleet of backpackers. Even heavyweight dealers from other parts of the country felt comfortable dealing with the Cartel, because the networks were already established. In London, the Turkish Connection felt so confident that it virtually stopped mass distributing heroin to anyone who wasn't part of the Cartel. All of its UK heroin was sent straight up to Liverpool, to gangsters like John Haase, and in smaller amounts to the Banker. John Haase was given virtual monopoly rights on the Turks' heroin. He then distributed the drugs to London, Scotland and elsewhere. What was strange was that the godfathers from these cities were happy to go along with the arrangement.

The Analyst said, 'If you're in London or Glasgow, why do you have to reinvent the wheel? You might not make as much money, but there's enough for everyone, and you share the risks. You're sitting there on your patch, and you've seen it become more organised over the years with the Liverpool criminals, with a greater propensity to travel. So it's a safe bet for you. From that perspective, the arrangement then seems to become logical.

'With regard to the Liverpool drug dealers, their life experiences of being in prison and meeting people from across the region inside jail helped in this respect, some of them being troublemakers who were shipped out of Liverpool prison to others around the country. It helped them. Or if they were arrested in a different city, they turned it into an opportunity. They were suddenly meeting people from different criminal groups and using it to enhance their local knowledge in that area, and experience, by learning from those people.

'They are effectively travelling to prison-based universities – universities of life. So, the Scousers spend their time in Strangeways learning from Manchester criminals. If they are in Haverigg, they are learning about Cumbria and so on.'

Some of the senior Cartel members began to behave like businessmen. The Banker gave £100,000 to start a community project for children. The donation had started out as an investment in a property-development scheme with a well-known former gangster, but it overran and suffered business problems. When the former gangster shelved the idea and said that he now wanted to turn it into a community project, the Banker agreed and waived the loan, saying that if it was going to a good cause then that was fair enough. Later the building became a successful resource for helping children from poor backgrounds. But other Cartel members were taken aback by the Banker's avarice. One said: 'The Banker was sick with money, he was that tight. He was fucking scared to lose it. Making money gives him a buzz every day. However, he's not a clown, and people love him even though he's someone who cannot be messed with. That's because he's made a lot of people rich as well.'

The rapid advance of the Cartel caught a lot of traditional gangsters off guard. A few refused to join on the grounds that dealing drugs was a taboo. For some, like doorman Shaun Smith, the culture clash would set him on a course that would nearly cost him his life, leading him to spend years involved in a vicious struggle with his enemies and, eventually, to a long prison sentence. For others, like the softly spoken hard man Paul Burly, staying independent of the Cartel and its tentacles would mean a life of careful politicking combined with extreme measures. Paul was a traditional street-fighter, a kind of underworld maverick who stuck by the old-fashioned code of respect. That code was, as far as Paul was concerned, set in stone. It was as if he drew a red circle around him, and anyone trespassing into that circle was expected to adhere to his way of life. However, Paul's bugbear – and Achilles heel – was bullies. He hated bullies, and whenever he could, he stood up to them. Once his reputation had been established, many ordinary people whose lives and businesses had been affected by intimidation approached him for protection, which he offered freely and without strings. Paul had started out as a general labourer, whose life in those days was dominated by casual labour: literally fighting for work with other job-hungry family providers on what was known as 'the Stand'. There were many such stands dotted around the docklands of Liverpool. He was known as a 'tough little bastard' and eventually ended up running some of the roughest pubs and clubs in Liverpool for years without taking liberties.

Although Paul had run-ins with Cartel founder Fred the Rat in the mid 1970s, he'd always left the door open for compromise so that an escape route could be followed if the heat of their disagreements ever burst into flames. It was due to those ever-open escapes that his conflicts were never seen as bludgeoning. His run-ins with Fred had shown the Rat that things could have been worse, which caused him to back away from full-fronted retaliation. Paul's policy was simple: to react ruthlessly if and when he felt intimidated by anyone, especially drug dealers . . . but an escape route was always open. On one occasion, he'd been caught in a fist fight with a certain Cartel family during which two of them had been severely hurt, but, knowing of their ways, he had organised some friends to come and help out. The tactic of that Cartel family was to storm a place, which they did, only to find it full of Paul's friends. As the door closed behind them, the sounds of their cars being destroyed outside could be plainly heard within the walls of that club, amplified by microphones that had been strategically placed in the street. The following clatter of their weapons sounded like an ovation of surrender as the floor became littered. He had won without a cut or bruise to anyone; they had chosen the door of capitulation. He was happy at that, for his friends had not had to put themselves in any more danger than they already had, and his enemies merely had to let the acid of humiliation dissipate.

When he was on the border of easy retirement in the early 1990s, Paul was faced with a dilemma. He received an anonymous threat written on a piece of paper. The message stated that his son was going to be killed. Paul didn't know the exact reason why. Was it because he had refused to join the Cartel? Or was it because he'd upset someone else in an unrelated feud? If so, which bloody feud had it been? Crime author Peter Stockley has written about the events that followed in his book *Extenuating Circumstances*.

His first reaction was to lash out at the enemies who were immediately around him. He put one man in hospital before deciding that he couldn't have written the letter, because he couldn't read or write. Paul then spent a lot of time and effort systematically assessing the threats against him. He thought about all of the people he had upset. He had served two prison sentences, but he concluded that the threat must have come from someone he had upset outside prison, and much more recently. After a brainstorming session with his underworld and twilight pals, he narrowed it down to three suspects with whom he had gone head to head since last coming out of jail. What became clear was that all three suspects were taxmen linked heavily to the drugs trade and the Rat's Cartel. The dilemma Paul faced was what to do about it.

Had the Rat allowed their upsets to fester while waiting for new beasts – beasts with no fear of firebrands such as Paul – to come along? The Cartel's new power base were doormen knee-deep in the nightclub E trade. Tony Sinnott was a machete-wielding hotheaded football fan who had blown up his TV set with a shotgun after England lost a game. He was forever involved in the many wars with rival door firms and always carried a knife with a straight edge for a smooth scar and a jagged one to make the mark look ugly. Paul had once disarmed and beaten up one of Sinnott's gang after he had tried to stab a customer at a pub where Paul ran the doors. It was hardly a massive thing, but to Sinnott it was an affront to the fearful power base that he had established. He then threatened to tie Paul up and rob him. Paul later waylaid Sinnott at a petrol station and grabbed him by the throat, lifting him off his feet. With the words: 'Never come near mine to rob me, otherwise I'll personally stick your knives up your arse and rip your innards to bits!' Paul felt the job was done. It was hardly a life-threatening thing and nobody had witnessed it, but Sinnott was the type of person to hold a grudge and threaten the easier target, Paul's son.

George Bromley was one of the new generation of 'taxmen'

who robbed non-Cartel-affiliated drug dealers. Paul had merely warned Bromley's brother over a row in a pub. The man had been threatening the bar staff and used his taxman brother's name as back-up. When George objected, Paul merely smiled in his face, saying: 'Lad, your enemies are ten times my number, don't double your problems by bringing me into your shitty world!' Only words, Paul recalled, as he and his friends reflected on that moment only to decide, unanimously, that Bromley was suspect number two.

Number three was voted in as Kevin Maguire, a nasty piece of work. He'd been a doorman at the Quadrant Park nightclub, where he'd honed his violent tactics. Maguire was hoping to leapfrog into the Cartel through hardcore violent acts, which they, especially the Filipino cartel who had recently hit the town, loved their enforcers to be capable of. Maguire was also taxing rival drug dealers with George Bromley. He was a formidable force whom few messed with. Maguire was known to be a bully. On one occasion, he kidnapped a police inspector's son and put him in the boot of his car. He was later jailed and claimed to have found God. One day, he picked on a used-car salesman and stole three cars from his forecourt. The car dealer had come to Paul Burly for help. Paul had humiliated Maguire merely by walking into his many known haunts with a cloth cash bag over his hand, demanding that Maguire get in touch. Mad Dog did so, thinking Paul to be looking for him with a gun. The cars were returned. Again, no blood had been spilled but face had been lost.

Burly now had the three possibilities in his sights: Maguire, Bromley and Sinnott – all psychopathic, all somewhat deranged and all had proven that they had no compunction about killing . . . even a kid if they felt like it. Paul started making plans.

Meanwhile, the underworld was booming, but the legit economy remained stagnant. Just under 40,000 people in Liverpool were still on unemployment benefits, representing 14.1 per cent of working-age people in the city compared with a national average of 7.8 per cent. Life on the streets was getting tougher, but there were glimmers of good news. By 1993, the Toxteth Triangle was ostensibly back under the control of the police, mainly because strategy, tactics and goals had all been changed – and the new policy was paying dividends. Drug dealing on Granby Street had been made *the* priority crime. On the ground, the Merseyside Police Toxteth Section had formed itself into Proactive Teams, each consisting of an inspector, a sergeant and 14 constables. Virtual round-the-clock cover was enforced. Between 8 a.m. and 2 a.m., drug dealers were relentlessly pursued, harassed and disrupted within the quarter-of-a-square-mile area of south Liverpool. The results were self-evident. In two months, the operation clocked up 106 stop and searches, 92 arrests and 74 detected crimes. The top brass liked the stats, but in the ranks there was a sense of gloom that was becoming hard to shift: a sense that it was already all too late.

The Analyst carried on regardless. He had moved on to a new position. He was able to study one of Curtis Warren's deputies up close, a notorious E supplier to nightclubs known as Johnny Phillips. Phillips's case was in a way symbolic of where the Cartel had reached.

The Analyst said, 'In 1993, I was the custody sergeant in Wavertree police station and Johnny Phillips came in. Phillips said that he was making a £100,000 a year, no tax. He was boasting, of course, but he was also explaining something important. There was an underlying message.

'He was talking about a change that had occurred – the message was that his form of criminality was now far removed from the street. He was almost describing himself in terms of a businessman, like a white-collar criminal, and that consequently he was not part of the world of a normal bobby.

'He said to me: "I will give you no aggression, nor cause you harm, because you don't affect my world. Uniformed officers are not a threat to me. You have got your job, and I've got mine."'

Phillips was very open about his activities to the Analyst, because he believed that a gulf had opened up between the Cartel and law enforcement. Phillips was almost saying that parts of the police no longer really mattered to the Cartel. The police spoke to him because it was a chance to gather intelligence – and to distract him from kicking off. The Analyst's conclusion was simple: the attitudes of organised criminals had changed completely.

Meanwhile, a uniquely violent incident gave the impression that the trouble had simply been displaced from the ghetto into mainstream society. On Christmas Eve 1993, in the State nightclub in Liverpool city centre, an altercation occurred between three punters and the doormen. Darren Delahunty and two friends threatened security. The doormen included experienced hands such as John Crokker and Paul Walsh, and all of them were well versed in dealing with mouthy hooligans. The upshot was a fight in which one man got his nose broken and another may well have been knocked out. All three troublemakers were ejected from the club. This was followed by the usual threats that the doormen were going to be shot. Threats were common on the doors and were usually dismissed as hot air; normally they were never carried out.

However, Darren Delahunty bore grudges. He returned to the State on the same night and could be seen acting very suspiciously outside. He was captured on CCTV trying to goad the doormen, in an attempt to lure them out of the entrance of the club and onto the street. After several failed attempts to engage his enemy, he pulled a gun out from under his top and let loose several shots at the doormen. In a few seconds, bouncers Paul Sergeant and Mick Naylor were lying on the floor. Sergeant was left fighting for his life. Mick Naylor had been shot once in the leg, the bullet passing out of his rear. Sergeant had been shot four times: once straight through the wrist, once straight through the knee and once each in the other leg and back. Miraculously, both doormen went on to make a full recovery.

Delahunty got 15 years in jail. However, the incident had far-reaching effects. The incident was to have wider notoriety than just in clubland: the CCTV footage of the shooting became a cult hit being passed around from person to person on VHS tapes. The story was shown on Sky News and made the papers. The images seemed to sum up the out-of-control atmosphere – and it seemed a portent for what was to come, a kind of propaganda video for the Cartel.

A clever DJ dubbed the soundtrack of the movie *Scarface* over the CCTV footage. Delahunty's voice is overdubbed with Al Pacino's. In the build-up, the haunting film score by Giorgio Moroder plays over scenes from the CCTV camera footage, which showed grainy shots of Liverpool on a winter's night. Before the shooting, Delahunty mimes the universal gangster mantra: 'Who put this thing together. Me: that's who. Who do I trust? Me.' Then he pulls out the gun. But it's the way he does it that's significant. He holds it with his right hand, cocked cockily to one side so that the gun handle is parallel to the floor. It is an iconic stance, for it would become the hallmark of the scallywag gunman of the next generation of Cartel *pistoleros*, copied by hundreds of other young lads who thought nothing of pulling out a gun on the spur of the moment. Just before he pulls his own gun out, Delahunty seems to say: 'Why don't you say hello to my little friend.' Then he fires off the rounds into the club door as the doormen battle to close it.

CHAPTER 22

KILLERS

1994

OLD-SCHOOL GANGSTER PAUL Burly continued to investigate three of the Cartel's most violent street enforcers. His method of intelligence gathering was crude but effective: 'swaps'. Every few weeks, he called together his most trusted friends who had been 'swapping' information about Tony Sinnott, Kevin Maguire and George Bromley. The scraps of intelligence enabled Paul to build up a picture of the lifestyles of the three men, particularly the parts of their lives they kept hidden. Paul was able to find who their enemies were and who they had robbed. He asked his friends to do more exchanges and then began to put his plans into operation. My enemy is your enemy. The basic premise was: feed their enemies with information that would further annoy them and send them proof of who had robbed them. Then he had similar-sized people use the methods of operation that those three used. Their MOs were not hard to duplicate; all one had to do was copy their mannerisms while hurting somebody who would bounce back with mean retaliation.

At the same time, Paul turned his own home into a labyrinthine fortress, a maze of corridors, some of which led to dead ends, others to exits. Paul lived at the centre of a large commercial building. The fortress contained several secret escape chutes. Every door had been deliberately made to squeak in order to alert him to intruders.

Paul soon learned that doorman Kevin 'Mad Dog' Maguire

had become an enforcer for a Cartel drug dealer. Maguire had been given the moniker 'Mad Dog' in honour of a particularly gruesome Northern Irish terrorist with whom he shared personality traits. With the Cartel's backing, Maguire felt confident enough to use extortion to win security contracts. His main strategy was called 'taking over a door': survival of the fittest in the cut-throat quasi-business environment of nightclub security. Put simply, it meant that one day a stronger company would oust a weaker one from a nightclub or pub using brute force, sometimes with the blessing of the venue's owner, sometimes not. The 'taking over' process often involved guns, knives, savage attacks, torture and, on occasion, murder. For Maguire and his allies, it was their bread and butter. Bullying was his stock-in-trade, the way in which he grew his business. It made Paul happy for, by now, Maguire had a list of enemies a mile long, which meant a lengthy list of potential allies for himself.

As Maguire expanded his business and the door wars grew more violent, he found himself mixing with a heavier class of villain: some allies, some enemies. George Bromley was a Bentley-driving gangster known as 'the Taxman'. Taxmen were the self-appointed duty collectors of the underworld, extracting tribute from drug dealers using torture. Bromley's modus operandi often involved bursting through the front door of a heroin trafficker's house with his three-man torture team. The targets were often independents, but sometimes rogue Cartel bosses used Bromley to attack rivals, or at least tacitly allowed him to do so, due to boardroom disputes and internal squabbles.

The target would often be stripped naked and tied up in front of his wife and children. Bromley's torture weapon of choice was the household steam iron. Why? Because every home has got one and steam irons do not need to be carried to and away from jobs, reducing the risk of being caught with an offensive weapon. In addition, steam irons were an extremely effective device for causing pain. In front of the terrified victim, Bromley would plug in the iron. His spine-chilling pay-off was: 'You have got until the iron warms up to tell me where you keep your money or drugs. If you don't, then I'm going to iron your bollocks off.' Bromley had no qualms about carrying out the threat and many victims who couldn't raise the money were burned. Other trademark methods of torture included stabbing victims up the anus, sexual abuse using a broomstick and shooting the calf muscles clean away from the bones of the men under his duress. Bromley made hundreds of thousands of pounds from taxing drug dealers.

Senior members of the Cartel were becoming worried by the antics of Bromley and his cronies. After all, it was their drug dealers whom Bromley was taxing, or at least some of them. It was their business that the out-of-control doormen were disrupting. A few Cartel members that had been hit were now being fed information of the identities of those who had hit them, now Paul's helpers were being fed inside information of certain people's movements. Paul soon learned of nearly all of Kevin Maguire's and Bromley's movements.

Maguire had turned into a full-time drug dealer. He had also become a born-again Christian. Later on, the church-going family man formed an alliance with Bromley, and then, along with his partner Nathan Jones, took up as a marauding taxman himself. They ensured that they didn't hit one another's intended victims. Their wider circle included Stephen Cole, a former Liverpool Football Club player turned security consultant. Another associate was Charlie Seiga, a safecracker and armed robber turned alleged contract killer. Though Seiga was not a Cartel drug dealer, police had wrongly linked him to a string of murders and accused him of carrying out assassinations for high-ranking traffickers. Though he was arrested and charged in connection with one high-profile gangland hit in particular, the police could not prove that he was a contract killer and the Crown Prosecution Service could not get a conviction at trial. Today he is a reformed character.

The door wars continued. One gang was known as the Wolf Pack. The firm was owned by a hard man called Stephen Clarke, a big operator and a very tough doorman. If club owners knew that their own door was weak and that doormen weren't throwing the troublemakers out, they often went to see operators such as the Wolf Pack to take over the door. Obviously, the existing team didn't like it, but their removal was carried out by force.

The culture of the door business was becoming more and more enemy-based. Nearly every firm treated competitors as enemy combatants to be destroyed at the first opportunity, their contracts gobbled up. Virtues such as extreme competitiveness, getting in there first and stealing the contract by force, were highly prized.

Then, after the admin was taken care of, the big pay-off was often selling drugs. Even though the divisions were internally destructive, several wings of the Cartel fuelled the door wars in a bid to sell more tablets and cocaine. They couldn't help themselves; it was easy money. The Cartel was often the ulterior motive behind a war.

It took many years for the police and the licensing industry to stamp out the door wars. Eventually authorities insisted that security firms had to have contracts with big brewery and leisure companies. In addition, the police began to inhibit drugs supply onto the dance floor. The resulting lack of big drug turnover, combined with a fall in the price of E tablets, meant there was less motivation for violence.

But for now, that kind of resolution was too many years into the future to worry about. By 1993, there were many doormen on major rave clubs making two grand a night selling tablets. Police found that convictions were hard to pin down. Evidence was near impossible to gather in the chaotic, close-knit world of loud music, laser shows and industrial-scale dry-ice machines. Costly, complex undercover investigations were set in motion. Nightclubs were raided and punters kept waiting for hours while their details were processed. Licences were withdrawn. Doors went in, Cartel bosses were nicked, seizures were made. But frustratingly, just before many of the cases came to court, witnesses mysteriously reneged on their evidence. Cartel drug dealers became experts at routinely perverting the course of justice by paying off witnesses. One Ecstasy dealer who'd been attacked by rival doormen was paid £40,000 to drop the charges.

In other cases, police got the wrong man. Former world champion kick boxer Alfie Lewis was convicted of supplying E at the Cream nightclub after 30 undercover police stings. But after three trials, the case eventually fell apart and he was released. Police had to settle for lower-rung doorman Amir Khorasani, who got seven years.

As the threat of conviction fell away, the bonds between the doors and the dealers strengthened. Drugs flowed into a club down a strictly controlled chain of command, just like a very efficient business. Some doormen formed mini-syndicates and started buying 50,000 tablets at a time in Holland for one pound each. The retail price was ten pounds each. Soon the doormen were eclipsing the bar take in the clubs that they worked on in terms of turnover. If they were lucky enough, if they could continue to shift drugs and keep a lid on the violence, some were invited to join the Cartel on an equal footing with traffickers and wholesalers. But this was a rare accolade: doormen were, in general, considered to be irrational and unreliable. In addition, it upset the balance within the hierarchy. Doormen were considered low level. The apex was reserved for traffickers. It would be a dangerous precedent to relinquish power downwards.

The dance scene seemed to march on and on. Millions of pounds poured into the coffers of the bullet-headed gatekeepers. A kind of rough career path was rationalised. First, doormen started selling the E. Once they'd got together a 'kitty' to fund bigger deals, they moved onto powders such as cocaine, heroin, speed and 'magic'. Next came the kilo batches. The graduation was often mirrored by the accumulation of showy assets. Suddenly, the old banger was traded in for a US-style super pick-up, a Ford Probe GT or a Lexus SC and paid for in cash.

Then with excessive surpluses of cash came the houses on the new estate, bristling with giveaway CCTV cameras, which became a signature fitting on gangsters' houses in the 1990s when few people could afford them. Investments in building firms were paid for, restaurants and hairstylist shops for their girlfriends acquired. Many invested in sunbed shops so they could wash their money. The Inland Revenue found it difficult to prove how many customers had been under the lamps.

Gyms were also favourite assets of the poor doorman made good. One door firm became so rich that they bought a theme park in Spain for cash. Another used a well-respected estate agent to buy nearly 40 dilapidated properties. The portfolio was bought through a front company with tax paid. However, the renovations, materials and labour were all paid for in cash. The profits on the sale and the rental incomes were all declared as taxable income. The property scam was a common money-laundering technique.

But with the Wild West-style land grab came pressure. With easy riches came easy losses. Security contracts were lost overnight. Clubs changed hands; new managers were employed; new gangsters came on the scene. The roller coaster lifestyle saw doormen go from penniless boxers to steroid-head multimillionaires back to drug addicts as the late nights and stress took their toll. The majority of players went on drugs, lost the contracts, were killed, maimed, blown up or shot at or just plain faded away. Some went back to living ordinary lives on council estates or in the suburbs. Many of them went under when the price of E's dropped.

One of the ones who had been determined to strike it rich was Kevin 'Mad Dog' Maguire. He had started in Quadrant Park taxing small-time dealers and selling Ecstasy. Maguire was short and stocky. His build was muscular and he had a ponytail.

Around the same time, there were calls in some quarters of the Cartel to have George Bromley killed. However, Bromley was a friend of Tommy Gilday, a Cartel legend who was allied to Scarface and Kaiser, Curtis Warren and a heroin baron called John Haase. Gilday was well connected within the Cartel, and to kill one of his mates would be a serious diplomatic problem. To some extent Bromley was protected, but it was also clear that he was living on borrowed time. Cartel members who'd been robbed by him repeatedly claimed that Bromley was too sly to have around. Ordinary street criminals complained to the godfathers that Bromley had stabbed and beaten them for little reason. Independents complained to their Cartel suppliers that their people had been shot in the legs by Bromley. He had been witnessed running into dealers' houses and battering them in front of their wives. One day Bromley had kicked a doorman to near death in front of his heavily pregnant wife. To prove how bad he was, she got battered as well.

The godfathers became more concerned when Maguire and Bromley became pals. It was double trouble. Maguire began carrying a snub nose Smith & Wesson pistol for protection.

Bromley and Maguire's behaviour went against the new look. The Cartel had spent a lot of time trying to create a business culture. Respect and trust were the new watchwords, underworld values that made giving and granting credit easy. But Maguire was only interested in spreading fear, which was considered bad for business. Other gangsters sprang up trying to emulate them. E culture meant that there was enough money around to sustain many gangsters who liked being nasty. The downside was that they were always getting killed. The door wars were even bad for the local papers. When a gangster got shot, there were usually hundreds of sentimental tributes posted in to the obituary section. When a family leader called David Ungi was shot a year later he had received so many columns of messages from the underworld that extra pages had to be added. But few felt sorry for the new breed of monsters when the time came. Few memorials appeared. Even close friends signed off tributes anonymously, out of embarrassment.

As the body count rose, a lot of people speculated that the doormen were being wiped out by professional hit-men. But most were just quarrels between individuals, disputes that were irrationally resolved, as opposed to contract killings. Hit-men had no empathy and often no association with their intended victims. It just came down to money. But most of the modern murders seemed gruesome and gratuitous: the new breed of taxmen had just stepped on the wrong toes and come a cropper.

Meanwhile, 550 kilometres away in Holland, a parliamentary committee had been set up to investigate organised crime. The Van Traa inquiry found that there were 11 foreign gangs operating in Amsterdam. Although the Brits weren't prominent, they had managed to enter into a partnership with a home-grown Dutch gangster called Klaas Bruinsma.

CHAPTER 23

REPEAT

1994

BY THE MID '90s, it seemed as though the authorities were losing the battle against the Cartel. Three cases exemplified the sense of defeat. John Haase, Curtis Warren and Ian McAteer were drug dealers and gun runners from three different factions. In three separate cases they'd faced justice. And in all three incidents, they had won and walked away free men. The trend illustrated not only how hard it was for the authorities to build complex cases against drug dealers but also how easy it was for a handful of incredibly wealthy people to play the system and in some cases pervert justice on a grand scale. For some, the cases of Curtis Warren and John Haase proved that the drug barons were now more powerful than the police.

During the previous year, on 27 July 1993, John Haase and his sidekick Paul Bennett had been arrested while trying to escape from a big heroin bust in Liverpool. They were charged with possessing and distributing 50 kilos of heroin, which was part of a much larger consignment. But during their time on remand, they pulled off an extraordinary escape plan. Instead of breaking out of jail by digging tunnels or scaling walls, they used a more cunning method. They ploughed hundreds of thousands of pounds into a corrupt scheme to obtain two Royal Pardons from the Home Office. It worked. The then Home Secretary Michael Howard was duped into granting the pair their freedom just 11 months into their 18-year sentences. The con involved smuggling a gun into Strangeways Prison and blaming it on a fellow inmate called Thomas Bourke to qualify for the Royal Prerogative, an ancient loophole which decreed that prisoners could win their freedom if they prevented prison officers from being attacked. Haase and Bennett falsely claimed that the gun was going to be used to kill guards during a breakout by Bourke, who was then on remand for murder – even though they had smuggled the gun into Strangeways in the first place. Haase and Bennett also fabricated 35 other gun caches and paid bribes, at various points fraudulently linking them to the IRA and phantom gang bosses.

Underneath the layers of lies and deceptions, there was also betrayal of their underworld pals. Haase and Bennett had been secret police informers, providing some legitimate intelligence, since 1992. They had been supplying the police and Customs and Excise with information on dozens of Cartel bosses, including Curtis Warren and one of his associates known as the Rockstar. Their role as agents of the state had helped them twofold: first, the help that they were giving the authorities in turn helped them to get a Royal Pardon each; and second, by taking down some of their rivals within the Cartel, the field was left open for them to take over themselves.

John Haase and Paul Bennett were released back onto the streets of Liverpool. They took up their positions once more within the hierarchy and began dealing drugs. To secure their power on the street, later they set up a door-security company called Big Brother. In addition, they began running guns and drugs to Scotland after linking up with Glasgow assassin Ian McAteer.

Like Haase, McAteer should have been in jail. But like Haase, McAteer was a master at manipulating the evidence against him and beating cases. Despite being one of Britain's most dangerous criminals, according to police, he had recently walked free from court. McAteer had recently been inside. He'd fallen out with a 26-year-old criminal associate called Jack Bennett (no relation to Paul Bennett) while in jail in 1994. Bennett's family claimed he was targeted because he rejected McAteer's homosexual advances. At first, McAteer put out a contract on Bennett's life offering '2 oz of tobacco and 50 temazepan tablets' to any inmate who killed Bennett on the wings. According to witnesses, these were McAteer's own words and they were later reported in court.

No one took up the offer. So McAteer swore that he would do it himself on the outside.

Both of them were released a short while later. By then, McAteer had become obsessed. Once he was out, McAteer hunted Bennett down. In broad daylight, Bennett was stabbed 57 times in a Glasgow street. The case against McAteer went to court, but the jury was not convinced by the evidence. They returned a 'not proven' verdict.

Overturning the odds had convinced McAteer that he was now untouchable. In the same year, just yards from where Jack Bennett had been stabbed, McAteer shot another man, blasting him badly while he was waiting at traffic lights. McAteer went on the run but was later arrested in Merseyside after going to seek help from the Cartel. But, once again, he escaped possible jailtime when the victim refused to make a complaint.

'His extreme violence made him notorious in the criminal underworld,' said Detective Superintendent Julieanne Wallace-Jones of Merseyside Police at a press conference reported on by the *Liverpool Echo*. Wallace-Jones later investigated McAteer for yet another murder. In Liverpool, McAteer repaid the loyalty shown to him by the Cartel: he used guns, knives, knuckle-dusters and baseball bats to suppress its enemies, according to police. McAteer became known by John Haase and the Cartel as the 'Mad Jock'.

The fact that Curtis Warren, John Haase and Ian McAteer had all beaten cases caused morale to plummet in some parts of the police. The Analyst remained stoical: he concluded that the police weren't tackling drugs as well as they should have been because the top brass were from a different generation who hadn't experienced the problem.

He said, 'Organisationally, we had people of Chief Superintendent rank who wouldn't have seen the drug problem as a priority simply because their organisational memory wouldn't have known drugs. Police officers tend to dwell on their early years of service probably more than their later years. They form opinions about crimes and what is important to them. The problem was that the men at the top at the time wouldn't have seen drugs as a problem, because in their early years drugs hadn't been a problem. That's because drugs had come upon us quickly in the 1980s.

'So the younger officers like me were seeing the changes at street level, but the senior officers probably didn't see it the same way. They weren't completely naive, but they didn't have the same understanding as others had.'

After having beaten his big case, within a year Curtis Warren was back dealing drugs. He'd learned a lot from the Customs investigation that had nabbed him a few years earlier and which later fell apart at his 1993 trial. Both the run-up to the trial and the case itself had been a fiasco for the authorities. Rot had set in early after an informant called Brian Charrington, Warren's former partner, turned out to be corrupt and unreliable with respect to the help that he had given the police. Moreover, to Warren's surprise, the case had been the subject of much high-level discussion between the Attorney General, the Paymaster General, a chief constable and an MP. Curtis was learning about politics. He understood that his newly acquired wealth and power could indirectly influence normally straight people in important positions. He had a certain mystique, which he began to use to his advantage. Staying cool and not saying much had the effect of making him seem more powerful than he really was.

Warren had also learned how to manipulate the press, employing a former con and tabloid journalist called John Merry to tip off the *News of the World* about stories that worked in his favour. The articles smeared both an MP, by linking him to backroom deals, and a rival gangster, by planting a story that he was a paedophile. After the trial collapsed, Warren went on holiday with the Banker's daughter. Colin Smith, who had been charged with the same offences, also got off. Their Cali contact Mario Halley was less fortunate. Halley had been nicked in Holland and got eight years in jail. But Warren and Smith weren't too bothered. They were confident that with their new power they could attract new Cali contacts at a higher level. Word had spread that even though they'd been arrested for 1,000 kilos, they hadn't said a word to the police. They were staunch, and that commanded a lot of respect.

When he returned to Liverpool, Warren reformed his drug-dealing network into a cell structure. He invested in a door-security company to cover his money. And he stepped up to become the Cartel's front man. He was going to jump right back on the horse – and this time he was determined not to get caught.

CHAPTER 24

CANNABIS KING

1995

FORMER HEROIN DEALER Dylan Porter was finding it difficult to make ends meet building sheds. Personal and family debts were mounting. One spring day in 1995, Dylan decided to dip his toe back into the drugs world. He told himself that he'd just do one or two deals – no more than three – to get himself clear financially and back on his feet. As an extra disincentive from getting too involved, he vowed not to deal Class A drugs.

Dylan said, 'I started getting back into it bit by bit. I didn't want to – but I needed money. I had realised how hard it was to make a living as a straight-goer. Plus there was pressure from the underworld. Every two weeks someone would come up to me and say: "Come on, Dylan, let's do some business." They knew I was decent and they knew I had the contacts, so they wanted to make money off me. So in the end I just gave in.

'At first, I was just doing weed: a little 40 kilos from Spain, here and there.' Though 40 kilos might seem like a lot of cannabis to a member of the public, to a smuggler, especially one as prolific as Dylan Porter, it is not a huge amount.

Business was also good for Poncho and his brother Hector. While Kaiser and Scarface were in Holland, he set about growing his mid-tier cocaine franchise back in England.

Poncho said, 'My brother and I started selling more and more in Birmingham, using the West Indian connections from the old days. We were selling cocaine to the kids of the fellers my dad used to sell weed to 20 to 30 years before, when the whole thing had started.

'This was now my full-time job. I had a hire car on permanent contract, three months at a time, up and down the motorways moving gear, twelve to eighteen hours a day. The money grew on trees: the best clubs, restaurants, silly-money clothes; we were bang at it. You think it's never gonna end. Even when bad things happen, you just think, "Not me."

'In 1995, we lost a few of our partners: they got nicked and got serious jail time. But we carried on. By that time, we'd both been traffickers, we'd been involved with smuggling at the international end with the cream of the crop, and now we were distributors, so we got a lot of respect.'

However, dark times for everyone were just around the corner. In May 1995, the Cartel was blown apart by an internecine gang war. Two rival factions from neighbouring areas were locked into a power struggle. One wing was predominantly black and headed by Curtis Warren. The other was mainly white and led by David Ungi. Both gangs wanted dominance in the drugs trade. But they were also fighting to retain their status on the street and within the Cartel. Both gangs saw themselves as top dogs and would not defer to each other. But there were also underlying tensions and it wasn't long before the anger on both sides soon brought long-held racial divisions to the surface. On the black side, street enforcer Johnny Phillips, who was one of Curtis Warren's deputies, was making most of the play. Phillips had been closely watched by the Analyst, so he was well known to police. Behind the scenes, Warren was more Machiavellian. He preferred to stay in the background, manipulating both sides, black and white, to his own advantage. While firing up Phillips on the one side by insisting that he didn't back down, secretly he remained friends with the white rivals, even serving them up with ten-kilo parcels of cocaine and heroin as a show of his commitment, showing them which side their bread was buttered. But soon even Warren's diplomatic skills were put under strain. As the threats escalated, Warren began spending more time in Amsterdam to stay out of the firing line and concentrate on business.

In April 1995, the DEFCON level went off the scale. Both sides had tried to stop all-out war by arranging a series of 'straighteners' between David Ungi and Phillips. But Phillips insisted on trying to buy a pub called Cheers, which Ungi argued was out of bounds because it was on his patch. Cheers was one of Ungi's locals.

On 1 May, David Ungi, one of the leading members of the South Liverpool Crime Group (a name given to them by the police), was shot dead at the wheel of his VW Passat as he drove through Toxteth. The father of three was killed after being ambushed at 5.30 p.m. The shooting was the catalyst for a string of tit-for-tat incidents. The murder sent shockwaves through the underworld and in many ways changed policing for ever.

The Analyst said, 'The murder of David Ungi was over a geographic power struggle. David Ungi used to drink in Cheers, which was perceived as a white area. They believed that the businesses that they grew into in that area were theirs. For instance, they bought another pub in a nearby street because that was owned by their own people there. There was almost a recognition and acceptance that you had your own area, that you worked it.

'Then Johnny Phillips comes along to buy Cheers from under their noses, and that's the reason for the straightener.

'That caused murders.

'Neither side realised the effect a gang war would have on business, because we ended up with a situation where the tit-for-tat shootings got completely out of hand.'

Gangsters started to behave differently. According to police they were influenced by the 'world of violence' on television, a false reality in which gangsters were running around with guns. Low-level criminals wanted to be perceived as gangsters because they were prepared to use a gun. Police recorded 32 firearms discharges in a matter of weeks. Opposing forces let rip with machine guns behind the Ungi HQ, a run-down pub dubbed 'Black George's' in Liverpool 8. However, it was the police that benefited most. Within a matter of months, the force was dragged out of the past and into the future. The irony was that the killing forced officers to switch to what are known today as disruption tactics.

Chief Constable James Sharples ordered armed police onto the streets: the first time armed routine patrols had been deployed on mainland Britain. Armed response vehicles became prominent.

The Analyst said, 'Before then, we'd had firearms officers who'd only come out on specific firearms operations. But now we had armed units on the streets. That's what changed.

'We didn't go in for the "let's arm everybody" strategy. But we adopt a coordinated approach: a very sophisticated approach, in fact. We'd bring all of our assets together from a number of different disciplines. We'd have a meeting with everyone there, all chaired by a chief super or an assistant chief constable.'

Each 'asset' was given a specific piece of work to do. One group of community intervention officers was sent to reassure a frightened neighbourhood. Disruption tactics against the criminals, like 'stop and search', were stepped up. Simultaneously, in the background, the murder investigation was taking place. Firearms units responded quickly. Key impact players (a policing term that refers to high-profile criminals with proven links to firearms) were dragged out of their cars at gunpoint on main roads so that everyone could see. They were searched roughly and questioned; Heckler & Koch weapons were pointed at their heads. A media strategy was formulated to deal with the national papers and TV that had declared Liverpool the capital of UK gun crime.

The Analyst said, 'We brought it all together under one banner heading, so everything was coordinated and everybody knew exactly what they were doing. It was the first time this had happened. The goal was simple; the message to the criminal was clear: we will disrupt the living daylights out of them by doing whatever we do.

'An intelligence picture began to emerge, to inform everybody of what they needed to know. We brought all that together: and all that came about because of the murder of David Ungi in 1995. It was a case of: "Now we have a good-to-fighting chance of defeating the organised networks," and we were determined to keep it up, not for it just to be a short-term measure. That was the view of the younger officers anyway, who saw this method as the future of fighting crime.

'We've fine-tuned that system over the years. No longer do we have a "knee-jerk" reaction to an incident.'

As a result of the police heat and underworld attacks, Johnny Phillips retreated into Toxteth to hide. His gang still believed that they controlled the ghetto. But by now the police had made sure that Granby Street was no hiding place any more. Officers boasted that they were 'all over it'. In August 1995, frustrated and under pressure, Curtis Warren vanished. He'd had enough of the gang war and its downward pressure on drug profits. No one could move gear about the city, never mind get drugs in, with so many armed patrols on the street. He went in search of a new, more low-key HQ.

His lieutenant Colin Smith decided to front it out. He stayed in Liverpool and opened a pub-cum-nightclub with his brother John Smith. The venue attracted the cream of the city's gangsters. At closing time, there were often fights outside. Lines of cars were smashed up, guns were pulled and gangs were chased through the streets with knives and baseball bats. Colin and John Smith had persuaded a TV soap star to front the business. As a high-profile criminal, Colin Smith could not have his name on the licence. But when the *News of the World* got wind of the set-up, they planned to expose both the sham and the celebrity frontman for selling cocaine and his links to organised crime. Smith had learned how to handle the press from his dealings in the Warren case. He knew the value of PR and had put a well-known PR firm on a retainer a few months earlier to keep his name out of the limelight. When the *News of the World* threatened to publish a story, his gang trapped their reporters in a hotel and forced them to negotiate with his PR representative. Smith's father John Smith Senior and his brother John Smith Junior also took part in the negotiations. The *News of the World* asked John Merry, Curtis Warren's old reporter friend, to negotiate on their behalf. He was flown to Liverpool to speak to the Smith family and ensure the safety of the reporters. The reporters were told they could go only after they promised not to run the story. Merry told them they were lucky. He said that Curtis Warren had offered to fly back from Amsterdam himself to sort out the problem.

On the party island of Ibiza, the Cartel was making inroads into the lucrative Ecstasy trade. For years, the Basque terrorist group ETA had secretly controlled the underworld on the island. Like the IRA, they used the drugs trade and protection rackets to raise money for the cause. But they understood little about the new dance culture and the superclubs that were popping up all over the island. Two senior Cartel members offered to take on the contract and front the sales for them. If ETA could help with security – including paying off corrupt officials – then the Cartel would flood the island with coke and E. A deal was struck and mid-level Cartel importers established themselves on the island. Some of them took advantage and did little to hide their operations, causing considerable embarrassment to the authorities. As a warning, one Liverpool-based trafficker was jailed in Spain for eighteen years for importation. Another Cartel member based in San Antonio got seven years but decided to inform on his associates. Back in Liverpool, his boss's house got shot up badly as a warning. One superclub owner, based in Ibiza but with strong Liverpool links, challenged the criminality. The proprietors were sick of having to pay huge amounts of protection money and having unwanted security companies thrust on them. When they sued the security bosses, the only information they had was the address of a Spanish solicitor. It turned out to be an unregistered PO box in the Basque stronghold of San Sebastián. The club did not pursue the case.

CHAPTER 25

SHADY GRAY

1996

IN LIVERPOOL, A senior Cartel boss called Eddie Gray embarked on a spending spree that would put a footballer's wife to shame. Gray was known as 'the Bear' because of his six-foot, seventeen-stone frame. In many ways, Gray was a typical drug dealer. He was driven by extreme levels of greed and ambition. His thirst for status, both within the Cartel and in wider circles, meant that he could not help showing off the trappings of his wealth. He spent lavishly on houses, cars and clothes, but behind the scenes he was a penny-pincher who shopped at discount stores and bartered over pennies with the grafters who sold him knock-off gear for cash. Eddie liked to feel like a big man amongst the normal people who lived in his neighbourhood, but in his mind he also believed that by mixing with the local scallies he was a man of the people. He could regularly be seen shopping at Aldi and Netto, loading plastic bags of discounted food into his £100,000 red Ferrari F355 Spider convertible, then squeezing into the bucket seats puffing and sweating like a man about to have a heart attack. Eddie wasn't suave, but he was known in the Cartel as a 'money-making machine'.

Another drug boss who had been around at the start of the Cartel with founding father Fred the Rat had several run-ins with Gray. He said, 'The thing with Eddie was that he was tight: every pound was a prisoner with him. That was unusual with that crowd – most of them had so much money that they could be generous. On one occasion, when a mate of ours was raising money for a good cause, to help local children, one of them gave me £100,000. The drug dealer didn't want to appear soft so he pretended it was a loan to get the scheme up and running. But he was never given it back and he was happy with that.

'But Eddie was a different story.'

Gray was also known as Fast Eddie, partly because of his fleets of sports cars but also because he could deliver large consignments of heroin and Ecstasy quickly and efficiently. Merseyside Police had him down as a 'top five' Cartel member. Millions of pounds flowed through his cricket-glove-sized hands. He regularly kept £50,000 in cash around the house for bits and bobs. Cartel bosses advised him to retire. But he was suffering from a disease that would take him and many of his associates down: greed.

The Flash Harry gangster spent money like water – but only on himself and his wife. Police officers who later put him under the microscope estimated that he blew nearly £500,000 over a 20-month period. His capital assets included a £250,000 villa in Spain and even stretched to £23,000 worth of personalised number plates on his cars. On the path of his five-bedroom house in Liverpool there was always a different car: an Alfa Romeo, a BMW convertible, a Lexus or a Toyota Land Cruiser. But Eddie was addicted to dealing heroin because he loved money.

Another Cartel criminal owned so many vehicles that he bought a private car park to house them. His fleet included a Ferrari, two boats, three jet-skis, a luxury caravan, a Winnebago mobile home, three motorbikes and seven 4 x 4 jeeps. But when it came to doing drug deals, Eddie would count his cash, and if it was £20 short on a £10,000 load he would wait until the full amount was paid up. A friend remarked that Eddie was so mean that he'd gone 'gray with greed'.

In a bar near Cartagena in southern Spain, Dylan Porter was sweating, his milk-white English legs reddening unevenly, embarrassingly. He had flown to Spain from Manchester airport to go for a drink with an old Moroccan friend. They chatted over a beer, Dylan sporting white nylon tennis shorts. Wimbledon was on the telly above the bar.

'What's happening?' Dylan asked the Moroccan.

'It's good to see you, Dylan.' They made small talk over olives and tapas before Dylan got down to business.

'What's the price on the weed?' Dylan asked.

'It's £475 on the kilo,' the Moroccan replied. 'How many do you want?'

That's how easy it was for a Cartel guy to get back in the game. Dylan was up and running in the big time again. For a few months previously, he'd been bringing in small 40-kilo loads to pay off his debts. Now he was preparing to upscale again, back into respectable amounts that'd get him back his throne within the Cartel. If he couldn't do that, then he'd settle for smaller, more frequent loads. It was swings and roundabouts. Dylan Porter didn't worship money like his associate Gray, but he was determined to make his new cannabis-smuggling operation a success.

Dylan said, 'Within months my cannabis business was booming. The price of rocky started going for £2,300 per kilo here in England, so it suddenly got very worthwhile. I could get it in Spain for £475 a kilo and get it home for £675. The transport cost me £200 a box.

'I knew people over there who were well established. My contact was a Moroccan guy I'd met at random years before. I'd saved him from getting a hiding from a bouncer once, and after that we became mates. The Moroccans wouldn't touch Class A's, but when I started again, he agreed to get me my pot. Another mate in Liverpool had the transport, so all the bits were in place. I flew over to Spain to sort it.'

The money to pay the Moroccans for the cannabis was sent out to Spain in a wagon or sometimes in a car. The cannabis was smuggled from Morocco to Tariffa. A Liverpool freelancer who worked for the Cartel drove the consignment up to Madrid. From then on, Dylan's transport would take over all the way back to the UK.

Dylan said, 'I was doing it in conjunction with my mate. He brought half a ton of cannabis back and another mate had another half a ton on the same lorry. When it got back to Liverpool they would lay half a ton on – that's give it to someone on credit. He killed it. They threw half a ton at you, just like that, as though it was nothing. I doubt anyone would do that today.'

Sometimes Dylan would monitor the consignment as it entered the UK to make sure they were not being followed. Just before Christmas 1996, Dylan went down to Dover to watch a lorry going through Customs. He travelled on a coach to avoid detection and then observed from a nearby hill. He was desperate to feel the old kick, the buzz of seeing a parcel 'get home'.

Dylan said, 'I was there to watch this kid bring in a ton of weed. It was exciting. We were all wanking on this. There were eight or nine of us on it, who'd invested in it: that meant someone would get 200 kilos, another 100, another 50 and so on. I didn't even know five of the other partners, but they were all Scousers. Basically, every one of us who was involved had a little bit of the parcel on the wagon. As usual I would get 40 kilos off this big amount.'

But just as the lorry was pulling out of the port, Customs officers stopped it, suspicious that the vehicle's load was heavier than the paperwork implied. The driver was ordered to put the trailer on the giant weigh station. According to Dylan, the driver asked the Customs officer, 'Can I go and get a cup of coffee?'

As soon as he was out of sight of the weigh station, the panicky driver phoned Dylan and his mate. They were on a hill watching from a car, but they couldn't be seen.

The driver asked Dylan's mate: 'It's on the bay – what should I do?'

The mate told the driver, 'I know; we're watching. You can fuck off now – but if you do and they don't find it, it looks guilty as fuck. Or you can go back, and if they find it, play daft. Say it's been put on by someone else at whatever warehouse on the way, nothing to do with you.'

The driver mulled it over and there was just silence on the other end of the phone. He was in a catch-22 position: there was the added pressure that if he walked away and lost the load, he wouldn't get paid. The truck would be confiscated and there'd be a lot of pissed-off drug traffickers waiting for him when he got off the train at Lime Street station back in Liverpool.

Dylan said, 'Then the driver thought, "Fuck it." We could see him from our vantage point on the other end of the phone, going through the options. Fair play to him: his arse didn't fall out and he decided to front it out. And he went back to the weigh station.'

'Are you finished?' the driver asked Customs.

The Customs guy nodded and said, 'Yes, mate: there's the keys.'

The driver snaked his way out of the port, and Dylan and his mate followed the load all the way back to Liverpool at a discreet distance.

Even though the cannabis took up a lot of volume, the bulk was hidden deep inside the truck within a 40-ft container. The process was repeated every month like clockwork. Each load made £22,000 for Dylan alone.

Dylan said, 'The beauty was that I never even saw it most of the time. After the first few goes, when I'd nursed it into Dover or gone to see it land in the warehouse, I didn't bother even getting involved with the transport side or going to pick it up at the end – I just took a back seat. When it landed, I was simply told the location of where it was being uploaded by my friend, which was usually at a place in Huyton. Then I rang up a third party, an employee of mine who did the running about for me. I told him the address, and he went down there and picked it up and stashed it until he got further instructions. Even before the cannabis had physically arrived in the UK, I'd usually sold it over the phone, like the way a trader would sell a ton of grain or something and reserve it. Then, after it arrived in Huyton, I'd simply phone the two lads who I sold it to, and I'd tell them it had landed. Then they would either collect it from my runner there and drop the money round to me the next day, or sometimes it got so that I didn't even need a runner. If I trusted the buyer, I sent them direct round to where it was being unloaded and they would take it off the wagon. It got so much like clockwork that I never even touched a bar.'

Meanwhile, Curtis Warren had relocated to a Dutch commuter town called Sassenheim. It was just far enough away from Scarface and Kaiser so as not to step on their toes but close enough to the action in Amsterdam to keep dealing drugs. He got a strong team of criminals around him from all over the UK and soon became the number-one trafficker in volume terms within the UK. It was another string to Dylan's bow: Curtis started supplying him with cannabis and other things as well.

CHAPTER 26

ROUND TWO

1996

THE HANDS-OFF APPROACH was common among Cartel operators. Once they had established their reputation, they could sit back and let others do the legwork without fear of being double-crossed, robbed or grassed up.

Dylan said, 'To do business that way, to have the confidence to delegate, you've either got to be physically tough, well liked or have an army behind you. I'm nothing special, but I'd like to think I was a combination of all three, in degrees at least. I'm not stupid and I am well known. I could have called on help quite easily, but I hated violence and I hated bullies. I've never been robbed, or bumped on a parcel, because I fly straight. And people saw goodness in me.

'It sounds mad, to use words like "good" and "genuine" in the drugs trade, but it's not all about being evil. People liked the fact that I was good, and they were attracted to it because there were bullies everywhere.'

But the virtues didn't wash with Dylan's wife. At night she used to say to him, 'It's dirty money: no good will come of it.' She was looking after six kids and hated the fact that her husband was a drug dealer. But the motivation was money, because Dylan was skint and he was too lazy to get a proper job.

Dylan said, 'You get used to a lazy man's lifestyle – always ordering food from the chippy or going to restaurants. Now I love cooking. But when you're a big drug dealer, nothing is a challenge. Book that holiday: three times a year, when you like. When my daughter was six months old, she had Moschino boots on, Moschino coats – and she couldn't even walk. It was fake. I was being showy but not realising it.'

Dylan's life was sedate, insulated from the outside world by a cushion of cash usually reserved for the highest-paid executives or top-performing professionals. Like a senior manager, he didn't have to deal with strife or get his hands dirty. For the successful Cartel member, it was like living inside an empire where the fruits of labour were available to the few.

But on the streets, an unprecedented gun war had been raging for almost a year.

Since the murder of David Ungi, around 44 shooting incidents had happened on Merseyside. The shots had started even before the funeral had taken place. Outside the Black George's pub in Toxteth, where the younger generation of the Ungis drank for two days after his death, a machine gun was fired into the building. It was an ominous portent of the bloody year to come.

In one incident, a hooded gunman had burst into a popular meeting place called Vic's Gym in Kensington and opened fire, wounding a 25-year-old fitness fanatic called Ricardo Rowe. On another occasion, a 31-year-old was found lying in a pool of blood in a road in Netherley, suffering from gunshot wounds to the leg. Five days later, a man called Paul Foster was shot at his home in Toxteth. The Cartel was imploding.

Police then issued an appeal for calm after five people were injured in another two shooting incidents. But it was roundly ignored: later that day, shots were fired into a house in Anfield. The tit for tat went on. Four days later, a man called Lee Parry was shot by gunmen in Toxteth. Things quietened down for a short while until shots were fired at the home of Kevin O'Rourke, then wanted for questioning in connection with the Ungi murder.

The net was closing on the main suspect, Johnny Phillips. When gunmen finally caught up with him, five shots were fired into Phillip's car, as it was parked outside his home. He had been charged with trying to kill Ungi, but, true to form, the case had been dropped.

In revenge, David Ungi's brother Ronnie was attacked and his home sprayed with bullets. A man named Jason Speed was shot at his home in Huyton. Unlike the First World War, there was no lull over Christmas. Instead, a full-scale gun war erupted, with five people being shot, one fatally, and a gun attack on a police shop. The new year started with a 16-year-old boy being shot four times in Princes Avenue, Toxteth. Hours later, a 27-year-old was badly wounded in nearby Upper Warwick Street.

Cartel godfathers took sides. All drug sales were put on hold as the police stepped up interceptions. Many Cartel members fled abroad. With the onset of the campaign season (drug dealers' slang for when business picked up in spring), full hostilities resumed in March 1996 when Phillips was shot again. This time he was fired at four times in Toxteth in front of his three-year-old daughter and his wife. He survived, but it was only a matter of time. A twenty-one-year-old woman was then shot in Granby Street, followed by a gun attack on six people. Even a copper was shot: PC Stephen Hardy was knee-capped after two masked men burst into his home in West Derby, and he was also shot in the arm. Police believed it was a case of mistaken identity. Four more attacks left three more victims shot. Finally, events came full circle. To mark the anniversary of Ungi's murder, a man called Owen Graham was shot dead in a betting shop – almost a year to the hour that Ungi had been killed.

The police needed to find a solution quickly. The new joined-up thinking that had been introduced after the Ungi murder had helped to stop things getting even worse. But disruption was only a tactic. Now a full-scale strategy was required. No longer could the police rely on backwards-facing, reactive policing. A new generation of coppers came to the forefront with new ideas. The time was right for a policeman like the Analyst to take up the reins from the old guard.

The answer lay in a fresh-out-of-the-think-tank philosophy called intelligence-led policing. Tested in the US, the new doctrine was built around risk assessment and risk management as opposed to individual incidents and types of crime. The jargon in a training manual defined 'a strategic, future-oriented and targeted approach to crime control, focusing upon the identification, analysis and "management" of persisting and developing problems or risks'. In canteen speak, it simply meant that the intelligence-gathering part of the police would, in future, guide operations. No longer would surveillance solely be called in to gather evidence after the fact. Now officers like the Analyst would scan the city in realtime and find out what was likely to happen next.

Calls for intelligence-led policing had started in the US after it was found that a conflict between law enforcement and intelligence had driven a wedge between the FBI and the CIA. As a consequence, cops were urged to become 'more like spies', according to Mark Riebling in his 1994 book *Wedge: The Secret War Between the FBI and the CIA*. That suited the Analyst just fine. Within ten years he would become Britain's top drugs secret agent, a kind of James Bond of drug enforcement, pitting his wits against the underworld, with a permanent target in his sight: the Cartel.

In order to harvest raw data, the police began to recruit more informants. One such was a criminal called David Parsons. In the summer of 1996, the middle-ranking heroin dealer claimed that he had become an informant for the senior officers and this would eventually lead to his working as a secret agent for the National Crime Squad (NCS). The NCS was a new initiative that was to lead the charge in the new era – and the attack on the Cartel. But the pressure was on. There was no time for grooming and vetting of the new army of narks: intelligence-led policing needed to be sorted now. Bargains needed to be struck. Devils needed to be danced with. Parsons suggested that his deal with the police was simple. He'd set up Liverpool drug barons for them to arrest, and in return the police would turn a blind eye to his own drug-dealing activities, as well as sweetening him up with cash rewards.

In effect, Parsons said he was 'pressurised' into becoming what is known as 'a participating informant': one that would not only feed inside info on drug deals but actively take part in the deals, and possibly steer them in the right direction. It was a dicey game for everyone concerned.

The first target was an out-of-town dealer called Mark Lilley. Lilley was an intimidating figure. He was six feet tall, powerfully built and had two prominent scars on his right hand. The informant said that he was allowed to buy drugs from Mark Lilley's gang and then with the knowledge of the police, he would sell the drugs on, so that the profits could be recycled back into the investigation, to cover the informant's expenses.

David Parsons said that the budget for his operation would be self-financing from the sale of drugs.

On one such deal, David Parsons targeted a low-level Cartel-related dealer. Before the police busted the dealer, Parsons scored off him, so that the 'hand to hand' – a police term for the part of a drug deal in which the negotiations have finished and the physical contraband is handed over – could be used to draw him into the police's net. Parsons said, 'I told [my cop handler] after the deal what I had bought and he told me to keep what I had.' The lines were getting blurred.

Meanwhile, a secret agent of a different nature was putting the final touches to his plans to involve people who would, inadvertently, be carrying out his wishes while reaping their own revenge. Friends of the taxmen's victims were whispering names into their ears during a complex operation to incriminate. Crime author Peter Stockley has written about the plot in his book *Extenuating Circumstances*.

Target number one was George Bromley as far as Paul Burly was concerned. After finding out that a leak was dribbling through to Bromley about death threats, Burly began to send messages out via his trusted people hinting that Bromley was planning something retaliative. This made those who wanted revenge very wary but also very much more determined. It was near the end of 1997 that Burly received a request for a bit more information, which involved finding out who Bromley's close associates were, along with telephone numbers and such. Conveniently, George Bromley had become friends with a former safe-cracker called Charlie Seiga, whom Burly knew well. Seiga had bought a second-hand car for his daughter from motor dealer Eddie Kelly: a close pal of George Bromley. At Kelly's garage, Bromley and Seiga had met and hit it off, and they began meeting regularly at Seiga's upmarket detached house in the West Derby area. Like an Italian mobster, former restaurateur Seiga was a good cook, and Bromley enjoyed popping round for a 'scran' early evenings, often to discuss the sale of stolen goods or contraband booze. Seiga began advising Bromley on property matters, and the Taxman revealed that soon he would be coming into quite a tidy sum of cash. Bromley boasted of selling up everything so he could live abroad. Liverpool was becoming too hot to handle after the

Ungi killing and the tit-for-tat shootings that followed. The plot thickened.

Meanwhile, in Liverpool, Amsterdam, and the Hague, UK police, Customs and Excise and the Dutch *politie* launched a joint investigation to catch Curtis Warren again. The Cartel superstar was now Interpol's 'Target One'.

CHAPTER 27

COLE

1996

ON WITH THE body count. It was a quiet Sunday night in May 1996. Like most doormen, Stephen Cole reserved Sunday nights for his other half: a quick drink in the local then off to town for a Chinese. The city centre was deserted on a Sunday night, and there was less chance of bumping into any wannabe gangsters: the bane of a doorman's life. But Stephen Cole was no ordinary doorman. He was a former Liverpool football player. He was the head of a very successful security company. However, of late he'd been dragged into one of the internecine gang wars that were threatening to destabilise the Cartel.

Within minutes of ordering a drink at the Farmers Arms pub in the Fazakerley district of Liverpool, a mob of 20-plus assailants burst through the pub doors and chopped him to death with machetes and meat cleavers. The attack was not only horrific, but there was also a touch of the surreal. The weird thing was that the killers chopped up their victim in front of his screaming wife. Even stranger was the fact that some of the other punters in the pub simply looked on as though it was normal. Some of them were gassed with CS spray, so they were not in a position to do much. But others who were unaffected looked on or moved out of the way. After the savage spectacle, they carried on drinking as though nothing had happened. People were learning to ignore, to normalise, criminality in communities where once it would never have been tolerated.

Cole was dead. The underworld tom-toms began spreading the news far and wide. Within hours, Poncho's phone was ringing.

According to Poncho, the caller said, 'I've got some bad news for you.'

Poncho was expecting the worst: that Scarface or Kaiser had been nicked abroad somewhere with a ton of cocaine on them.

Poncho said, 'What is it, lad?'

The caller said, 'Stephen's been macheted up in a pub: he's dead.'

Poncho was devastated. Stephen Cole, a father of two, was a trusted ally. Poncho didn't wait for the details. All he could think of was what Scarface and Kaiser would do. Would they take revenge and declare war on his murderers?

Later, detectives investigating the murder believed that a tightly controlled death squad of gangland mobsters had been 'called out' to carry out the slaughter. Officers believed that the hit team was an A-list gangster outfit that included several serial killers, a few professional hit-men and members of a notorious crime family. Most of the team had close links to the Cartel in one shape or another. Police managed to pick off some suspects later: a 42-year-old jobless hard man called Robert 'Evil Roy' McCarthy, a 48-year-old Kirkby bouncer called John Riley and a 37-year-old about-town toughie called Raymond Navarro.

Underworld watchers believed the hit was planned not only to kill Cole but also to send out a message to the wider community. Cole, who was head doorman at the world-famous Cream dance club, had been hacked to death in public in front of his wife and numerous witnesses. The message was simple: a new benchmark of violence had now been reached. The perpetrators were unstoppable and untouchable. The new bucks would stop at nothing to punish enemies and were so powerful that they did not care how they did it or who knew it or who had seen it.

No one would dare to testify against any of the attackers, named, rumoured or otherwise. No one could challenge the supreme power of the doormen on the street: not even the law. Door teams were now unstoppable in their marauding savagery across the cityscape. A well-known national crime figure from Liverpool who knew both parties revealed that the attack was a turning point in underworld lore, signifying the zenith of the door team as the most powerful organised-crime unit on the streets. The villain, who refused to be named for fear of repercussions, said, 'The attack on Cole was like nothing that had ever happened before in its ferocity, but also, more importantly, in its arrogance.

'It changed the face of things in many ways. In the vast majority of hits, the attackers try to disguise their identities and do the actual murder with as much secrecy as they can, for obvious reasons. With Cole, they chopped him to pieces in front of a packed pub, knowing that people would not report anything to the police.

'Even though it was premeditated, they chose to do it that way. The message was: "We don't care about the police. They are an irrelevance compared to our pull in the local area." That's very scary.'

Cole was 36 but back in the day had played for Liverpool reserves in the '80s. After his football career fizzled out, he became a security consultant for several pubs and clubs in the Kirkby area. The tension between his operation and a rival outfit exploded into open warfare over a seemingly trivial incident, but the underlying battle was about control of lucrative contracts. Cole had gambled on a pre-emptive strike, savagely assaulting an enemy boss in a surprise raid on his turf. In addition, it was alleged that he had shot a friend of the gang in the mouth. He was convinced that his quick actions had won a decisive blow and that the rivals would be too terrified to retaliate. On the night of the murder, he was quietly celebrating his gangland victory, enjoying a drink with his wife in a local pub. But Cole had become too confident: he'd forgotten that his main allies within the Cartel, Scarface and Kaiser, were abroad and weren't around to protect him. Little did he know of the incredibly horrific fate that awaited him.

The main eyewitness to the slaughter was Lorraine Cole, the deceased's wife. To stun her, the assailants sprayed tear gas in her face. Other drinkers were also deliberately gassed and couldn't see. Mrs Cole later stated that even though the gas went into her eyes, she had repelled most of the chemical by putting her hand in front of her face, thus enabling her to witness John Riley, a middle-aged man with greying hair, attacking her husband around the 'the bottom half' of his body. Fighting back the tears in the interview room, she also described how a young dark-haired male aged between 25 and 30 attacked her beloved husband, delivering the *coup de grâce* with a baseball bat. This was the killer blow. According to the pathologist's report, Cole died as a result of a blow to the head from the bat, as well as multiple stab wounds.

Later, at the trial, Preston Crown Court heard that Riley and McCarthy had led the 20-strong gang, armed with knives, machetes and baseball bats. They'd laid into Cole and carried on hitting him even after he was dead. His leg was nearly severed and his arms were mangled by deep incisions and slashes. Many of the weapons were never found. As the assailants sped off in a convoy of cars, many drinkers in the Farmers Arms who had witnessed the murder simply picked up their drinks and took them to the pub across the road called the George.

Although the pub was busy at the time, police initially found a wall of silence created by witnesses' fear of the killers. This was the new code of the street. *Omertà*, the code of silence originated by the Mafia, had now spread from the underworld into the lives of ordinary people. The grip of the Cartel on everyday communities was tightening. One politician privately likened the Cartel bosses to 'warlords' and 'feudal kings' who carved the city up into a 'mediaeval fiefdom'. Later he spent many years campaigning against organised crime in the city.

After the case, Detective Superintendent Russ Walsh, who led the inquiry, described the murder as 'barbaric slaughter'. He said: 'We will not tolerate the gratuitous use of violence by any members of the public and will diligently pursue anyone who resorts to this type of behaviour.'

However, the constant feuding and debt settling meant that the city became a magnet for hit-men from further afield. Assassins flocked to Liverpool from London and Glasgow to help the Cartel godfathers solve their problems. A crack team of former IRA button men known as the Cleaners – because of their reputation for devising innovative death plans and for removing all compromising evidence from crime scenes – reputedly carried out six hits in one spate of contract killings. One of their alleged victims was Warren's right-hand man Johnny Phillips. Phillips had been accused of helping to murder David Ungi. According to underworld sources, his personal cocaine supply was allegedly laced with poison. It is not known whether the alleged murder attempt was successful, but Phillips was eventually found dead in a safehouse in mysterious circumstances.

The Cleaners were awarded the contracts not because they were better than everyone else but because of simple logistics: they lived in Ireland and were able to get in and get out of the UK fast, vastly reducing their chances of being caught. A clean intro and getaway is the key to a successful underworld hit, according to a former Cartel enforcer. The conditions were right for criminals like the Cleaners to make a fortune. A leading assassin for the Cleaners allied himself with Warren's number two, Colin Smith.

But not everything was going well for Curtis Warren. Even though he was well out of the way in Holland, he was unexpectedly dragged into what he'd been fearing the most: a war with out-of-control doormen back in Liverpool. Senior detectives believed that Warren had put out a £100,000 contract to kill a doorman enemy. The alleged target was called Joey McCormick. Joe Mac, as he was known, worked the door of a Beatles-themed bar called Rubber Soul, among others. The row had erupted after the Banker's son had pulled a gun on McCormick in a drunken dispute. As the Banker's main protégé and now virtually his son-in-law – Warren was living with the Banker's daughter – Warren had felt obliged to sort out the situation. In the end, the contract was withdrawn and Warren paid £50,000 to keep everyone quiet. McCormick withdrew a police statement he had made incriminating the Banker's son. The matter seemed to be settled and everyone was preparing to move on. However, during the complicated negotiations that had taken place between various members of the Cartel and other criminals, a serving police officer had been asked to help tamper with evidence relating to the case. Inadvertently, the corrupt policeman, named Elmore Davis, was dragged into the mess. Davis had become well known on national TV after taking part in a reality show about Merseyside Police's murder squad. No one knew, including the senior officer, that the anti-corruption branch of Merseyside Police had been tipped off and had been listening in to the phone conversations. It was a relatively minor indiscretion by the Cartel, in their terms at least, but it had allowed the police an opportunity to get deep inside.

McCormick had a son: he turned out to be the teenage gunman who would shoot Rhys Jones a decade later. McCormick's son was a fourth-generation Cartel foot soldier.

Then things went from bad to worse for Curtis Warren. In October 1996, as he prepared to take possession of a massive load of cocaine, Warren and his gang were arrested in Holland. Six houses were raided in the 'Flat Place' and twenty in the UK. Among goods recovered were 1,500 kilos of cannabis, 60 kilos of heroin and 50 kilos of E's, as well as several caches of weapons and hundreds of thousands of pounds in cash. Just a short while later, Warren was named as Britain's 461st-wealthiest person in the *Sunday Times* Rich List under the banner 'property developer'.

CHAPTER 28

BROWN

1997

AFTER A COUPLE of years of trafficking weed, Dylan Porter was feeling comfortable – too comfortable. He itched 'for a new challenge'. He was battling to control his inner demons. The temptation to get involved in heroin again was strong. Soon his mind was made up for him. The cannabis operation went 'tits up' after Dylan's partner got into an argument with the transport boss.

Dylan said, 'I was working with a feller on the pot and he got into a dispute with the main man with transport. And the transport man turned around and said: "Fuck that. I'm sacking it." And he walked away from £100,000-a-month wages, just like that. My cut was between 20 and 30 grand a month, and I lost it. The cannabis was no more, just like that.'

Dylan went to see his brother-in-law, a senior Cartel smuggler close to Curtis Warren.

In June 1997, Warren was jailed for 12 years in Holland for drug smuggling. Even so, the cell structure of his organisation had survived. Warren was still running drugs from behind bars. Soon the remnants on the outside were back up and running.

Dylan had been introduced to Curtis Warren before his arrest, as well as to the other lads that formed part of the South Liverpool Crime Group. Through Curtis Warren, Dylan had then started getting 'bits' over from 'the Dam'. When Curtis Warren was jailed, Dylan switched to dealing with his underlings.

Dylan said, 'I had a link over in Holland for heroin, but,

crucially, my mate had the wheels. On the first one, we got twenty-seven kilos home and I got five or six kilos of that, and my partners shared the remaining twenty kilos. We agreed that was the deal, and my brother-in-law and Curtis's people were happy.

'As usual, we set it up for a monthly import and as usual, it was run like a military operation. And we smashed it, month after month after month. Even though only five or six kilos were mine, I organised the distribution of the lot so that there'd be no fuck-ups.

'Eventually, I took over the other 20 kilos and where that went. I franchised that out to a contact in West Yorkshire. So even before it landed, all 25/26 kilos were spoken for. My original five would go to someone I'd sold it to, and I would send twenty to Bradford. But I would never touch any gear personally. It was all guided by me over the phone and physically moved by workers.'

Dylan's profit from his own six kilos was £36,000 a month. But he also had a silent partner, a financier who'd helped put money up initially and helped with logistics, who got six grand of that. That left Dylan with net wages of £30,000 a month.

Dylan said, 'But soon I got another cannabis link in the Dam. On top of my £30,000-a-month take-home pay, I would get home 200 kilos of "wood" [cannabis resin] – that'd get me a little extra £5,000 a month.'

But soon, all was not well. Dylan's new transport boss was doing deals on the side. He was the brother-in-law of a notorious Cartel boss known as Cagey, now based in Amsterdam. With the help of his relative, Cagey was loading up Dylan's transport with extra supplies without anyone knowing. Later, Dylan found that Cagey had swindled him out of 27 journeys' worth of heroin and cannabis, without paying.

Meanwhile, in Thatto Heath, St Helens, hapless petty criminal Frank Smith had finished his research into the manufacture of designer drugs. He'd spent years reading books, doing test runs and supporting himself by small-time drug dealing. Now he felt confident enough to approach the Cartel for backing. His plan was to manufacture speed and methamphetamine on an industrial scale. He needed money and the Cartel's distribution network.

Smith was introduced to a mid-ranking member of the Liverpool mafia called Charlie Corke, from Huyton, in late summer 1997. Corke agreed to approach the Cartel with a proposal. In early November 1997, Frank Smith met up with reps of the Cartel to discuss a potential business deal.

'We make it – you sell it,' Frank told the godfathers. The Cartel was not convinced that Frank had enough practical experience to pull off the venture. To close the deal, Smith told the Cartel that there was a man called Roger Benson, a convicted speed maker, who would act as a consultant. Now the backers were happy: there was an expert who could produce the big quantities required to make the venture viable. The Scousers agreed to finance the venture with an initial £20,000 investment to buy base chemicals and glassware. They would also supply illegal ingredients. More importantly, they agreed to provide protection and a sales force to shift the product in Liverpool and London once it was completed. The Cartel's rep was a mysterious fixer known as Mr Big. He was described as one of the main men in Liverpool and that he would be supplying the BMK, the key chemical involved in the process. Benzyl methone ketone is a forensic chemical that is not available to be bought on the open market without authority. BMK is one of the main ingredients of amphetamine.

Charlie Corke reassured Frank Smith that the main gang behind the finance had access to 50 gallons of BMK: a huge quantity that would make a vast amount of amphetamine. To disguise the illegal operation, Frank set up a company on an industrial estate. The firm posed as a soil-testing laboratory and would be used as a front to buy restricted chemicals and equipment.

Frank said, 'I needed a building where all the chemicals would be delivered and no one's suspicions would be aroused.' Most of the people involved were poor or pretended to be poor. Charlie Corke owned an anonymous maroon Ford. The offside headlight was smashed, a small transgression that was a common problem with criminals involved in much bigger illegal activities. Research later carried out and taken on board by Merseyside Police found that serious criminals involved in drug dealing and firearms offences often engaged in petty crime. For instance, a specialist anti-gun unit found that hardened organised criminals would often not pay for road tax or insurance on expensive cars. This gave the police the opportunity to carry out stop-and-searches and later formed the basis of a tactic called 'disruption'.

The lab was used for the preliminary processes of the speed production. But the second stage of production was often moved to a rural 'venue' because the strong smell of ammonia would risk giving the game away. Coincidentally, a travelling network had become established in Cumbria, where it was selling drugs and getting to know the local villains. A small village called Wigton was identified as an ideal venue for the speed factory.

Frank said, 'To save time, I decided to carry out the first process at the laboratory. This process is called refluxing and involves boiling a number of chemicals in a reaction vessel until they react together and turn into a golden-orangey colour. The reflux mixture was then put in plastic petrol containers and transported up to Cumbria.'

The Cartel had roped in a local publican to supply soft-drinks containers to store chemicals. He also acted as a general dogsbody on the job. The publican agreed to rent a holiday cottage in Bowness-on-Solway for £5,000 a week. The cottage was isolated and the chemical smells would be easily dissipated.

The Scousers offered Frank £90,000 for every ten gallons of pure amphetamine produced. Frank was confident that they would pay because the Scousers always boasted that they had the market to sell the finished product. Two other members of the gang included BJ and Trapper. Trapper was to pose as a gardener at the cottage so he could keep a look out.

A steam-generating machine was bought from an industrial caterer. Frank was proud of his technical prowess: 'The Instanta machine was required to carry out a process known as steam hydrolysis . . . which involves passing steam through the mixture and lifting the amphetamine out.'

But sometimes Frank's theories did not always work out in practice. One day, the makeshift laboratory exploded.

Frank said, 'We took the container outside and poured in sodium hydroxide and ran away just before the container erupted and cleared the height of the bungalow in a massive reaction.'

The explosion set the team back and much valuable product was destroyed. To make up the loss, the gang worked on another container of liquid and ended up working through the night.

Frank said, 'We weren't tired at all. This was because the steam escaping from the apparatus and the amphetamine mix was intoxicating us. Through the night we had completed about three "cooks" and had to separate the amphetamine oil from the water using separating funnels.'

But the operation was beset with more problems. The bungling chemists had bought the wrong acid, which would not turn the oil into the required paste. The Cartel was becoming frustrated with Frank and his chaotic gang.

Frank said, 'Charlie Corke was so annoyed that he started to threaten us. He told us that the people behind the financing would not be happy at all if all the amphetamine sulphate wasn't produced and told us what they would and wouldn't do if we weren't successful.'

For Frank, the venture had started out as a bit of a laugh and a chance to earn some money on the side. Now he was finding out what happened to civilians who got mixed up with Britain's most ruthless drug dealers. The Liverpool gangsters blamed Frank's technical consultant Roger Benson for the mishaps and threatened to attack an elderly lady he was living with at the time if he didn't pull his socks up.

By now, Charlie Corke was getting really angry with Roger Benson. He was shouting about what was going to happen when the main men found out that there were wastages and delays. In desperation, Frank and Roger then tried some different acids to turn the oil into paste. Luckily, the reaction worked. Their fear was overwhelming, so much so that they tried some of the speed themselves, to make sure the Cartel would be happy. When the substance worked, and proved non-poisonous, they began making more for their Liverpool bosses.

Meanwhile, in Liverpool officers began to put intelligence-led policing into practice. They launched an investigation into a businessman called Phillip Glennon, who had close links to Curtis Warren. The police suspected that he had evaded £1 million of tax in a fraud operation that involved burying money in his garden.

The 66-year-old former docker lived in a beautiful house in West Derby, an area popular with football players and showbiz stars. According to intelligence reports, police suspected that he was involved in tax evasion, money laundering and false accounting. More than £3 million worth of assets under his control could not be linked to legitimate income. When the police raided his home in September 1997, they were proved right. Officers dug up nearly £1 million in used and foreign notes buried in his garden. Many were guilders from Holland.

The raid led them to an acquaintance called Robert Jarvis, who was also involved in tax evasion, money laundering and false passports. Almost £500,000 of Jarvis's property could not have been purchased legitimately, police said. The police were on to something, even if it skirted the main issue. But they were ordered to keep on going. Gently they started prodding further, to see if they could properly infiltrate the Cartel.

CHAPTER 29

SETTLING SCORES

1997

THE SELF-MADE MILLIONAIRE Paul Burly now knew that things were in place for Bromley's demise, and he waited. He now worked on the other two suspects by informing their enemies of misdemeanours that had affected them perpetrated by Maguire or Sinnott. To be on the safe side, he had whispered truth and stated actions that had left victims, and now he was passing times and whereabouts to those who were clamouring for the chance to even things up.

A Liverpool mafia godfather called Charlie Seiga had befriended Bromley. Seiga had told Bromley that he was selling his big house, knowing that Bromley had become obsessed with it. The property had a heated indoor swimming pool. Cynical underworld sources have suggested that this was a ploy by Seiga to lure him into a trap. For the people who wanted him dead, this was an ideal scenario. One underworld source said that there would be an extra benefit for Seiga. By pretending to sell the house, Bromley would have to come up with the money. This would give Seiga an opportunity to steal the cash as well as kill him. That was the reason, underworld sources suggested, that Seiga was dangling a false transaction in front of Bromley. The theory was straightforward: Bromley would have to sell his assets to raise the cash to buy the house. The cash would then be hanging around until the deal was done – ripe for the taking. Bromley could not purchase the house in an orthodox way. He would have to purchase it under the table using untaxed, unwashed money. Whatever the underhanded scenario, gangland watchers said that Seiga was pulling a classic, convoluted, streetwise double con to set Bromley up, with a view to taking his money, and Paul helped fuel those rumours by having his friends add to them. In the meantime, Seiga continued his friendship with Bromley totally unaware that he was in some way aiding the forthcoming execution.

An excited Bromley started planning to remodel Seiga's house. The mountain-bike-riding fitness fanatic envisaged a sauna and a gym. He drafted in none other than Kevin 'Mad Dog' Maguire, the nightclub doorman and physical-training obsessive, to help him design the gym. Their world had become incestuous.

Just after Seiga and Bromley had agreed on a price for the house, the tax extortionist revealed a sinister secret. The Serious Crime Squad had told him that there was a £100,000 contract on his head. Had someone got wind of Paul's efforts to set him up? The police are often duty bound to tell potential targets if there is a serious death threat against them. There was some speculation that it was a separate contract placed on his head by cocaine baron Curtis Warren. On the same night that Seiga and Bromley went out to celebrate the house sale, in a casino they were forced to repel an attack with a 12-inch knife and a gun, for which they were arrested.

However, Seiga and Bromley's friendship continued to blossom. Tuesday, 18 November 1997 was a typical rainy Liverpool winter's day. Just after 3 p.m., an underworld acquaintance popped in to see Seiga at his home for a chat and quick read of the early edition of the *Liverpool Echo*. Ironically, the murder trial of the men accused of killing Stephen Cole was going on. The story had gripped the underworld. Local gangsters were desperate to see if there were any stories about it in the paper. Charlie had a laugh and a joke with his visitor then asked him to leave because Bromley was coming over and didn't like sharing his private moments with anyone.

At 4 p.m., Seiga phoned Bromley to confirm that he was coming for tea as usual at around 5–6 p.m.

Bromley duly arrived at 5.50 p.m. and carried his mountain bike into the hallway, saying, 'This is worth a couple of grand, and I don't want to leave it outside in case it goes missing.' As

Seiga went to put the kettle on, Bromley sat at the kitchen table and got stuck into the Cole story in the local papers. According to an account given by Seiga, Bromley declared: 'This crowd are going to get life for this murder. They've got no chance.'

Little did George know that his last words would be about a gangland murder. Little did he know that while he was reading that story he would undergo the same fate as Stephen Cole.

What happened next is a mystery, but later the police came to the conclusion that a hit-man had got into Seiga's house and shot Bromley in the head. The police initially believed that Seiga was in on the act, and that he and others were working as a contract-killing team that had set Bromley up.

But Seiga denied involvement, claiming that three to four minutes after Bromley sat down there was a ring at the door. Seiga opened it and was told by a masked gunman to get back into the lounge. The gunman then ran towards Bromley in the kitchen and fired three shots. Seiga heard the discharges as he was making his escape through the patio doors into his own garden, in which he hid until the scene went quiet. He assumed the gunman had fled.

'I saw George Bromley lying on his back on the tiled kitchen floor,' Seiga later told police. 'He was in a right mess. Part of his head had been blown away. There was blood all over the floor. It was a miracle he was still alive. He started making gurgling sounds, still breathing heavily. I picked up my phone and called 999.' Seiga also revealed the events in his 2002 book *Killer*.

Bromley's execution was cold, clinical and silent: three taps to the head, end of story. It was a textbook contract killing that was a world away from the blood-curdling frenzy of the Cole murder. The police found it hard to believe Seiga's account of the murder, especially when they started to examine his intelligence files. The records stated that Charlie Seiga was a known gangland hit-man, a 57-year-old tough guy whom Merseyside police intelligence had dubbed a 'killer'. His planning was known to be militarily precise.

The police had no idea of Paul Burly's secret plot to incite Bromley's enemies. Neither did they know of Paul's game of 'swaps' with Bromley's enemies, who also wanted him dead. They believed that the motive was simple: as usual it came down to money, police concluded. Intelligence reports stated Bromley had a £100,000 price on his head for upsetting cocaine baron Curtis Warren. They suspected that Seiga had taken up the contract on behalf of the Cartel. In addition, police had already warned Bromley that a second and separate execution order from a different gang had been issued. This contract related to Bromley taxing a local drug dealer. Only the real killers knew.

Paul Burly was thankful: one of his worries was dead and there was not one piece of evidence that could be connected to him. He had used the information route wisely.

Bromley had upset so many people that there were a myriad of motives for his murder. He had been an underworld extortionist who had many enemies. One victim, Jimmy O'Callaghan, was confined to a wheelchair with a colostomy bag for life after he was disembowelled. Bromley had blamed the tough Irishman for shooting him, and another man called John White for setting up the attack. In revenge, Bromley stabbed O'Callaghan in his behind in a pub. He then blasted the lower half of White's leg off so his leg was severely mutilated. They later became mates again and Bromley affectionately referred to White as 'Skippy' for his severe limp. Neither O'Callaghan nor White had anything to do with shooting Bromley. However, there were potential enemies who had a motive to kill Bromley all over Liverpool.

In another attack, Bromley and Kevin Maguire had fired more than 100 gunshots into a victim's house, causing his pregnant wife to miscarry. Another pregnant woman was nearly kicked to death while her husband was tortured. Another of Bromley's tricks was extreme psychological torture. On one occasion when he was trying to extract tribute from a young couple, he forced the female to lie down inside a body bag to give her an idea of how death felt. Another young man was kidnapped for two days and raped with a broomstick in a darkened cellar. Countless others were burned with irons, stabbed and shot.

Soon after Bromley's murder, things started to calm down. Business got back to normal. Colin Smith took over Curtis Warren's role within the Cartel. Another cell within the Cartel had discovered an excellent way of smuggling in drugs – bananas. Phillip Brown was a serial drug trafficker, later described by a judge as a 'nasty piece of work'. But he fancied himself. He'd moved to an upmarket part of the Wirral and reinvented himself as an independent financial consultant.

Brown was the mastermind behind a travelling network heavily linked to Curtis Warren that had sealed a partnership between Cartel legmen from Liverpool and villains from London and Lancashire. They'd been bringing in cocaine, but the plan now was to do some groupage: smuggling in superload cocktails of every drug they could get their hands on abroad.

They put together the team. Michael Melia was an unemployed driver from St Helens. Melia was a main Liverpool distributor. Gary Hunter, from East Peckham, Kent, was the manager of a distribution depot; the warehouse was used to unload the drugs. Melvin Radford, from Burnley, Mark Riley, from Liverpool, and Charles Hoskins, from Basingstoke, were in charge of storage, transport and security. Joseph Noon, from Liverpool, was another dealer. The gang sourced cocaine and cannabis from Europe, hid it in crates of fruit and began driving it into the UK. Things were moving. Police believed that at least ten other Liverpool crime groups were operating similar schemes. The Cartel was prospering once again.

But it was a case of one step forward, many steps back. Halfway around the world, in Curaçao in the Dutch Antilles, the Cartel was about to receive a major blow. One of its main suppliers was about to be unmasked and interned. Lucio, the Cali Cartel godfather who'd given Scarface and Kaiser their big break nearly a decade earlier, was about to be taken out. He was travelling on a false name using a fake passport in the name of Mr Lonzano. The Dutch police were pretty confident that they could identify him by his real name.

He was travelling from Bogotá, where he'd first met the Scousers, to the Caribbean, where he was to spend Christmas with his brother. But the Dutch authorities had been tipped off. When he landed in the Dutch colony, he was picked up on a hastily arranged warrant by spotters disguised as baggage handlers. On Christmas Eve, the DEA in Washington faxed over a set of fingerprints to confirm the ID of the suspect. It matched. The crack Dutch Prisma anti-drugs team had their man. His real name was Arnaldo Luis Quiceno Botero, known in the Cali Cartel as 'Lucho' and as 'Lucio' to the Scousers. To Curtis Warren, to whom Scarface and Kaiser had introduced him, he was known as Mr L.

Botero was put on a plane back to Holland and sent for trial on numerous international drugs charges.

Poncho said, 'We were gutted. No one could believe it when we heard that Lucio had been nicked. But at the same time, we couldn't believe our own luck, in as much as we'd seen it coming and trusted our instincts and got out before it all came on top. Me and my brother were in the UK, and Kaiser and Scarface had been laying low. They were still in Holland, but they weren't doing anything with Lucio.

'Luckily, after Curtis had got in with Lucio, they had taken a back seat and decided to find some more links. They'd known that they couldn't ride Lucio for ever and they'd had a good run and decided to branch out to some new pastures.

'After Curtis had got nicked they'd been doubly cautious. So by the time Lucio got done, they were well off the scene. Well under the radar.'

CHAPTER 30

DYLAN MARK 2

1998

DESPITE THE SECOND wind, by 1998 the Cartel was falling out of love with Amsterdam. Internal disputes had led to several shootings. Too many run-of-the-mill villains who were on the run were turning up in Holland looking for graft and a place to crash, expecting to find work within the Cartel. At one point, there were so many Liverpool criminals quartered in the city that they had their own football teams based around their postcodes back home.

The Cartel workers settled into a lazy life: shopping in Marks & Spencer for Chinese chicken wings and tea bags (they couldn't do without home comforts) and drinking away weeknights at the City Bar. Saturday was reserved for the Escape nightclub, which made them homesick for Cream. Meetings were held in the nooks and crannies of the Irish bars and the *bier kellers* in and off Dam Square. Soon there was a surplus of young criminals looking for 'work'. When the Cartel couldn't oblige, they turned to street crime.

Poncho said, 'I started to go back out there to graft. I didn't want to, with all the commotion around Lucio, but I had to. My cocaine round in the UK was petering out, so I was back doing stuff with Kaiser and Scarface over there. But it had changed quickly in the time I'd been away. By that time we knew the Scousers had fucked Holland, because too many of them had been hiding out there and were doing snatches and robberies.

We were one of few firms who saw the writing on the walls. Even our lads, who'd been there for a decade, were starting to stand out and attract heat. That was because of what had happened to Curtis and Lucio.

'Our people were black and mixed race, so we played the ethnic card and moved out of the city centre. We stayed anonymous in the minority districts. For instance, the Moroccans thought I was one of them when I was over there. By that time, the British police had spotters in Amsterdam and even they thought I was a foreigner, so it was OK.

'Then I went to the Dutch Caribbean for a while and sat out there. I slipped in there easily because they thought I was West Indian, which I was.'

On another subject, Poncho, Scarface and Kaiser had decided to let the murder of Stephen Cole go. For a start, they didn't know who had ordered the hit or carried it out. It just seemed like a load of grief between doormen. To go after the perpetrators now would bring heat on them at a time when the police were on them, or at least waiting for them to make a mistake, anyway. Now was the time to stay on the move, not to pin themselves down with a gang war.

Since the imprisonment of Warren, other Cartel cells had decided to give Holland a wide berth. They were now so powerful that the Colombians would come to them. The Cali Cartel sent a UK sales representative to set up shop full-time in London, to make it easier for the Scousers to place their orders. A former Venezuelan shipper called Ivan Mendoza di Giorgio started to get himself busy on the King's Road in Chelsea. Two of his first and most trusted customers were Spencer Benjamin and Edward Serrano, hardcore Cartel drug dealers who had come down from Liverpool to talk shop over a light lunch. They agreed that London was a safer meeting point than the Dam. They frequently shared afternoon tea in a Bayswater hotel.

Meanwhile, Dylan Porter was watching the money roll in. Above him was a mysterious Mr Big, a senior Cartel drug lord who dressed like a businessman and lived on the Wirral. Dylan had acquired a partner called Martin Neary, and they were seen as lieutenants of equally high rank. Neary's job was more hands-on than Dylan's, but still he never carried drugs himself. However, Neary frequently travelled to Europe to set up deals using a stolen car with false number plates. The car was always a ringer: the phoney registration numbers matched those of a car of the same make parked legitimately on a garage forecourt in Liverpool. So, to anyone watching, it always looked like the car stayed local. Meanwhile, Neary drove abroad via the Eurotunnel. One of the gang's main customers was Glasgow drug lord Ian McAteer. Every week he bought four kilos of heroin from Dylan's outfit for £40,000. Like clockwork, McAteer sent down the money with a courier called Warren Selkirk, who Dylan knew, trusted and had even grafted with. The four kilos were sent back up to Glasgow using a separate courier. The whole set-up ran like clockwork, which was partly down to Dylan's experience.

Dylan said, 'But it's a false feeling, earning 30 to 40 grand a month. I'd've felt better about myself earning £2,000 a month, in a normal nine-to-five, I really would.

'But the overwhelming feeling you have, the first feeling that stays with you, is the relief you experience when a parcel has landed. It's home: you've put money on it, and now you're happy because the investment is in safe hands.'

One of the key couriers bringing the drugs in was a 53-year-old disabled family man called Carl Emerson Frederick. Registered disabled, he exploited his condition as cover. Frederick even used a car he'd bought on Motability finance to travel to France. As an added distraction, he took his wife and children with him and placed his wheelchair – which he did not use – in the boot.

Dylan said, 'Twice a month the gear got dropped off. But the strange thing was, when you'd get the profit in a few days or weeks later, it would be an anticlimax. I'd come home with a Tesco bag full of cash. I'd say to my wife: "D'you need anything new? Have we got enough three-piece suites and tellies? Do you need any new clobber?" I still lived in a council house because we didn't want to show out. By then, the days of buying a house for cash were over. The police used to let you go if they caught you with cash; now it was criminalised, and if you went into a bank with cash, it triggered an alert. So I made sure my house was done up inside like *Dallas*. All in all, it was a pretty hollow way of life.'

Dylan said that he never had the 'brain' to invest in money-laundering scams. Partly out of guilt, he started giving money away to family. He said, 'They used to call me Robin Hood. I'd knock at my family's doors and go, "There's two grand." I got pleasure out of that.

'My brother worked for British Rail, and one day I showed him £180,000 in a bin bag in someone's loft, which I used as a kind of bank. But he was unimpressed. I will never forget what he said: "It's not worth a shilling because it's just gathering dust. You will never enjoy it."

'And he was right – it was a false economy in the sense that you never really benefit fully from the money because either you waste it, people charge you more for things such as cars because they know it's black money or you have increased expenses because you can't pay the bills in the normal way. Or you can't spend it: it doesn't seem real.

'I had spent tens of grands on the back kitchen, had all the back turfed. I'd done it up boss. I couldn't buy a bigger house with cash and I was too paranoid to go and see a money launderer. I just thought the money would be there for ever. So you just spend it on shit, sit down on the couch and change the channel. Just waiting for the next call from someone saying: "All good, lad," meaning that the last consignment had made it home.'

By now, Dylan's cell was a well-organised and tightly run operation. Within months, they felt comfortable enough to expand. Smuggling was stepped up to bi-monthly trips to the continent. After returning to Liverpool – to depots mainly located in the Toxteth and Dingle areas – the bulk of the heroin was sent to Cartel hubs in West Yorkshire and Scotland.

Dylan organised his end like a small business. Each member of the gang had his own role. Some were couriers, others arranged cars and accommodation. The top individuals, like Dylan, acted as 'facilitators', ensuring everyone knew what to do.

However, unbeknown to Dylan, there were already dark clouds gathering. The new policy of intelligence-led policing was reaping its first harvest. A new branch of the police called the Major Crime Unit was set up specifically to go after the big guns: dealers just like him. The net was being drawn tighter. After a tip-off, officers began to collate data on suspected heroin gangs. Within weeks, they identified a number of separate drug-smuggling cells, which were acting independently but had close links. Basically, they had mapped out one section of the Cartel that revolved around Dylan.

The investigation was soon formalised under the banner Operation Kingsway. Simultaneously, the MCU were targeting another branch of the Cartel, the crew that was meeting the Cali Cartel in London. But in Liverpool they concentrated on identifying the hierarchy around Dylan.

Bingo! It didn't take long for the MCU to hit pay dirt. They locked on to the Cartel boss above Dylan and quickly put a name to him. He was ID'd as Paul Lowe, a shadowy businessman figure that lived on the Wirral. The bonus was that the police soon discovered Lowe's smuggling route: he brought the drugs in through France. Dylan and Martin Neary were soon identified as his lieutenants. Below them, the police uncovered an elaborate chain of couriers and go-betweens that did most of the dirty work, making Lowe stand out but, at the same time, making him a difficult man to take action against.

At first, it was hard to believe that they used a disabled courier. Carl Emerson Frederick looked the most unlikely candidate to be a heroin smuggler, but soon the police had linked him to at least 11 trips to the continent, bringing heroin back to the UK and up to Liverpool.

Astonishingly, the police had been able to follow the trail even further. Once in Liverpool, the drugs were stashed away in two safehouses. The main one was the sparsely furnished home of a 30-year-old called Anthony Ellis on Toxteth's Upper Parliament Street, smack bang on the edge of Toxteth Triangle and a post-riot haven for drug activity. A second safehouse, run by a courier called Jason Smith, was found in a place called Wood Lane at the opposite end of the city, in Prescot. Under instructions from Dylan, Smith also acted as a local courier, taking the drugs to meeting points to hand over to link men from other cities.

Dylan organised distribution of the heroin throughout the Cartel's network. His contacts book was a Rolodex of Britain's underworld. His buyers in Glasgow included one of Scotland's most feared gangsters, a 40-year-old hit-man called Ian McAteer, who was also friends with another wing of the Cartel run by John Haase and Paul Bennett. Dylan had got to know McAteer through another Cartel bagman called Warren Selkirk. McAteer and Selkirk had met in prison. The incestuous spiderweb of connections was a sign that the Cartel was maturing, but it was also a weak spot that the police could use to knock down cells like a row of dominoes.

In Bradford, police learned the name of Dylan's link-up. He was supplying to gang boss Mark Davey, a 35-year-old operator who'd carved out a niche among the Asian gangs and the white mobsters from nearby Leeds. Often Dylan would cut them a deal. If the Glasgow and Bradford gangs sent their own couriers to Liverpool, he slashed a discount off the top of the kilo price: anything between £500 and £1,000 on a £20,000 wholesale purchase. Dylan didn't need the hassle; drivers were notoriously flakey. 'Stack 'em high, sell 'em cheap' was his motto.

At the coalface, the intelligence-led police operations were going well. But the Analyst never took his eye off the big picture. The property boom of the late 1990s was affording the Cartel an unmissable opportunity to legitimise their money on a grand scale. A new phenomenon appeared on the streets: sunbed shops, strings and chains of them on posh parades and in the middle of sink estates, kitted out to an incongruously high spec with few paying customers. The Banker was believed to have set up 30 sunbed shops in a money-washing scam. He also bought a large proportion of a city-centre site in Bold Street, including a shopping arcade.

A Cartel godfather called Dennis Kelly began working on a plan to import huge amounts of cocaine from Spain. As an in-joke, he bought a pub for a laugh: it was called The Dealers. He was based in Garston in south Liverpool. Garston was well connected because it was between Liverpool airport and the docks. The area was well served by several Cartel heavyweights, including Colin Smith, Stephen French, a notorious crime family and a professional hit-man. The locals were known as 'mudmen' and the Sunday League football teams turned out with boots full of guns in case it kicked off.

The Analyst said, 'More and more people in the criminal hierarchy were becoming more and more established. So across the city, there were a large number of individuals becoming more and more involved. For instance, if you look at just one example, Dennis Kelly, who was later locked up for a big importation of cocaine, he was gearing up in the late 1990s. In the early 2000s, he brought himself into a police investigation called Operation Copybook, the job that eventually brought about his demise.

'He was a first-generation drug dealer and then he brought his son into the family business. You looked at these people, who seemingly haven't had a lot of money, but then you started to see more and more wealth. First he bought the Dealers pub in Garston. I was thinking: "How are they able to buy a pub outright? Where's that money come from?"

'Then they started to live in nice houses in places such as Menlove Avenue, as opposed to back-to-back terraced houses on Heald Street in Garston.'

The Analyst knew what had to be done. He was determined to rise through the ranks, to attain a position where he could start using his encyclopaedic knowledge of the Cartel to more effect. He wanted strategic control.

He said, 'Everyone aspires to get to the rank where you can make those decisions that will bring down the likes of Kelly. I kept at it because I was confident that one day I could really go at the networks like they'd never been attacked before.'

CHAPTER 31

MAJOR CRIME UNIT

1998

ON A WARM mid-September day in 1998, a 34-year-old businessman walked into a gym in the Waterloo area of north Merseyside to work out. Darren Becouarn was not a member of the Crosby Health and Leisure Studio, but he seemed respectable and pleasant enough, so the manager allowed him to pay a visitor's fee for a one-off session. A quick round of exercise was all that he wanted. A harmless-enough request.

Becouarn quietly got on with using the machines and the free weights, casually chatting to regulars in between sets, politely following gym etiquette by asking other weightlifters if benches were free before using them himself. Everything was cool and he fitted in.

No one really noticed that as Becouarn pumped iron, he was discreetly eyeing up the layout of the building, paying particular attention to entry and exit routes. In street (and police) terms, he was 'casing' the joint to understand how the gym worked and who did what when. Were there any CCTV cameras? Was there any security? Were the exit doors locked with chains? Or could he break them open in the event of an emergency? All the time he was smiling, letting on and swapping pleasantries. Now and again, he even lent a helpful hand to fellow bodybuilders. Becouarn seemed like an ideal customer. Afterwards he had a shower before saying goodbye and leaving.

Over the next fortnight, Becouarn returned two or three times more to work out. He became a semi-regular, becoming familiar with the ebb and flow of the club: the punters, the culture, the floor map.

Meanwhile, Merseyside Police's Major Crime Unit was running several concurrent operations: a bid to swarm the Cartel by attacking drugs activities on several flanks. The Analyst noted that the force was becoming much more sophisticated in targeting criminals.

In 1998, two members of the South Liverpool Crime Group were doing particularly well from cocaine and heroin. Brothers Ian and Jason Fitzgibbon were related to the family with the Filipino heritage. They were importing drugs with a gangster called Pepsi Smith. In May 1998, police intelligence experts identified the Fitzgibbons as key players on the crime scene. Operation Black was launched, aimed at bringing the pair and their cohorts to justice. The police soon established that the Fitzgibbon brothers made up one of the most ruthless and dangerous crime gangs within the Cartel. The police investigation would turn into one of the biggest operations ever mounted by Merseyside Police.

Jason and Ian were second-generation Cartel bosses. Consequently, they were determined to be more violent in their approach than the older ones had been. The wars between rival door teams had led to a situation where each one tried to outdo the other in terms of who could be the most violent. Now everyone had to be bloodthirsty in order to penetrate the distribution cells and keep them in line. The police would have to rely on their own data gathering, such was the fear of giving evidence. People dared not complain about the gangs. To some extent, the brothers lived with *omertà* as an insurance policy.

The police learned fast. Like predators, the behaviour of the police began to mirror that of its prey. They adopted a similar set-up to the Cartel's structure. The MCU set up 'syndicates' of officers, which began a painstaking process of intelligence gathering that would continue for 18 months. The scale of the Fitzgibbon cell was bigger than anyone had imagined. They were supplying large amounts of heroin across Merseyside, Scotland and the Midlands, bringing it up from London, where they had forged their own links with Turkish gangsters.

Jason and Ian had learned from the mistake of first-generation barons like Eddie Gray. 'Don't be flash' was the motto. They bought themselves suburban homes in a middling area called Prescot, for around £80,000 each: hardly millionaire mansions but not bad for men with no declarable income.

Their only weakness was expensive cars, which they changed regularly. Like Dylan Porter's, their homes were modest but expensively furnished, and they travelled abroad a lot. At the heart of the cell was the sidekick gangster Peter 'Pepsi' Smith, who lived out in Runcorn.

The trio were at the centre of a hub linked to around eighteen homes and business premises in Liverpool, three in Scotland, two in Manchester and one in Cheshire. In July 1998, police watched Ian Fitzgibbon as he picked up one load from a single address – ten kilos of cannabis worth £72,000.

On the police side, the new watchword was 'patience'.

The Analyst said, 'It took time to investigate them because of the way they lived and operated. Similarly, we would give the police teams time. So they had the ability to start building a case over time, to prove the wider conspiracy. We started taking out seizures and shipments along the way, until we got sufficient evidence to convict, when the time came. This is when we started to cross the geographical boundaries of our force and move across into Europe.'

Merseyside Police was the only force outside London to have developed international capability: the resources, the know-how and the permission to carry out complex, cross-border investigations in foreign countries. For the first time, a new generation of coppers like the Analyst, who'd been brought up through the rank nicking drug dealers, were making the decisions that mattered.

The Analyst said, 'Before David Ungi's murder, we knew about drugs and we did target it. But now we had to put ourselves in a position of saying that we couldn't allow it to continue any more. I'm not saying that at any point in the past we ever acquiesced to it. But from now on, it was a case of saying: "Our focus is on this now – drugs – and we've got to stop this from developing." We got to stop it potentially going to the stage that it could have done. That's when the Major Crime Unit started targeting that level of criminality. I don't think the timing was right to do it before then, if I'm being honest. But it was only when we hit that threshold, around the David Ungi killing, that we realised that things were different.

'We started asking the questions: "How has it got to where it is? And what do we need to know?" So that led to a greater emphasis on intelligence. This coincided with being told by the government, in the late 1990s, that intelligence-led policing was the way forward.'

The force stopped talking about drugs and started doing something. Community intelligence was prioritised. Beat bobbies were ordered to find people who were prepared to talk and groom them. The motto was: 'Start small, then go after the big guys': a bottom-up approach that hit the Cartel at its weak points – poorly paid street dealers. The Analyst was a pioneer in this new approach. The Analyst began to run teams in two police stations, specifically targeting street-level drug dealing. Every house that he went to, every person he arrested was now shaken down for secret information about the Cartel. Someone, somewhere was bound to fold – and when that time came, the police, for the first time, were in a position to do something about it.

The Analyst said, 'My role was to say to the team, every one of those arrests is a potential informant: start speaking to them and see what they've got to tell you. One in ten would probably talk to you about criminality. They would probably give you the person who supplied to them.

'So then we'd step up a little bit and start looking at the first-level suppliers. And every one of them we did, we'd start to get a little bit bigger, and then those dealers would probably give you the person above them.

'And by the time we'd finished a piece of work, within 12 months we were taking out multi-kilo seizures as a little local team.'

The system worked. The Analyst may have been like a minnow gnawing away at a whale, but at least it was a start. Little did anyone know that his system would be the beginning of a police campaign that grew into the biggest anti-drugs force the country has ever known.

The Analyst said, 'Our interrogation was straightforward. Our goal was simple: "Where did your stash come from? You're going to jail for X number of years: if you help us, we can help you." Legally, there's an opportunity for text.'

Text was the police term for a secret report that could be written by an officer in support of a criminal going to trial. The text would detail the cooperation given to the police by a drug dealer and would be given to a judge before sentencing, in the hope that the criminal would get time off.

The Analyst said, 'More often than not, the dealers would take the bait and bite – and give you the next dealer, one up the rung. You'd get your operation together – we'd have to be more sophisticated with each bigger catch because they were more sophisticated. But we'd literally be hitting safehouses with multi-kilo loads inside, with thousands of pounds of cash hidden, as opposed to the situation we were in a couple of years before, when we'd take the door off a house and there'd be 15 sticks of cannabis in someone's bedroom that they're selling on their doorstep. At last we were getting where we wanted to be.'

The Analyst soon had two of the worst districts on lockdown. Street dealers knew to beware, that if they set up in his locale there was no point. Trouble would come their way. The Analyst would come and get you within a matter of days. But the Analyst always had to keep an eye on internal politics. Patiently, he'd gather intelligence until he knew that a safehouse was full of drugs. But it wasn't enough: he wanted the safehouse above that, and the one above that, so he held off and continued the watch. But the older officers, unfamiliar with the way it worked, wanted a quick hit, instant glory, drugs on the table.

The Analyst said, 'The safehouse is gonna be the key to tumbling the whole crime group. Politically, the senior officer wants a big hit. They want to publish a story; they want the drugs and guns out. They just want the glamour. But the team says no – you've just got to bear this through.

'The senior officers say, "No." They end up seizing the drugs and guns. No prisoners and they burn that line of inquiry for good. So the bosses get what they are after: the limelight for 24 hours. But it scuppers the operation.

'However, we soon learned from those experiences and said sometimes you've got to play the longer game for the greater benefit.'

There was also a greater emphasis on visibility: showing the community practical examples of how dealers were being taken down. The Analyst's squad went after the mid-ranking dealers who had the stone-lion statues on the corner of their gates. He busted them to prove a point. Within months, the house was up for sale. The Mercedes was gone from the driveway.

The Analyst: 'That's when it started to have the wider impact, when people saw that the police were actually doing something about this problem, taking them down, at all those different levels of criminality. You can do more at the lower level than you can do at the more sophisticated level – so you've got to express that physically so that everyone can see it.'

But as the intelligence got more heavyweight, the Analyst was faced with a new dilemma: the supergrass. Supergrasses were great because they were prepared to blow up a whole criminal infrastructure. But the problem was that much of their intelligence was historical. By the time they were sitting down in front of the Analyst, they'd half extracted themselves from the crime group. Therefore, they were less useful.

CHAPTER 32

SET UP

1998

COMPARED TO INNER-CITY Liverpool, Crosby was a relatively prosperous area and much quieter in terms of guns, gangs and drugs. Compared to other gyms, Darren Becouarn's new haunt was civilised and there were fewer gangsters. Becouarn settled in. He looked like a young professional with a salary to spend. He didn't speak with a Scouse accent, wore smart clothes and lived 'over the water' on the other side of the River Mersey, on the Wirral. Of course, he gave no indication that he had four previous convictions. His record for robbery was never mentioned. When other customers gossiped about the crime splash in the *Liverpool Echo*, Becouarn shied away. An awkward conversation about the fact that he just got out of prison on early release was to be avoided at all costs. He didn't want to go there.

During the sessions, like most gym users, he broke off for regular breaks and a drink of water. He took the opportunity to speak to those nearby. He was paying particular attention to two muscular men doing sets together: 36-year-old Kevin Maguire from Thornton, a feared nightclub doorman known as Mad Dog and sometime associate of the late George Bromley, and his sidekick, a younger man called Nathan Jones, who was only 24 and from a nearby estate in Crosby. Becouarn engaged them in conversation and shared the odd joke.

Maguire and Jones were ferocious bodybuilders. They worked out at the gym for between one and two hours most days, following a punishingly rigorous routine to boot. But they were happy to join in the locker-room banter with the newcomer. After all, Becouarn seemed genuine – and he was no threat to them.

Meanwhile, Merseyside Police were determined not to make the same mistakes that other forces and Customs and Excise were making. Intelligence-led policing was a powerful weapon, but it had a big weakness. First, much of the intelligence was from criminals. So could it be trusted? And could you use those criminals, who'd grassed up their mates, to go a little bit further, a little bit deeper, to set them up as well? This area was a legal and ethical minefield. Customs and Excise were learning that informants would and could fabricate evidence for their own ends: sometimes, like John Haase, on an industrial scale. In addition, there was a risk that so-called 'participating informants' would entice targets to commit crimes that they wouldn't normally have got involved in. Soon the underworld had dubbed intelligence-led policing 'the Judas system'.

The Analyst said, 'We never really got drawn into the supergrass system. We never used informants for evidence, only intelligence.'

Technically, informants were known by the acronym CHIS: covert handled intelligence source. Two years later, the good practice and methods pioneered and developed by the likes of the Analyst were codified-in-law. The management of informants was governed by the RIPA Act (the Regulation of Investigatory Powers Act 2000).

The Analyst said, 'Informants give you the edge when you start the case, but it's about the art of exploiting what they give you. You may never have known who that person was. If you take the example of Marks & Spencers in Amsterdam, the supergrass may say: "A dealer goes to Marks every morning for his croissants." That's the trigger for the operation and then you're up and running. The trigger leads to a safehouse. The safehouse leads to surveillance opportunities. Surveillance leads to associations: finding out who the target knows and meets with. Associations then go on to mobile phones. Finally, if you can attribute identities and information to mobile phones, then you've got a distribution network. This in turn leads to more safehouses to watch, which will reveal how and when the importation of the drugs take place.'

But once the drugs were over in the UK, that's when the

hard work started. The police mounted surveillance on distribution in the UK and began to link everybody through to someone else in the chain. As the operation as a whole came together, it was important that the police took their time and built the case stage by stage.

Customs and Excise were criticised in an official report called the Butterfield Review, which was sparked by the collapse of the famous London City Bond warehouse prosecutions in Liverpool. The cases fell apart after the court heard Customs officers had encouraged the offences in a sting operation. One informant had become a witness in the case, confusing the various roles.

The Analyst said, 'If you have a person who gives you information, he's called a confidential contact, and you can only meet them a couple of times. You can task them, but you can't involve them in the suspected crime, or the investigation side of things; that's asking them to do something wrong. If the relationship goes further, the confidential contact has to be registered as an informant. This protects them, and their rights are secured under Article 2 of the European Convention on Human Rights.

'Butterfield was the review of a case involving evasion of duty. You can't let someone become an informant when they are calling themselves something else in the case, just to make life easy for the investigation. Everything we do is robustly underpinned by legislation.'

As the big police operations had an impact, some Cartel members tried to switch sides to save themselves. But the Analyst was careful. He perceived the supergrass as a particular type of informant, like in the Northern Ireland situation, who went into the witness box and into the evidential chain. During the Troubles in Northern Ireland in the 1970s and '80s, the police and army had been successful in 'turning' former IRA members and converting them from intelligence sources into witnesses who gave evidence in court against their former comrades. The witnesses became known as 'supergrasses'. The Analyst refused to go down that route, no matter how tempting it was to burrow deep inside the Cartel. It was a frustrating decision, considering that he'd been building up to this point with the lower-level operations. But the law was the law, and he had to abide by it no matter how tempting the short cut was.

The law later allowed some informants to give evidence. But even that legislation, which allowed supergrass evidence under strictly controlled conditions, didn't come along for another seven years. In 2005, sections 71 to 73 of the Serious and Organised Crime and Police Act allowed police to use people as informants and as witnesses, to give evidence.

The Analyst said, 'But even back then in 1998, everything we did was underpinned by legislation. There was an authorising officer whose job it was to be independent and impartially decide whether it was legal, necessary and proportionate. There's a difference between informants and CHIS, who are prepared to give evidence.

'We use informants, and on occasion you can use participating informants, who can become involved in the low level of the criminality. But there are really strict rules about that, so that participating informers can only be peripheral. They can't incite the criminality. That meant that we couldn't use informants in isolation, just rely on them for a case. You've got to use them collectively, along with surveillance and your case building.

'You can build a conspiracy case. For instance, in Amsterdam, wiretapping or telephone interception is legal. So you can use it as evidence over here. If the dealers are involved in drugs trafficking in Europe then that's how they get caught: that's where Curtis Warren fell foul – because the prosecution used the telephone evidence from Europe in this country. If it's lawfully obtained in another country, it can be used here in British operations.

'There's a debate in this country about using wiretap evidence in court, but I don't think there's a will to do it. I think the problem lies around disclosure. If you wanted to use a conversation as evidence in court, you might end up with 1,000 hours of phone calls to be disclosed in evidence. You might only want to use two hours, but sure as eggs is eggs, the defence will come on one and want to know what's on the other nine hundred and ninety-eight hours. "Can we have a transcript?" Logistically, you just couldn't do it, could you? And if you just hand over the tapes, there might be something on there that is sensitive. So wiretap evidence is not as good as it seems.'

In April 1998, six regional squads were brought together to form the National Crime Squad. It was going to deal mainly with organised and major crimes. For this reason, the NCS reporting lines were streamlined. No longer would officers be hindered by having to report to their aging constabulary bosses who knew little about drugs. They would report directly to the Home Office, which was theoretically singing from the same hymn sheet: it was in their interests to make intelligence-led policing work. The NCS had nationwide and international jurisdiction but didn't have to get bogged down in security or terrorism matters.

The Cartel bosses were worried. The NCS's brief looked like a Cartel to-do list: drug trafficking, contract killing, gun running, money laundering, extortion, kidnapping and murder relating to any of the above. Crucially, the NCS could support regional forces like Merseyside Police. The NCS consisted of 1,656 full-time personnel, spread over three regional command units, including five Directors, 1,169 seconded police officers and 280 civilian police staff. Their resources were unprecedented, including a property portfolio of offices that would rival the Cartel's.

The new mood of optimism was accompanied by several successes. In late 1998, a top Cartel money-launderer called Ussama El-Kurd went down in history as the first person to be convicted solely for money laundering. El-Kurd had run a West London bureau de change estimated to have washed £70 million in dirty money, much of it linked to Curtis Warren. One of Warren's runners, Peter McGuinness, was jailed for ten years. Two of Warren's E dealers who had helped export drugs to Australia were arrested at Warren's old house and later jailed for ten years. During the previous year they had made £800,000 from the Oz connection, wired back to the UK in over 200 money transfers.

Joseph Noon and Michael Melia, who had set up a drugs run importing drugs in plantains from Antwerp Fruit Market, were nicked and jailed. Many believed that they had been set up by John Haase, who was seen close to where they had been arrested and was still feeding information to Customs and Excise.

The biggest fish was yet to be landed. In October 1998, Luis Botero, aka Lucio, was jailed for six years and fined one hundred thousand guilders: not much, considering his position, but the Dutch prosecution could only muster one highly incentivised paid-for witness, such was the fear of going against him. Lucio was sent to the same Dutch jail as Curtis Warren, which was ironic, as he was believed to be the mysterious man called Mr L who Warren had been heard referring to on Dutch wiretaps, although Warren and his lawyer denied there was any link.

Scarface and Kaiser were devastated for their old pal Lucio. Without him, there wouldn't be any Cartel. But at the same time, they had to count their lucky stars that they had not been drawn into the investigation. The whole Curtis Warren thing was turning out to be a mess and they felt guilty that they had introduced Lucio to him in the first place. Scarface and Lucio believed that Lucio had been caught because he'd wandered onto the Dutch wiretaps as the mysterious Mr L.

Despite the obvious successes, some police officers were still not happy. They became frustrated at the amount of red tape that some believed was holding them back. Crime groups weren't bothered by legislation, laws or rules, and if a plan didn't work they simply found a way around it. However, the rules surrounding informants were only a fraction of the legislation that the Analyst had to consider before getting down to the real laws: those concerning the offences under the Misuse of Drugs Act 1971 and the various related conspiracies. In addition, most of the Warren-related cases – which included a total of 80 arrests and the seizure of a staggering 4,000 kilos of drugs – were done under a joint police–Customs and Excise banner known as Operation Crayfish. The investigation was a model of cooperation, but Merseyside Police wanted its own capability.

CHAPTER 33

MAD DOG DOWN

1998

UNUSUALLY, KEVIN 'MAD Dog' Maguire had allowed Darren Becouarn the privilege of some small talk during his small number of visits to the gym. They were getting comfortable. Maguire was usually nasty and uncommunicative, according to those who knew him well. To some extent, Mad Dog was letting his guard down. The gym was his comfort zone. Maguire felt totally at home there. Like it was for most doormen, it was, in fact, a second home.

As a senior security boss, his whole livelihood depended on his being muscular and fit. Maguire had been training nearly all of his life. In the gym, he felt on top of his game, supremely confident and safe. He knew everyone in there, and a casual visitor like Becouarn seemingly had nothing to hide. He had come openly with a smiling face, revealing his full and true identity.

A lot of business between doormen was conducted in gyms. Being 'on the weights' had turned into a self-contained underworld subculture. For the Cartel's growing power base, gyms were the new churches. But as far as Maguire was concerned, with Becouarn it was just pleasure. He was a distant associate at most. An irrelevance.

Meanwhile, in April 1998, the Cartel nursed the country's biggest-ever speed factory into production. Using Cartel-supplied base material, amateur chemist Frank Smith had completed the first phase of the amphetamine-making process. This had been completed at his front laboratory. Now it was time to move out and upscale the operation for the final phase. This phase involved cooking up the intermediary chemical in a makeshift distillery, siphoning off amphetamine oil and then converting it to speed paste. For this, the Cartel had rented out a cottage in a chocolate-box village in the Cumbrian countryside.

However, within days the operation had descended into farce, more *Carry on Cartel* than Britain's most sophisticated narcotic facility. The team had given themselves daft code names. Charlie Corke was known as 'Bollocks'. Tony Johnson was 'Casey'. Chris Willows was 'Katie'. (Tony and Chris were middle-ranking members of the speed-making gang.) During the telephone calls, the front laboratory was dubbed 'the supermarket'. BJ was 'the neighbour'. Like most drug dealers, they talked in a form of crude code, as though that was going to fool anyone listening in. In reality, it did little more than bond the group – and they needed all the help they could get, for things were going wrong.

A helper called Terry Cheshire had brought his dog along to the cottage, but instead of guarding the entrance, the pit bull terrier kept eating the valuable amphetamine oil as it dripped out of the condenser, spilling on the floor. The dog got high and suddenly went berserk. Terry Cheshire had to take the dog for a long walk until it calmed down. Terry was worried in case his dog overdosed and died. The episode was a source of great amusement to the gang, who were working 24 hours a day, in sweatshop conditions. The rooms were filled with deadly fumes. But the stress was even harder to cope with: the gang were under constant threat of violence from the Cartel godfathers.

Each production cycle was known as a cook. The first cook produced 12 kilos of pure speed paste. A Cartel fixer called Charlie Corke bagged up each kilo. The most powerful, potent part of the paste was known as the 'brain' and sold for £2,600 a kilo. The non-rump standard paste sold for £2,000 a kilo.

The different-strength pastes were taken to Liverpool. They were given to a specialist 'bashman': a subcontractor who was able to dilute the pure speed with bulking agents, a specialist job that took a reasonable degree of skill. Each kilo of pure paste was cut in the ratio of seven-to-one with lactose sugar, meaning that in total one original kilo produced eight kilos. Each 'bashed-up' kilo was wholesaled for £1,000. The first cook generated £96,000 in kilo sales.

One day, a few of the Cartel bosses paid a visit to the Cumbrian factory to see how the operation was coming along. The group was led by Mr Big, who seemed to be in charge. Frank Smith felt as though he and his team weren't getting a fair share of the profits. In a bid to bargain up their fee, the workers plotted to give Mr Big 'a taste of what they had been through'.

Frank Smith recalled, 'You have to realise we were working with respirators, with caustic soda all over the floor and ammonia in the air. It got so bad that at one stage we filled the bath with water to allow us to stand in the bath to stop our feet burning, because the chemicals were eating through our trainers. The ammonia was burning our lungs.'

Frank and the workers played a trick on the visiting dignitaries by deliberately blasting them with the ammonia. It was a dangerous ploy that risked agitating Mr Big and the other Cartel bosses – some of them were high up and strictly hands-off – but there was a hidden agenda. Frank was scared that the factory was inefficient. They had used a whole three gallons of BMK, the raw material given to them by the Cartel, for the first cook: much more than had been budgeted for. Frank was worried that he'd get punished for wasting too much; he wanted to show Mr Big that the error was down to the dangerous conditions as opposed to waste or theft.

Frank and his team had been promised a flat fee of £90,000 for making the speed and a bonus of £5,000 for the bad conditions. Therefore Frank and the team were expecting a total of £95,000. But instead of being given £95,000 for the first cook's revenues, they only received a total of £25,000 in cash. That worked out at £3,500 wages each for the seven-man team that Frank was responsible for (which included himself) and £500 left over for sundries such as food and drink. In order to get avoid paying the balance, the Cartel argued that a total of £65,000 had already gone through Frank's account at his laboratory. This was true, Frank agreed, but he argued that that money was not wages but expenses and had been spent on equipment and chemicals and various other things such as cleaning gear and office supplies. Frank argued that he hadn't been reimbursed for this; hence he wanted the full £90,000 plus his bonus. The Scousers refused and said that he'd have to bear the cost of expenses. To add insult to injury, he later got a message from Mr Big refusing to pay the £5,000 bonus for bad conditions. Their ploy at demonstrating how hard it was to work in the ammonia-filled atmosphere had fallen flat. Frank was learning how the Cartel short-changed its suppliers and tricked them out of money. The horse-trading left Frank confused. When he and the workers complained, Mr Big threatened to have them killed.

On the second cook, Frank and his team were promised £140,000 each, plus £90,000 expenses. But the Scousers were contemptuous of the 'woolybacks' (the term that peole from Liverpool used to describe out-of-towners) and constantly played them in complicated Indian giving deals, where they pretended to give with one hand but took away with the other. The Scousers enjoyed horse-trading like the professionals they were, because as expert drug dealers they had the advantage of knowing the cost and sale price of all the materials, and they often left the amateurs bewildered and frightened during the complex trade-offs.

On one occasion, Frank Smith was conciliatory. He agreed to reduce his £90,000 fee claim by £20,000 in order to pay for a chemical called formamide (which the gang wrongly named 'formahide') that was urgently required. The Scousers laughed: they were never going to pay the £90,000 anyway, and Frank was getting deeper and deeper in debt with his legitimate suppliers, a liability that he was personally responsible for.

The rip-offs and the petty backstabbing continued. On another occasion, Frank discovered that he had some formamide hidden in the laboratory's stores. He tried to get the Scousers to pay for it in a ploy to recover some of his expenses. They promised £18,000, but he only received £1,500. The front laboratory was sliding into insolvency. Behind his back, the Cartel plan was to secretly 'long firm' the business: bleed it dry of all the registered chemicals it could buy, then bust it out and saddle Frank with the debt.

To pretend to help Frank, one of the Scousers proposed a side deal of supplying five gallons of BMK that would get them an extra £140,000 worth of speed to clear the debts. The Scouser said that they would make the extra speed on the side and not tell the Liverpool bosses.

A new team of amateur chemists was drafted in, including an

old mate of Frank called Tony Johnson. Tony Johnson had been involved earlier but only on the periphery as a kind of advisor. Now he was brought in full-time as a hands-on 'cook'. In the next, more efficient cook, the gang produced forty kilos from ten gallons of BMK and a further twenty kilos from Charlie's own side stash that he'd been given by one of the Scousers to clear the debts.

The Liverpool bosses arranged for their 40 kilos to be taken to the bashman. The helpful Scouser agreed to take away the unauthorised 20 kilos as well. Frank was reluctant to part with them, but he had few options; he had no alternative method of distribution. The drugs were transported away from the cottage in false-bottomed propane gas cylinders. But the containers leaked and the drivers got so high off the fumes that they went too fast and missed the turning on the motorway. Eventually they arrived in Liverpool. The Cartel converted the whole of the 60 kilos of pure amphetamine into 480 kilos of diluted drugs by adding seven kilos of adulterant to one kilo of pure chemical. Therefore one kilo of pure gave eight kilos of diluted speed. They sold the 480 kilos almost straight away. The profits were great: 60 times 8 times £1,000 = £480,000. But, as usual, Frank's share was low, even though he'd been promised an under-the-table bung to clear his debts. He and a couple of other workers got £7,000 each. Frank was furious.

CHAPTER 34

OPERATION PIRATE

1998

SOME GYM USERS described father of four Kevin Maguire as friendly and approachable. In the outside world, it was a different story. Maguire had risen to become a feared underworld enforcer for the Cartel. Even so, the top drug bosses didn't like him. But, for now, it was better to have him inside the tent rather than having him turn on them. Maguire was a stalwart on the cut-throat door scene and a frequent participant in gang wars over security contracts. But he was disliked, many believing that he threw his weight around and bullied weaker people to get what he wanted. He didn't even follow the general underworld rule that most Cartel villains lived by: Maguire seemed to target both criminals and law-abiding civilians alike, not caring whom he stabbed and shot. Maguire was of a new breed of arrogant, ruthless villains who considered everyone fair game in his battle for wealth and power.

Maguire had a previous conviction for a disorder offence and had been jailed in 1995 for the kidnap and assault of a 21-year-old student whom he stabbed in the leg with a pitchfork. His sidekick Nathan Jones, though younger, was a rising star in the door world and had previous convictions for a public order offence and assault.

As Maguire and Jones laddishly swapped quips with Becouarn, their killer waited calmly and smiled; he had them relaxed and totally unaware, and all he had to do now was wait for the right moment in order to make each shot count and therefore ensure the success of his hit. The lady who worked in the gym had to be out of the way so nobody else was to be endangered – that was an order from Becouarn's controllers, according to Paul Burly. Becouarn had been contracted by a middleman on behalf of someone who had been severely wronged by Jones and Maguire. But who that someone was Paul Burly had no idea – for he had sent a lot of information out to their victims via his network of reliable 'squeaks'. That was Burly's term for the gossips and underworld propaganda merchants who worked on his behalf. Burly was too careful to become directly involved. Burly could well have done the job himself he claimed, but he had no wish to risk a slip-up that could send him away to prison once more. Even though he felt it was a moral right that Maguire should it killed, of course it would be classed as a wrong in the eyes of the law. Time was now running out for Maguire and Jones, who had killed and maimed so many during their underworld careers. Many of their victims would see their murder as natural justice. Now Becouarn was awaiting his final orders to execute the important stages of the plan. In the meantime, he continued to nonchalantly familiarise himself with the scene of the action.

When he felt the time was right, his hand reached into the bag and unwrapped the towel . . .

Meanwhile, in Cumbria, things at the speed factory were going from bad to worse. The Liverpool drug barons were manipulating the men they had hired to make the amphetamine. One of the Scousers, Charlie Corke, offered another 'side deal' to help Frank get out of debt. The unauthorised cooks yielded thirty-five kilos from ten gallons of non-Cartel-sourced BMK.

But, again, Charlie Corke didn't pay them. He claimed that the final product made by Frank was substandard, blagging him that the crystal was turning black and brown. However, it was just an excuse. Frank's speed had been good. The brown sample that he showed Frank as proof of poor quality was someone else's that Corke had switched. Charlie was passing off somebody else's bad speed as Frank's in a ploy not to pay him.

To soften the blow, Charlie Corke offered Frank one final superdeal: he said that he had personally bought forty-five gallons of BMK from Holland, off his own bat, without Mr Big knowing.

He said that it cost £80,000 but if Frank made the speed 'on the side' again he could sell it back to the Dutch, with a sell-back price of £1,200 a kilo. By keeping it in a Dutch loop, the Cartel needn't ever know, Charlie bluffed. It was a testament to Frank's expertise that the Dutch criminals were now wanting to buy speed that he made rather than buy stuff made in Amsterdam.

Frank realised that 'things were getting bigger and bigger, and there was less and less chance of getting out alive after paying off all of the bills'.

A new worker called Taff Shipman was brought in, a computer student at Liverpool University. Taff was a specialist at making methamphetamine, a souped-up form of speed that commanded higher prices. They also discussed how to make a hallucinogenic designer drug made out of skunk oil and LSD. Seeing a way out of his predicament in methamphetamine that sold for a premium, in desperation Frank offered Taff research facilities at the laboratory. But Taff Shipman preferred messing about than getting down to business: he simply filled the office computer up with Internet downloads, emailed people about making drugs and eventually broke the hard drive.

The locals in Cumbria were becoming suspicious of the speed factory in their village, so the Cartel bosses demanded that a new factory be opened at a secret location, preferably nearer to Liverpool. Through Charlie Corke, the gang eventually found an old car mechanic's garage on a quiet road called Coal Pit Lane in Atherton. The venue was ideal because it had a car-spraying room attached equipped with a powerful extractor fan that could be used to disperse the fumes.

Frank's men pulled together, organising themselves like a 'gang' on a building site or in a coal mine. They were more amateurish than professional tradesmen, but they had a can-do, casual pragmatism which seemed to pull them through. They wanted to present a united front to the Cartel in a bid to negotiate harder. They threw themselves at the new work, hoping to get themselves out of debt.

The Liverpool bosses paid £10,000 for six weeks' rent on the old garage. The owner, who was called Carl, seemed to know that his garage was going to be used illegally, and he tried to cover his back by getting a legal contract drawn up so that he could blame anything on the renters. It was a long shot if things went wrong, but the Cartel bosses persuaded him that it was a get-out-of-jail-free card if the premises were raided.

Computer boffin Taff Shipman was rehired. He worked in a tidy area separated from the main factory by a black curtain. His job was to make higher-quality methamphetamine. Some people within the Cartel had become obsessed with 'crystal meth'. The drug had swept through several cities in the US like a typhoon, and it was hideously addictive but dirt-cheap to make.

When he was not watching porn on the office computer, Shipman had done lots of research into so-called 'super speed'. The Cartel bosses became fascinated with a story of how Nazis had used methamphetamine during the Second World War to fight combat fatigue. The Cartel wanted Shipman to make powder that they could press into pills for sale in the clubs. But they found out that the Nazis had laced chocolate with methamphetamine, which was popularly known during the war as *fliegerschokolade* (flyer's chocolate) or *panzerschokolade* (tanker's chocolate) to keep soldiers awake while operating heavy machinery. The Cartel had already done their market research. The reason why they wanted meth was because it fitted neatly into a niche, between downmarket normal speed and designer Ecstasy. By 1998, the bottom of the E market had fallen out because of the low quality of MDMA. Consumers were wary of cheap imitations, but they were no longer prepared to pay between £10 and £25 per tablet. If the Cartel could peddle a meth tablet at between £5 and £10 a pill, they were convinced they'd strike gold. What's more, if they could add it to chocolate or sweets, then it'd be a gimmick that'd fit into their demographic. To protect the brand they would have to keep one story about meth a secret: Adolf Hitler had become addicted after receiving daily injections to overcome depression and tiredness.

Shipman got busy and was granted unlimited resources and special privileges to work on the secret project. He worked like a scientist, and the people next door were impressed that he made a 'catalyst' to hurry the reactions along.

Frank said, 'His methods were extremely clean and quiet. His method involved dropping a chemical at two drops per minute.'

Eventually Shipman produced 520 grams of methamphetamine, which he said would cover his wages. He was promised £10,000 but only got £6,000. Charlie Corke came to collect the meth and took it away to the cutter. But, once again, he came back later complaining that it wasn't as good as the standard amphetamine that Frank was making. The Scousers were playing different parts of the gang off each other.

Frank said, 'I took this to be Charlie Corke lying to us again, so he could cream some money off the organisation.'

Frank got on with his part of the bargain. This time he honed the chemical process down to a fine art, with imported equipment and a new recipe. But still his workers made mistakes.

He said, 'The refluxing was carried out in giant 25-litre flasks. While we were doing the separations of the amphetamine oil and water, Terry Cheshire was being intoxicated by the fumes and was getting confused and pouring the wrong chemicals into the wrong containers and generally messing up.'

The third cook made 60 kilos of pure amphetamine, which generated £480,000 at wholesale. Frank hoped the Cartel would show mercy and pay him the several hundred thousand pounds he thought he was due.

Frank said: 'I can recall at Atherton that Charlie Corke paid £5,000 to everyone. Before I had even had a chance to count the money, he said he owed someone £13,000 and was £5,000 short, so he needed to borrow the money back from me.'

Instead, all of the money was handed over to the Cartel Mr Bigs. They included a gangster with close links to John Haase, another villain called John Byrne (who had no links to Haase but was known to police), and a Cartel speed expert called Terry Yates. He was a cook who specialised in producing speed using an efficient, high-pressure method.

CHAPTER 35

SPEED KING

1998

ON 28 SEPTEMBER 1998, a few days after one of Becouarn's visits to the Crosby gym, a 36-year-old mature student called Neil Green said goodbye to his girlfriend. He left their flat in nearby Aintree and went out. It was the last time he would be seen alive.

Just over 36 hours later, on 30 September, his body was found face-down in sand dunes on the beach at Ainsdale, near Southport, Merseyside, by a man walking his dog. A bag of cocaine with a street value of up to £50,000 was discovered in Green's Vauxhall Vectra car, which was found less than 50 yards from his body. There were no signs of a struggle, Green did not appear to have been robbed and there were no signs of foul play. Green was a social studies student who had no visible links to the underworld; even though a small amount of drugs was discovered in his car, it was probably not enough for police to suspect the usual motive: that it was a drug deal gone wrong that had resulted in a murder. The mystery deepened when detectives admitted they were baffled by the death on the popular stretch of beach.

The underworld rumour mill ground into full gear. Some gangsters believed that Green had been unwittingly recruited as a low-level drugs courier by the gang currently at war with Maguire, or that he at least had some loose connection to them. Because Maguire and Nathan Jones knew Green well from around the neighbourhood, they had then decided to 'tax' Green by stealing all of the drugs and money he had, an unspeakable double-insult to his enemies. They lured him to a meeting on Ainsdale beach to force him to hand over the drugs. Even though he had £50,000 worth in his boot, a terrified Green refused to tell Maguire and Jones where the drugs were for fear of upsetting his own bosses. If he handed them over, they would be sure to kill him. He was caught between a rock and a hard place. Maguire and Jones began to torture him, possibly by forcing his head into the sand or seawater so he couldn't breathe. Suddenly they went too far and Green died. Maguire and Jones quickly left the scene, not even caring to search his car in case a passer-by stumbled upon the murder.

Other underworld speculators said there was a similar but simpler explanation. Green had unwittingly got caught up in the drugs business and was paying protection money to Maguire. When he failed to pay, he was killed: whether it was on purpose or by accident was irrelevant. In disgust, Green's furious pals then ordered revenge by asking for help from the gang that Maguire was at war with.

Whatever the truth, it was a matter of underworld semantics. The facts were simple: Green's sudden death seemed to be the alarm that triggered the gang bosses controlling Becouarn to send him into action. One of the other gangs behind the order was rumoured to be the cocaine cartel run by Curtis Warren – the richest criminal in British history, worth £200 million. Though Warren himself was serving 12 years in a Dutch jail for massive coke smuggling, underworld sources claim that members of his gang back in Britain, on the outside, had put a £100,000 contract on Maguire's head.

Underworld contract killings are rarely that straightforward. Had Paul 'piggy backed' onto Warren's execution order by passing on badly needed information and a phone number via a trusted friend? Did he now want the other two dead, and if so, was that the reason he was already in touch, in the same way, with a few of the victims that Maguire and Sinnott had left littered around the city?

Meanwhile, back at the speed factory in Atherton, the cook was producing a huge amount of dangerous toxic waste. The dirty barrels – two forty-five-gallon drums and twenty five-gallon drums – were also full of incriminating evidence. Instead of getting rid of them carefully, the gang disposed of the waste like they did in Mafia films. Some of the criminals who worked for Frank were so desperate for cash that they wanted to steal the waste to recover extra amphetamine residue.

Frank said, 'I was later horrified to be told by Tony Johnson that he had seen the barrels at the side of the road and was thinking about recovering them to extract the oil. I was worried in case the barrels leaked into the water system.'

The cutter, or bashman, lived above a pet shop on the High Street in Skelmersdale, a town on the border between Merseyside and Lancashire. He mixed the drugs with the bulking agent in large blending machines that he had in the rear of the shop. Under the instructions from the Cartel, he sealed the drugs with a vacuum-packing machine in bags used to wrap bacon for supermarkets.

One day, Frank and Charlie Corke went to drop off three kilos at a Cartel Mr Big's house in the plush Sandfield Park district of Liverpool. Frank wanted to use the opportunity to go over Charlie's head and appeal directly to the big boss for a better deal. But he was naive to think that he would be granted an audience. Charlie stashed the drugs in a skip near the boss's house and then said to Frank that Mr Big lived in one of the big houses on the estate. Frank was amazed at the size and splendour of the mansions.

The Cartel demanded that Frank expand and franchise out his operation. A second factory was set up in Cumbria. A third was planned at a farm in Knowsley. The farmer said he would take the kids away for the summer in exchange for a huge fee. But Frank was getting increasingly desperate and confused.

Frank said, 'In short, I was fearful that I could have been killed: dead men don't talk.'

One day he overheard the Mr Bigs having a meeting. 'The figures they were talking about were astronomical: in their millions,' said Frank shaking. Frank Smith was becoming scared for his life, so he hatched a plan. He went on holiday to Majorca, but he was planning to use the opportunity to disappear. Before he fled, he hid all of the lab equipment and chemicals in a container on an isolated farm, effectively bringing the Cartel's speed operations to a standstill. He'd got it in his head that he'd hold the Cartel to ransom: 'Pay me what I'm owed and I'll tell you where the equipment is.' The threat was foolhardy to the point of suicide. He was planning to blackmail the gang bosses into paying him what he was owed, as well as the debts at the front laboratory. If they did, and gave him assurances that he wouldn't be punished, he'd come back to work and give them the equipment for the new factories. If they didn't, he'd disappear.

But the Cartel wouldn't play ball. The gang threatened to track him down and shoot him. In addition, they made it clear that they'd kill his son, who was back in the UK, if he didn't stop messing about. Panicking, Frank flew back from Spain to try to sort things out. But he was too scared to meet them. He lost his bottle and ran off to a safehouse in Cornwall.

At this point, the situation got very messy and mysterious. One of Frank's old mates called Tony Johnson, who had been one of the cooks in Cumbria, had decided to branch out on his own. He knew where Frank had hidden 'the glassware' and the other vital ingredients needed to make speed. Tony saw no reason why he couldn't set up his own factory in Frank's absence. After all, the makings were just sitting there doing nothing and he was skint. All he needed was some backing. Crucially, he needed a partner with access to distribution. Without any guidance from Frank or the Cartel bosses, it wasn't long before he was out of his depth and walking into a big mistake. Tony Johnson joined up with a local villain called David Parsons, who promised him cash, free supplies of BMK and access to dealers to sell the finished product. But Tony was heading into a trap. Parsons was working for the National Crime Squad, as an undercover participating informant. The National Crime Squad were desperate to get an 'in' within the Cartel. As the first speed operation imploded in Frank's absence, they saw a chance, amid the confusion, to pick off the weak links: hence Tony Johnson. They hoped that by the time the next cook got underway, they'd have one of their snouts close to Johnson and at the heart of the production.

Through Tony Johnson, Parsons was quick to bleed him dry of all the Cartel secrets he had learned over the past few months. David Parsons also found out from him that the Cartel had just set up a new factory in Cumbria that was bigger and more productive than the first one, which had been set up by Frank. Frank's ploy had not stopped them from making speed. They'd simply gone out and bought more glassware and employed new technicians to operate it. Parsons passed the information up the chain. Within days, Charlie Corke and the Scouse operation were arrested in Cumbria. Tony Johnson's independent factory wasn't busted, and Frank was still on the run.

In his safehouse in Cornwall, Frank had got wind that his mate Tony Johnson was hanging around with a suspicious new contact called David Parsons. He'd also heard that the second cook in Cumbria had been busted. It didn't take him long to put two and two together. He concluded that the Scousers had been blown up by David Parsons, who had suddenly and conveniently appeared on the scene.

He was right. Parsons's motivation for informing was simple: he wanted credit from the police. First, he claimed that he benefited by police turning a blind eye to his own drug dealing. But there was also a more perfidious type of self-interest at play. By taking out the Cartel's newest speed factory, he hoped to capitalise by exploiting his monopoly on the market. He had got a share of Tony Johnson's speed production. Now he had manipulated a gap in the market that the Scousers had once filled. Effectively, he was using the police to do his dirty work for him and take out the competition.

In a statement to police, Parsons said, '[A big drug dealer called] Michael gave me 15 to 20 kilos of bad Ecstasy tablets that had gone wet and formed into a mash. I told [my police handler] that I had obtained tablets off Michael and gave the handler a sample of the tablets for him to test to see what they were. The NCS said they had a high percentage of amphetamine.'

By this time, Parsons had also come into possession of some lab equipment, some of which was probably technical glassware that had been hidden from the Cartel by Frank Smith. Frank's original glassware had been hidden in the steel container by Tony Johnson, who probably tipped off Parsons as to where the valuable equipment was. Instead of handing it over to the police as evidence, Parsons claimed that he told his National Crime Squad handler, who agreed that they could use it in a sting on Frank Smith, in what was rapidly becoming a very convoluted exercise.

David Parsons said, 'My handler at the NCS then told me to use the glassware I had obtained (this was obtained to set a factory up in order that we could set up Frank Smith, who was another person my handler was after at the time) and turn these bad E's back into amphetamine so that I could buy BMK to set Frank up.' However, the police officers involved later denied any wrongdoing and were never found guilty of breaking any rules or the legal codes governing investigations.

Parsons was crossing the line. As an informant, he was doing everything that the Analyst had warned against. Effectively, Parsons was saying that the NCS were allowing him to set up a drug dealer at their behest, using E tablets and equipment that he had obtained from the underworld. Then he was going to sell the reconstituted E tablets to fund the purchase of speed-making chemicals, to then set up a drug dealer whom the NCS had expressed an interest in catching: exactly the type of bad behaviour from participating informants that The Analyst had warned about.

David Parsons said, 'I was telling my handler that it was costing me a fortune in expenses running about and buying the BMK. He also told me to take some of the BMK to make a paste to cover the expenses that I had paid out. The handler also used me to set up Frank Smith. Both myself and the handler were looking for places to rent in order to set up a factory to get Frank Smith cooking. On one of my meetings with the handler, he brought with him some papers of properties to rent in Wales and enquired about them from his own mobile. Eventually, a place was booked and I sent the deposit down for the rental of the property. The intention of this was to set up a factory so that we could get Frank Smith cooking so that [my handler] could bust the factory and catch him.

'I have already mentioned about some bad Ecstasy tablets that my handler told me to turn back into amphetamine after he tested them. In order to do this, the handler told me to set up a factory as we already had the glassware and the chemicals.'

At the last minute, the venue was changed from Wales to the north-east.

David Parsons added, 'He was also aware of the fact that he would make a profit on this factory, but this stage was never reached, as we were unable to reverse the tablets, so they ended up getting buried.' Once again, the police officers denied certain allegations made by Parsons and were never found guilty of doing anything wrong.

Frank Smith was lured out of hiding by David Parsons's offer. Parsons promised him that he wouldn't tell the Liverpool gang and that if they set up a speed factory together, it would be run as an independent and the profits would be shared equally.

Frank helped him set up the factory in the north-east on some land that had been sublet to them.

Frank said, 'When we went to Durham, there was myself, Tony Johnson, David Parsons, a man I know as Neil Carter and a huge man called Mark who used to be a bouncer.'

Neil Carter, according to informant David Parsons, was a big drug dealer who liked guns. Carter was also being protected by the NCS. Mark was probably a drug dealer called Mark Lilley, whom the NCS were also targeting and had previously asked David Parsons to bring down. Detectives bugged Mark Lilley's home in a bid to obtain more evidence. It seemed as though David Parsons was bringing together all of the targets that the NCS wanted so that they could be arrested in one swoop.

There is a slight difference between David Parsons's story and the account given by Frank Smith. Previously, David Parsons had said that the mushy Ecstasy mixture had been buried. But Frank claims that Neil Carter dug the sample up again. He brought the 25 kilos of damaged E's, which he described as a 'large amount of brown sloppy material similar in texture and appearance to clay'. Frank said that they set up a cook and were successful.

'In fact, we did recover the MDMA and obtained a thick brown oil,' he said. 'We then cleaned the oil using steam and ended up with 700 ml of MDMA. This was mixed with the cleaned bulking agent, which had been removed and turned back into powder.'

Technically, the police were now able to link Mark Lilley to drug dealing, no matter how spurious and set up it seemed. Even though the MDMA base had been supplied by the informant David Parsons, it could still be used against Mark Lilley as evidence. His house was raided shortly afterwards and he was charged with drugs offences. Cocaine, heroin, Ecstasy, amphetamines and cannabis resin totalling £1.2 million were seized from him. Firearms were also recovered. From the outside, it looked like a dream bust and Lilley was facing a long time in jail. But later he skipped bail during a trial at Bolton Crown Court and fled to Spain. In his absence, Mark Lilley was sentenced to a 23-year jail term for conspiracy to supply drugs, but he has never been brought to justice. Lilley still remains on the Crimestoppers' list of the Most Wanted Spanish-based fugitives, known as Operation Captura. Despite several appeals, he has refused to come back from Spain, claiming that his case was corrupted by the police's bad handling of its wayward informant David Parsons.

Elsewhere there were other criticisms of the police for allegedly inciting crimes during investigations, one involving Curtis Warren's friend Phillip Glennon. In a court case involving a corrupt police officer being paid by Warren, Glennon was described as 'a very wealthy man as a result of drug-dealing activities from which he amassed a fortune'. Glennon hit back in a statement he made public through his solicitor after the court case, accusing the police of 'consistent and cynical breaches of the law', blaming 'senior officers at an international level'. Even so, the case was a success: the corrupt copper and two of Warren's cronies were jailed.

CHAPTER 36

THE BUST

1998

ANOTHER CASE WAS also coming to a conclusion. It was 11 a.m. on Thursday, 1 October. Two days after Neil Green's body was found on a beach near Crosby, Darren Becouarn paid a final visit to his new gym. He handed over the visitor's entrance fee as usual and entered the weights room. Both Kevin Maguire and Nathan Jones were working out. Maguire's common-law wife, Linda, was also in the gym, as were the premises' two owners, Carl Tierney and Mark Scott. A couple of other customers were hanging around. There was a total of eight persons in the area, including Becouarn, making it a quiet time of day.

Becouarn pumped iron for half an hour and chatted to Maguire, his wife and Jones. He was a cool customer. Becouarn did a few more sets before exchanging more small talk. Suddenly, he reached for a canvas bag and pulled out a long-barrelled handgun from inside. He aimed the revolver at Maguire. At close range, he blasted the doorman with one shot. Maguire was killed instantly. Naturally, Jones was terrified. He immediately began running towards the door. Coolly, Becouarn moved towards him, took aim at his heart and fired. The wound in Jones's chest was massive but not instantly fatal. However, Becouarn was not interested in hanging around to find out whether Jones would live or die. A third shot was fired before the assassin made his escape.

Nathan Jones managed to stay on his feet. He staggered into

a changing room before collapsing. He lived for a few more minutes but later died on his way to Fazakerley Hospital. Before the alarm was raised, Becouarn ran out of the gym and got on the back of a black Honda Trials motorbike that was waiting outside. Quickly he was driven away by an accomplice. At nearby Victoria Park, the assassin and his getaway rider abandoned the bike. Police believe that at this point they were met by at least one of the Mr Bigs involved in the hit: the senior hit-man who had planned the whole operation and oversaw its implementation, a Mr Big who had insisted on split-second timing, and observed the unfolding events from a short distance away.

Detectives believed that at this point Becouarn and his motorbike man jumped into a dark-coloured car and that either the Mr Big or another accomplice drove them to safety. The killing had all the hallmarks of a professional slaying. It was a three-part pattern of events: triggerman – motorbike-getaway – car. It is a tactic that has become standard within the underworld and in political assassinations.

The use of the motorbike in targeted killings had first been used by the Mafia in Italy in the 1970s: simple, cheap, deadly. From a tactical standpoint, the technique ticked all the boxes of a textbook attack: speed, aggression, mobility. On the street, Mafia *pistoleros* had liked it because both the identity of the getaway rider and armed pillion passenger could be hidden using helmets during the escape. In this case, although Becouarn's ID was known, the bike driver's wasn't, which made it difficult to link the shooter to anyone higher up the chain. The bonus was that after a racing exit from the scene, the assassins didn't have to torch the bike. If they were using a car, the standard practice was to burn it out later. Motorbikes, however, are much less recognisable by witnesses and fewer forensics stick to them. Consequently, the bikes could either be disposed of, as they were in this case, or hidden and recycled on the next job. Not having to petrolise the getaway vehicle and set it alight saved hassle and money. The principals who contracted out targeted killings may have been wealthy, but like many 'businessmen' they were greedy and liked to keep costs down.

During the 1980s, the model had been exported and adapted by IRA terrorists, Colombian drug cartels and crime outfits worldwide, such as the North London Adams family who had made it their trademark method of slaying. The tactic had been modified with back-up cars, triangulation of fire and weeks of preparation: just like with the Becouarn hit. The Cartel had become experts in rubbing out their irritants.

A murder investigation swung into action. Officers were convinced that the Maguire/Jones double-hit was a contract killing from start to finish. Among other theories, they suspected that the Mr Big had been awarded the contract by Curtis Warren's gang, which wanted the pair dead. The Mr Big had then subcontracted the job of triggerman to Becouarn and wheelman to his mysterious motorbike-riding associate, also providing them with the firearm, the know-how and an idiot's guide to how to carry out the plan.

Meanwhile, hapless amphetamine king Frank Smith was getting busy setting up a new drugs factory in County Durham. Foolishly, he had decided to set up independently of the Cartel, even going behind their backs. Smith had double-crossed his Liverpool mafia bosses and they had people searching for him in various parts of the country.

The second big mistake Smith had made was to find a new partner. The third was that he chose a police informant called David Parsons, who'd been tasked by the National Crime Squad to infiltrate the Cartel. Though Smith had fallen out with the Cartel, the NCS's plan was to concentrate on the peripheral associates in the hope that they would serve up the big bosses at a later date, possibly by giving evidence against them in court.

So desperate were the NCS to get into the Cartel that it was claimed that they had allowed their nark far too much scope. There was too much incitement to trap Smith rather than let the crime run its natural course. Parsons claimed his police handler allowed him to source the equipment to help Smith build a factory and the E tablets to set Smith up, and that the handler had even helped check out properties. However, later the police officers denied any form of malpractice or corruption and were never charged or convicted with any allegation of abuse of office.

The policing tactics may have been questionable, but Smith and Parsons's new factory quickly became a roaring success, so much so that they carried out five separate productions of amphetamine at the Durham site, one after the other: a major feat in underworld terms. In total they manufactured an estimated

30 kilos of very high-grade synthetic drugs. The active ingredient was then bulked out to eight times its original weight, giving a distribution mass of 240 kilos. Each wholesaled for £1,000, yielding a total of £240,000. Finally, Frank thought, he was getting the rewards he deserved.

Much of the profit was Frank's and he was very pleased with himself. Now he wanted to set up a second factory with Parsons. All of his suspicions that Parsons was a grass were gone. He was getting more and more confident, so much so that Smith said that the gang could even use his old house in Thatto Heath as a cook venue. The location was a big risk for Frank. Not only was it in a built-up area where the fumes might hassle the neighbours, but also the comings and goings at all times of the day and night might attract heat from the police. In addition, the area was close to Liverpool, where the Cartel had put a price on his head. He'd be working in their backyard.

'Fuck them,' he told the gang. 'We can do it without the Scousers, and the last place they'll look is right under their noses.'

Smith also convinced his top cook Tony Johnson that he could manage the fumes using better technology. Frank was getting high off his own abilities.

Frank got busy making plans. He asked David Parsons to source some of the chemicals. Parsons said he could get the BMK. As good as his word, he soon afterwards came back with the drums full of illegal chemicals. Later, this cache of BMK would cause great controversy. Parsons claimed that the police had given it to him to give to Frank, effectively inciting a crime and propping up a speed factory that would not have existed otherwise. To make matters worse, Parsons also claimed that the police had got the BMK after raiding another speed factory in St Helens owned by the Cartel. Parsons was claiming that the police were recycling illegal drugs and evidence from one case into another. If true, it was a highly dubious practice.

However, Parsons was less successful in sourcing other chemicals needed for the process. He got confused and made elementary mistakes. He ordered a solution called formaldehyde instead of what Frank had requested: the usual formamide. The error set them back several days, forcing Smith to hang around longer at the factory than was necessary, waiting for Parsons to come up with the right stuff to add to the BMK. During this phase, Smith was particularly vulnerable: a sitting duck. Had Parsons made this mistake on purpose and planned the hiatus deliberately?

'I was sat on their settee waiting for the phone call from David Parsons at around 11 a.m.,' recalled Frank, 'when the front door was forced open and I was arrested by uniformed police officers.' The police had caught Frank red-handed with his cooking gear and BMK, bang to rights.

To his horror, after being charged, Frank was put on remand at HMP Liverpool in Walton: a jail full of Liverpool drug dealers and notorious for violence. The Cartel was still after him, not having forgiven him for running off with their chemicals and equipment, and he knew he was vulnerable. The Scousers also hated Frank more after finding out that he had chosen Parsons as his partner, the snout they now suspected of grassing them up. Smith cowered in his cell, hoping that no one would recognise him. But things got worse. News reached him that the Scousers from the second Cumbrian cook were in Walton. And he wasn't the only person who had been nicked during the latest round of arrests. All of the rest of the original gang – including several Liverpool bosses going back to the first round of cooks in Cumbria and Coal Pit Lane – had been swooped upon as well. It seemed as though the police had been watching them for months, and Smith's arrest was just one part of a big operation. In all, nineteen men were rounded up from all over the country, including three from the Wirral. Astonishingly, it turned out that the police had been watching them for ten months, between 1 February 1998 and 11 November 1998, at all the locations that had produced amphetamine, as part of a massive joint operation, codenamed Pirate, between police forces on Merseyside, Cheshire and Cumbria and the National Crime Squad.

The pieces of the jigsaw began to fit together. The alleged Mr Big was an appropriately named 41-year-old Liverpool boss called Frederick Cook. He was so high up that Frank Smith had never even met him. All the other suspects were there in prison, including Charlie Corke and John Byrne. After Frank Smith had left the Cartel operation, Cook had ordered the remaining members of the gang to set up a new factory in Cumbria. They'd chosen West Mead cottage in Bowness-on-Solway. This time, Cook declared, he wasn't interested in ten- or twenty-kilo batches.

He wanted them to take the expertise that Frank Smith had given them and produce amphetamine on a hitherto-unknown industrial scale. Now that dance drugs were in decline, the Cartel were plotting to flood the UK with cheap speed and turn the towns and cities into US-style crystal meth wastelands. The police had smashed down the door of the cottage on 17 September 1998 in a bid to stop this new frightening phase in its tracks. They found chemicals and components that made 750 kilos of drugs, just like Cook had wanted.

Rumours were flying around the jail that the Cartel bosses were 'straightening out' all of the lower-rung members of the gang. One target included Brian Jefferson, whose decision to dabble with the Liverpool underworld had nearly cost him his life. BJ, as he was known, had been the caretaker of the speed factory. Now he was being threatened by the drug lords to shut up. Later he was put on an isolation wing for his own safety.

Frank Smith prepared for the worst. If the Scousers were in the same jail, surely they would want to kill him as well. After all, he'd done much worse than BJ. They'd want revenge for pulling out of the deal. They might even blame him for getting them nicked. The Cartel was becoming trigger-happy.

Astonishingly, when they finally got to Smith in his cell, the Scousers came to him with smiling faces. They were friendly. They even tried to help him. They offered him money, intelligence and legal advice from one of their top lawyers. 'What the hell is going on?' Smith asked himself.

A Liverpool fixer called John Byrne, who had been a manager in charge of the Cumbrian cook, explained that if Smith remained loyal and did what he was told, then everything would be OK. But if he continued to misbehave and stay on his own, then there might be trouble. Byrne said that himself, Smith and the others had been nicked as part of a great conspiracy. Byrne revealed that they had worked out that they had all been set up by an informant called David Parsons. Parsons had been sent by the police to bring them down, he said. But the upside was that if they could prove that Parsons had behaved badly, gone above and beyond the call of duty, had broken the rules of being an informant, then the case against all of them would collapse.

'So what's this got to do with me?' asked Smith, terrified that he was getting out of his depth again.

'Because you know Parsons best,' said Byrne. 'He got right into you. He actually grafted with you in Thatto Heath and Durham, so you know how he works. All the time he was setting you up – so you've got to expose this.'

'Why can't you?' asked Smith.

'Because Parsons never got near to us. He got to us once removed by going through Tony Johnson and tapping him up and then you. You were another weak link, and he went after you direct to get at us.'

The Scousers wanted Smith to do their dirty work for them. Smith may have been the weak link, but now the Cartel needed him badly. Suddenly, Smith had gone from being on their hit list to being a prized asset. Smith felt scared.

Frank said, 'John Byrne told me that there were some tapes in existence which showed that I had been set up by David Parsons and that the BMK that David had brought me had been given to him by the police, and that the police had got it from the Scousers' lab in Widnes for which they had been arrested.'

The 'Scousers' lab' that John Byrne had been referring to was a speed factory that the Cartel bosses had set up after Frank Smith had deserted them. They had set it up inside a catering shop in Widnes that was owned by a corrupt businessman called Stan James. The shop was raided. James was later convicted for allowing the amphetamine factory to operate on his premises.

A lot of long-serving Cartel bosses and foot soldiers were facing jail as a result of Operation Pirate. But instead of taking the pain and letting justice take its course, the Cartel did what it always did when caught red-handed: they tried to wriggle out of it, blame the crimes on someone else and manipulate their non-Cartel co-defendants into taking the rap. The methods had been perfected by Cartel godfather John Haase. Despite having been arrested for 50 kilos of heroin, he'd spent his time on remand plotting and scheming his way out of the charges. He was sentenced to 18 years in jail but had miraculously got out after 11 months. It was the same with Curtis Warren in 1992, the same with Ian McAteer on his violence charges and the same with countless other drug-dealing Liverpool mafia bosses who thought they were above the law. Their lying and cheating had worked. Many of the defendants involved in Operation Pirate knew John Haase and Curtis Warren and had learned from them.

Now they were trying to cause a big manipulation in their own cases. As usual, it involved covert tape recordings of sinister conspiracies, set-ups and allegations of corrupt police informants.

The Cartel bosses claimed that they had a tape of Frank Smith talking to David Parsons about setting up the Thatto Heath factory before it was busted. If authentic, the tape might prove that Parsons, a de facto police agent, had behaved illegally and the case against the Cartel might fall apart.

In order to control Frank Smith, the Scousers wanted him to change solicitors to their own. Kevin Dooley was a notorious Cartel solicitor who worked for Curtis Warren and numerous other drug barons. He was later bugged by Merseyside Police and struck off for links to money laundering.

The Cartel wanted Frank to blame everything on David Parsons. Inside prison, Charlie Corke got busy trying to keep everyone in line. He tried to persuade some of the non-Cartel workers that it was in their interest not to go against them. He even offered some of them work. He admitted to Stan James, the owner of the catering firm that had been busted, that he was still working for the Liverpool gang. If James stayed onside, they would give him work, Corke promised. The Cartel always took care of their own, he crowed. The Cartel were interested in manufacturing perfume and he could have a piece of the action and get rich quick once they were released – if he stayed onside, that is.

CHAPTER 37

DOOMSDAY

1999

HIS FACE WAS covered by a mask. His weapon was covered by a balaclava. But when the assassin got close to his target, he revealed his weapon of choice – and it was one that was difficult to mistake. The MAC-10 sub-machine gun is one of the most instantly recognisable weapons in the world. Lauded in popular culture. Starring in more Hollywood blockbusters than any other gun in history. Counterfeited by more underworld gunrunners in the UK than the AK-47. More hits on Google than Jesus Christ.

But the assassin had chosen his instrument of death appropriately. The target was a difficult man to pin down. He was alert and jumpy because of his cocaine habit. Just a few weeks before, he'd outrun a machete-wielding attacker, living to fight another day. His state-of-the-art body armour had saved him from more than one enemy. A spray-and-pray machine gun was ideal for the job. If precision wouldn't kill him, then overwhelming force would.

Several years had passed since Paul had sworn a vendetta against the three men whom he believed had threatened his son. Two of those suspects were now dead: George Bromely and Kevin Maguire. A third man, Nathan Jones, had been killed by association. But few in the underworld felt any remorse – Jones had revelled in some of the violence and suffering that had been handed out by his mentor Maguire. It was also strongly rumoured that Jones had taken part in the killing of the young man Neil

Green who'd been found dead on Ainsdale beach near Crosby just a few days before Jones had himself been shot. Underworld sources said Green had been force-fed sand before being killed, and Jones had been named as his torturer. The upshot was simple – in the eyes of the underworld, Jones had been found guilty by association with Maguire. According to Burly, it was a case of 'run with the dog, die with the dog!'

Though Paul Burly had never dealt drugs, he'd had to befriend some of the Cartel's men in order to create the conditions for the hits to be carried out successfully. Burly said, 'I had to create an atmosphere for my goadings and innuendos, which were necessary to form the illusion of truth.'

The first two 'contracts' had been the subject of much secret negotiation. Paul Burly was an old hand at underworld intrigue. To minimise the chances of being associated with the killings, it was alleged that allies of Paul had 'swapped' several hit-man contracts with members of the Cartel. They would kill Paul's targets if the Cartel would kill theirs. Therefore there'd be no link between Paul's allies and the two dead suspects. And if and when Paul's associates returned the favour, there'd be no link between the Cartel and the people that he ironed out for them. The exact details of the plot remain a mystery, but to this day Paul Burly denies any direct involvement with the hits and says that if his associates made any agreement with the Cartel they did it without his knowledge.

But just one problem remained: thirty-nine-year-old former boxer Tony Sinnott. Sinnott was the third suspect on Paul's alleged hit list. He was also a Cartel drug dealer but one who was unpopular enough for his death to be sanctioned by others. Paul Burly's associates had taken counsel from his enemies. Sinnott was out of control on drugs, they said. They also wanted him dead. If they did him for Paul's friends, Paul's friends could do one their enemies for them. Or so it was alleged. Once again, Paul Burly later denied direct involvement.

Many people had suffered at the hands of Sinnott, according to Paul Burly. The full story of the plot to kill Sinnott is explored in detail in Peter Stockley's book *Extenuating Circumstances*. They began to hear stories of more hurt coming their way because Sinnott, it was widely thought, could not be stopped. Some concluded that they could no longer rely on the law. The system had let them down badly, they claimed. One judge who'd sat in judgement on a case in which Sinnott had been accused of violence had dismissed Sinnott with these words: 'You will leave this courtroom without a blemish on your character.' To many of his victims, that meant Sinnott virtually had a licence to do whatever he wished. He was becoming increasingly arrogant.

To create a conspiracy against Sinnott, Paul had to target those who had been Sinnott's victims. But he had to be careful to select those who had the bottle to exact revenge. Paul Burly said, 'Or those who were so scared that they had become mice; but even mice can turn into vicious things when they feel overly and wrongly threatened. If telling somebody the truth, even though it led to another's murder, was a crime, then half the world would be felons.' Paul smiled as he made his first phone call . . .

On 23 April 1999, a masked gunman confronted Sinnott at a garage on his home turf in Speke, near John Lennon airport. The assailant levelled his 9-mm sub-machine gun and fired 22 shots at him. A hail of 18 bullets cut Sinnott's steroid-pumped frame to pieces. Only four bullets missed their target. Three heavyweight enforcers with links to the Cartel were suspected of overseeing the murder, but they were too high-up and hands-off ever to get blamed. The execution only took two seconds. Only one getaway car was used: a Ford Fiesta XR2 that was car-jacked at gunpoint from a passer-by. Zero guilty persons have ever been convicted. The case is still unsolved.

A pair of low-level associates were eventually tried for the hit, but even they walked free after a trial. One of the men charged was the owner of the garage who, it was alleged, had lured Sinnott to the industrial estate. A number of other gangland figures were roped in for a go-around in the interrogation room, but none folded under questioning. Paul went back to his life, looking after his family and running a charitable organisation.

Paul smiled and resumed his life knowing he had done a lot to help put right situations that the law had seemed unable to prevent in the first place. His smallholding could now be enriched with tame wildness now that the wildness that had threatened it had been tamed.

Across the city in Kirkdale, door supremo Shaun Smith was sleeping in his pub. The popular local wasn't really a business. For Shaun, it was more of a home and hobby. He'd built up a massively successful security company that employed hundreds of men. He also provided close protection and back-up for VIPs, underworld figures, football stars and businessmen. Part of his empire crossed over into a nightclub operation run by his in-laws. The jewel in the crown was a rave club that had become hugely popular with the mainstream crowd that couldn't get into Cream.

By night, Shaun patrolled his doors, settling scores and dealing with troublemakers. In the early hours he returned to his oasis, the pub over which his wife and young baby slept.

Shaun Smith said, 'One night I was in bed. At 4.30 a.m., a window downstairs was smashed. Someone had thrown a tyre iron and spare wheel through the glass and got off in a car. What the fuck was that about?'

Shaun wasn't too bothered at first. Scores of petty disputes simmered under the surface of a life on the doors. Little did he know that this wanton act of vandalism would drag him into a decade-long gang war: a savage struggle that would involve the biggest explosions of bombs on mainland Britain since the fall of the IRA; the first gangland dispute in which the police would become a legitimate target; a fight for power that would threaten the old order on which the foundations of the Cartel were built.

Shaun Smith began to investigate. He replayed the overnight CCTV images on the giant music video/karaoke TV on the stage at the side of the bar. Shaun couldn't believe what he was seeing. Through the grainy image, he could see two young men getting out of a car, opening the boot, removing the tyre iron and lever, and lashing it at the plate-glass windows. Momentarily, Shaun was taken aback: for he knew the exact make and model of the car and, astonishingly, he recognised the figures in the images. The car was driven by a local teenager called Kaim, who lived in the next street and had been coming into the pub since he was a kid. Kaim's dad was a close family friend.

Shaun went to see him. 'Your Kaim has smashed the pub window for some reason,' he told him. 'I don't give a fuck why he's done it. Get £1,500 off him and I'll call it quits.'

Fines and compensation were a quick and easy way of solving local disputes before they spiralled out of control. But after talking to his son, Kaim's dad came back to see Shaun and said that the compo wouldn't be forthcoming. Hostilities were likely to continue, he added.

'I'm sorry, mate, but it runs a little bit deep,' Kaim's dad told Shaun. 'My lad was with his mate called Terry that night. They'd been thrown out of one of your clubs for wearing trainers. The doorman was called Big Nose. Terry had fumed: "Who the fuck is this Big Nose, the cheeky twat – I'll plug him."'

Big Nose was part of a family that Shaun knew very well. Shaun ran the family's large portfolio of pubs, clubs and security contracts. But the new generation of tearaways didn't respect status, money or power. They had realised two things. First, that the multimillionaire gangsters who ran the underworld had cushy lifestyles and loads of assets, such as businesses and big houses. That made them vulnerable because they couldn't hide: they were tied to their treasures, reliant on their highly visible assets.

Second, it didn't matter how big and tough you were, there was a new equaliser in town: the gun. The new generation of teenagers realised that they could take on an 18-stone, steroid-fuelled doorman on equal terms if they were armed with a 9-mm pistol or a side-by-side shotgun, bought for £200 from the local estate.

The third characteristic of the young bucks was their sensitivity. They were hotheaded and quick to anger, highly irascible when it came to 'respect' issues. Being knocked back from a pub was a matter of huge humiliation, which had to be avenged by death if necessary. Many of their mums and dads had been smackheads and crack addicts. From an early age, the kids had been plonked in front of the telly, watching *Scarface*, while their parents chased the dragon on the couch. Their kids weren't socialised. No one had ever taught them how to control their anger in public.

That night, after they failed to find Big Nose to shoot him, in desperation they smashed Shaun's pub window, simply because he had a connection to Big Nose.

Shaun said, 'They only did it because I was closely connected to the family. Terry and Kaim, they were kids, they were fuming, snorting their brains out, driving around, looking for someone to take it out on – so getting at me was just a way of letting off steam.'

To stop the dispute escalating further, it was decided that both Terry and his doorman enemy Big Nose would have a straightener.

Shaun said, 'The kid was game, to be fair. Terry had a bit of arse on him, so it wouldn't have been a pushover for Big Nose, who was around the same age. But Big Nose had more to lose, so it made the whole thing a bigger risk for him. If Terry won, the arse would have fallen out of his business. He would have lost the seven doors that he controlled, because being on the door is all about reputation. And if you lose a straightener, then someone will realise that you're weak and take your doors off you.'

But suddenly the fist fight, which was due to take place in a boxing ring attached to the club, was called off.

On the following Saturday night, Terry and Kaim's gang were celebrating, as if the fact that the fight had been called off was a victory. They drove past the nightclub, determined to rub it in. They threw bottles and cans at cars belonging to Shaun and the family, threatening to torch the pub and nightclubs of Shaun that were run by Big Nose.

By now, the row was getting out of control. A foot soldier loyal to Shaun Smith decided to take matters into his own hands. Without Shaun's go-ahead, he got two squirty bottles and filled them full of petrol. He went to the back of Terry's mother's house while the family were asleep at 10.30 p.m. on a Sunday night. Four squirts of accelerant were fired through the letterbox and into the bin. The fumes were lit and the fire took hold silently. As a small sign of underworld empathy, the gangster booted in the door to deliberately wake Terry's family, giving them time to escape. The message was clear: 'This is a warning. We let your mum escape. Next time we'll nail the doors and windows shut and burn her alive.'

Shortly afterwards, Terry phoned Shaun. But he wasn't calling to surrender. 'You've torched me ma's house,' Terry screamed. 'My family was in there. You're fucking dead.' He made more threats against Shaun's family.

Shaun: 'The firebombing was done totally without my knowledge – it wasn't my style. I settled my disputes man to man. But I'd been dragged into the situation because Big Nose would not have a straightener. And that was the start of the nightclub war, which went on for years and destroyed the lives of many.'

The nightclub was the jewel in the family's leisure empire. Terry's gang made their next move: they attacked the club when it was filled with dancing teenagers. They sprayed bullets at the Halfway House pub, which was also owned by Shaun.

Meanwhile, in an unrelated case, a mid-ranking Cartel dealer had just been released from prison after serving four years in jail for supplying drugs. Warren Selkirk vowed to make a fresh start. He told friends that he'd never touch drugs again. Some of his pals weren't so sure that he'd stick to his word. Selkirk was surrounded by Cartel peddlers. Temptation was a mobile-phone call away. Dylan Porter was an old mate who'd served him up heroin before now. Scottish drug dealer and Glasgow enforcer Ian McAteer was also a friend. John Haase and Paul Bennett were also contemporaries – all heavyweight Cartel VIPs.

Selkirk needed money fast. To keep his promise, he said that he would no longer get involved in hands-on distribution. But he was prepared to make himself available for support activities, such as running money and general dogsbodying. He soon picked up a job as a Cartel courier, ferrying cash, up to £30,000 at a time, from Scotland to Liverpool to fund drugs deals.

Colin Smith's brother John Smith Junior was also climbing up the ranks of the Cartel. Around 1999/2000, he began making trips to Amsterdam to set up deals. By the late 1990s, John and Colin had got themselves well established. Life was good in the world of international drug dealers.

CHAPTER 38

OPERATION KINGSWAY

1999

FOR DYLAN PORTER, business was also booming. As a middle-to senior-ranking Cartel distributor, he was pulling in between £5,000 and £20,000 per week. But little did he know that the police were already on his case. The secret operation against him had now turned into a huge deal: the biggest operation of its kind ever mounted by Merseyside Police. If it failed, the consequences would be catastrophic, potentially bringing the whole philosophy of intelligence-led police into question. The future of the new generation of officers was riding on it.

In a bid to move Operation Kingsway along at a faster pace, the police mounted a crude undercover operation against Dylan. To date, they'd had his movements pinned down with covert surveillance, but they were desperate to 'get a body next to him' that would enable them to pick up better, real-time information. The icing on the cake, if feasible, would be to sting him with a hand-to-hand – to catch him red-handed with a controlled purchase of drugs by an undercover cop, captured on covert video that couldn't be dismissed in court. But Dylan was careful. So far, his outward appearance had given little away to the long-lens snappers and listening probes that the police had directed against him.

One officer disguised himself as a low-level smackhead, pretending to sell shoplifted clothes to cash-rich dealers: a kind of door-to-door salesman of the underworld. To make the cover story stack up, he was introduced to Dylan by another local grafter whom Dylan knew well. As they chatted away in Dylan's front room, suddenly the undercover copper asked Dylan whether he could get any coke. The question was probably a touch premature, and the copper might well have done better to hang back until he'd got his feet under the table. But the pressure was on, and it was always a tough judgement call, to balance the pressure from superiors to get the job done and the subtler operational requirements of the job.

'Fuck off, I don't get involved with that,' Dylan rebuked him, meaning that he couldn't be bothered selling bits of gear to smackheads. The direct question had been inappropriate, ill timed and too direct, according to Dylan. It left him feeling spooked.

'I was selling kilos, hundreds of kilos, to other big dealers,' Dylan explained. 'I was a well-known operator. I wasn't a street dealer. Why would I suddenly turn around and serve up a few ounces of charlie to a complete stranger, who was roasting anyway? The feller was bang on, and I knew he was a busie. I was quite wise to all that, to be fair. By that time, I'd already been targeted by Operation Garrison, an investigation into the sale of stolen goods. I'd been caught in a kind of sting. But I'd got out of that in the end, because I'm not a bad feller, I've always been a nice feller, and five women gave evidence on my behalf. But I wasn't about to be turned over by a plainclothes busie again, so I fucked him off.'

The run-up to Christmas was traditionally a boom period for dealers. Punters were queuing up to stock up on drugs over the festive period, when customarily deliveries slowed down for a few days: a period known in the trade as the 'Christmas drought'. But this year, there was the added bonus of the end-of-the-millennium party. Every type of drug was flying out.

A senior Cartel dealer called Cagey wanted to cash in. Cagey was part of Curtis Warren's crew. He'd once been partners with Johnny Phillips. Cagey had been living in Amsterdam and was linked to several shootings there. Dylan Porter refused to name Cagey, Warren or any of his criminal associates; however, the author was able to piece together the network from other sources, including court reports and other documents.

Dylan said, 'Despite all the ups and downs of normal business, and despite the fact that I suspected the busies were on me, I was still grafting away and I was doing really well. The run-up to Christmas was steady but was building up. One day in December I'd sent ten kilos of brown to Bradford. The money came back sweet, no problem. It was business as usual.

'Then this kid I knew, called Cagey, turned up at my door, and said: "Can you do anything with tablets?" He had 10,000 Doves – E pills – which he wanted to sell quickly.

'But I said, "I don't do nothing no more like that." I'd stopped doing little deals on the side. E's, weed, speed: in general, I swerved it, because it was hassle and I didn't want to compromise my day-to-day business. I just stuck to my Bradford stuff, or stuff that came through the big, normal channels kind of thing. Don't forget that I had an inkling the busies were on me after the undercover copper tried to get me to sell charlie, so I didn't want to take any risks.

'But Cagey kept asking me, hassling me, so as a favour, I phoned my mate in Bradford and asked him whether he wanted the E's. In the conversation I also told him that I had a few kilos of heroin left over, if he wanted them.

'To my surprise, my Bradford mate said: "Listen, send me your last three kilos of heroin and I will take the ten thousand tablets."

'So I thought, "Why not? It's a nice little Christmas bonus, and I was going to have to send the heroin to him anyway and it'd get Cagey off my case." So it was killing two birds with one stone.'

By this time, Dylan had rationalised his heroin dealing in such a way that it no longer affected his conscience. He justified selling heroin in the same way that most dealers do: by convincing himself that he wasn't actually serving up to heroin addicts directly. That was the domain of the 'creatures' lower down the food chain, whom he looked down upon. He considered himself to be a businessman, and drug dealing just seemed like an extreme form of capitalism no different from corruption or price fixing or overselling substandard goods. Businessmen, corporations, out-of-control bankers and boardrooms seemed to do what they liked. It was boom time. Blairism and globalisation were the dominant ideologies. A concept that would later be identified as disaster capitalism had come in from the cold, and was now widely accepted as a force for good. Selling heroin was no different from sweatshop slavery in the Third World, Dylan concluded, or wars for oil, or loaded free markets imposed on loan-saturated countries by economic hit-men. He may have been right in some respects, but like so much criminal psychology, the reasoning was flawed and self-serving. However, it enabled him to carry on.

'I sent the heroin and tablets to Bradford. But the courier who was taking them for me to Bradford in the car got nicked. "What the fuck's going on?" I asked myself.

'I immediately went down to see Cagey and said to him: "Those tablets have gone down."

'But he was strangely calm. He said: "I already know, I've seen it on the Teletext."

'That made me a bit suss, because the kid who'd been captured wasn't named on the Teletext report that was flashing up on his TV. It just said a man had been arrested on the motorway with some drugs. So how could Cagey have put two and two together so fast and assumed it was our man? It could have been anyone: quite a few people got nicked on that stretch every few months. Call me paranoid, but that got me suss that Cagey either had inside info off the busies or knew it was going to happen because he'd tipped them off. In other words, I started to suspect that Cagey had set me up.'

To make matters worse, Cagey then told Dylan that he'd have to pay for the E tablets, even though they'd been seized on the way to Bradford. He owed him £11,000, Cagey warned.

Dylan said, 'That's how he snared me, there and then, that's how he reeled me in for what he had in store for me in the future. Of course I protested. I said, "Fucking hell, Cagey," arguing that it was unfair and too much dough. Sometimes, if a load went down, you just wrote it off, or split the cost in half, because it's no one's fault, really, just part of the job. But Cagey wasn't arsed.

'He did give a little bit of slack in the end, saying: "Don't worry, you can work it off, you don't have to weigh me in now." Meaning that on the next deal that we did, he would deduct the £11,000 from my share of the profits. So that's how he snared me, that's how a one-off deal suddenly became two or three deals, cos I was in debt to him – from now on I was beholden to him.

'I should have given him the 11 quid [£11,000] there and then, as it wasn't a lot of dough, but it was kinda nothing, just one of those things, and I let it ride.'

But on 19 December 1999, the plot thickened. Dylan got a phone call from a Cartel insider, tipping him off that Cagey had just 'taxed' an independent dealer for 20 kilos of heroin: that is, stolen the drugs from him. The insider told Dylan that Cagey was on his way to see Dylan, with a view to getting him to sell them on his behalf. By now, the Cartel had developed a wide-ranging and efficient intelligence system that passed important info on to favoured members. Dylan was tipped off that Cagey wanted to sell him the stolen 20 kilos of gear – and this was the deal where Dylan could 'work off' his £11,000.

Dylan said, 'As if on cue, Cagey turned up with a sample and made out that he had 100 kilos instead of just 20. "There's as much as you want," he said.

'But I knew he was lying – because I knew he only had 20. He was trying to blag me, in the hope of striking a better price. Or maybe there was another agenda, I don't know. But he'd also come to me, I said to myself, because this was the deal on which I could pay back the 11 grand that I owed him, and make some on top for myself. It was all a bit mad, but that's life as a dealer. You take what comes; you buy and sell. I was a one-stop shop, a walking stock exchange for heroin, so it's just another day, and you're thinking not only can I make a few quid but I can get him off my case as well. So I said to him: "Go ahead – sound. I'll sort it."'

Dylan got the scratch: the scraping of heroin sliced off the consignment as a sample. He sent the small bag up to his mate in Bradford for testing, in order to get the percentage purity, which would determine the eventual selling price.

It came back 'sweet', meaning high quality. That night, the Bradford dealer phoned Dylan back. He was buzzing: 'That gear is the bollocks, I'll take whatever you can get.' It was an ideal, unexpected stop-gap to plug the Christmas drought.

With an order in the bag, Dylan immediately phoned Cagey to close that side of the deal and take care of the logistics. Cagey was well known for being a 'tough negotiator' who 'charged through the nose' for his 'tackle', according to Porter, who described him but refused to identify him by name. But, unusually, on this occasion he settled for a relatively cheap wholesale price:

an enticing £17,000 per kilo, which Dylan jumped at straight away. Dylan was surprised that he hadn't been hit for £20,000 or more, but he assumed Cagey wanted to get rid of it quick and was happy to cream his 11 grand bonus.

Dylan said, 'With the buy-price sorted, I then phoned my mate in Bradford, and he told me that he'd take 20 kilos at £18.5 K. So my cut on the whole thing, as the middleman, was 20 times £1,500 profit = £30,000, which was half-decent, to be fair, for a few phone calls and a couple of hours on the couch. I did the maths: I'd give Cagey the £11k that I owed him for the E's that went down on the previous deal. After that, I'd be left with 19 grand, which would take care of that week's wages.' That year's Christmas must-have toys were Pokémon and Furbies – Dylan could afford to buy a whole shopful for his kids on this deal alone.

But within hours, the best-laid plans had been scuppered. The next day, Dylan's mum died unexpectedly. The heroin baron was left 'cabbaged' in the house, grieving and making arrangements for the funeral. He decided to put everything on hold while he got his head together and took care of family matters.

Dylan said, 'I told Cagey and my mate in Bradford that I wasn't doing any graft and switched my phone off. Cagey had just lost his ma a month before, so he said he understood the situation. He made out that he wasn't that worried about the deal.

'I was devastated for five days.

'On Christmas Day, Cagey phoned the house out of the blue. Not to do the deal, he said, but to console me type of thing. He said: "Don't be afraid to cry, lad."

'I told him that me ma was getting buried on 29 December. I invited him to the wake and all that. But he said that he couldn't come because he was on bail for a murder at the time.'

However, Cagey told him that he would come and see him in the new year to finalise the 20-kilo heroin deal. Dylan was surprised that he hadn't got rid of the gear yet and that the deal was still on the table. He took it as a sign that Cagey was loyal to him. On the night of the funeral, Dylan went out and got rotten drunk.

Dylan said, 'The next day, I wasn't going nowhere: just sat off on the couch while my wife was looking after the kids, who were all running around while my head was exploding with a hangover. I had no plan to do anything that day, never mind pick up the baton on a heroin deal from a few weeks earlier. I was just going to watch the telly, I was still mourning type of thing.'

At 4 p.m. that day, 32 police officers were scrambled to watch Dylan. Surveillance was redoubled and the team was put on red alert, having received a tip-off that something potentially big was in the offing. How did the police know? It was the day before the millennium. At Liverpool's riverside Pier Head, the Cream nightclub was putting the final touches to its New Year's Eve extravaganza. In London, the Millennium Dome was gearing up for the Queen's visit. Meanwhile, an observation post was videoing the front of Dylan's house. In one scene, once again they captured a local heroin addict selling shoplifted sundries door to door.

CHAPTER 39

SEIZED

1999

AT 3.55 P.M., Cagey and another well-known dealer called Mealy, two of the most prominent members of the Cartel, unexpectedly knocked at Dylan's door. The police video did not record the visit.

Dylan said, 'Cagey was all business all of a sudden. "What's happening, lad, and all that?"'

Dylan, his face white and with a sheen from whisky and grief was surprised to see the dealers on his doorstep. His mother had been in the ground for less than 24 hours and already he was being dragged into graft.

Dylan said, 'Sound, mate. What's going on?' Dylan didn't knock them back or tell them to come back later. He was always polite but this time doubly so – he was conscious that he still owed Cagey 11 K. To boot, he was slightly weak and paranoid from the booze. Cagey could be exceedingly violent, if push came to shove. On one occasion, he had escaped an assassination attempt by one of the country's most-feared hit-men. An internecine dispute had erupted between two wings of the Cartel. One group had contracted the services of an extremely violent gangster from Scotland who specialised in contract murder.

The Scotsman had planned to ambush Cagey outside his house near Runcorn Bridge. He'd brought with him a small arsenal of weapons, including several handguns, a shotgun and a fast-firing sub-machine gun. What followed was a bizarre scene in which the Scotsman ambushed Cagey as he came out of his house, letting loose with everything he had: first the pistols, then the rest. But coolly, Cagey got out of his car and began to return fire in the suburban street, in the middle of the day. No matter how much firepower the Scotsman rained down on his target, Cagey would not go down. Eventually the Scotsman gave up and went back to see the principal, the Cartel boss who'd put the contract out on his enemy.

The Scotsman told him that Cagey was like the man they couldn't hang. He refused to die and, for that reason, he must be protected by a higher force. The conclusion was that the Scotsman could not fulfil his obligations under the contract. The Scotsman wouldn't be making a second attempt, as is standard practice. He handed back the weapons and got off back to Glasgow.

Now the bulletproof gangster was standing before Dylan on his doorstep. Dylan wasn't intimidated, but he did want him out of his life as quickly as possible. Once inside the house, Cagey told Dylan that he still had the heroin. Cagey claimed that he hadn't sold it yet because he was staying loyal to Dylan. Plus, he wanted 'to help [Dylan] out' with the £11 grand he owed him.

Dylan said, 'I was still half drunk, but I couldn't turn them away. I told him that I could do it, but he'd have to help with the logistics. I told him that I'd make all the calls and set up the handover. I told him to sort some transport and send the heroin over to Bradford, hand it over to my people there. I told him to do the handover at a landmark they both knew. And five minutes after the Bradford people had taken possession, they'd come back with the paper.' 'Paper' was the term that Dylan used for money.

But Cagey didn't like it. The Cartel drug lord refused to take responsibility for shipping the gear to Yorkshire. He made it clear that he wouldn't be laying on a car and a driver. Cagey got the number of the Bradford dealer from Dylan. Bullishly, he phoned the Bradford dealer himself and told him that he'd have to come to Liverpool to collect if he wanted the 20 kilos. They could pick up ten kilos on tick, and once they'd paid for that they could have the balance of a further ten kilos the day after.

The MO was well out of the ordinary for both Dylan and the

Bradford crew. But, his head wrecked by a hangover and under stress, Dylan reluctantly went along with the plan. It wasn't his usual method, certainly; it involved far too many strangers and variables. But what could he do? His mind was elsewhere. Foolishly, in his haste, Dylan persuaded the Bradford couriers to reveal the make and model of their handover cars over the phone – a Honda Legend and a Suzuki Bandit – so that he could tell Cagey what to look out for. It was a strict breach of protocol, but he just wanted to get on with it. For anyone listening in to the phone calls, it was a godsend. The police now knew what cars to look out for.

The plan was actioned quickly and the Bradford end agreed to come to Liverpool. A few hours later, the Bradford crew were in Liverpool. They picked up the first ten kilos from a suburban street called Chelwood Avenue in a quiet neighbourhood called Childwall, which dated back to the Domesday Book. The handover went well. But within minutes, things weren't looking so rosy. On the way back from the rendezvous, on the M62 going towards Bradford, the heroin-carrying cars were pulled over at the first service station. The whole Bradford team was nicked. Dylan claims he wasn't at the handover and was still sitting at home while the drama played out without his knowledge.

However, within minutes he got the call. *Bang!* Action stations. On hearing the news, Dylan was immediately convinced that he'd been set up. But there was only one suspect – and that was Cagey. It sounded too hard to believe: Cagey was a hardened, respected Cartel veteran who'd been there right at the beginning. He'd funded his first deal by ram raiding over a decade before. Now he was a hard hitter with Curtis Warren's backing. Had Cagey turned informer? Was one of the most trusted members of the Cartel now working for the other side? Dylan couldn't believe what he was thinking.

Dylan was further confused by Cagey's response. The following day, Cagey expressed grave concern. He told Dylan to get rid of his phone. He referred to the bust briefly, though he seemed to be going through the motions. He said it was 'hard lines' for Dylan, but that's where his empathy seemed to end. Suddenly, he turned. Cagey now demanded more money and compensation for his lost 20 kilos of heroin. He presented Dylan with a bill, saying that Dylan now owed him an extra £127,000, including the £11,000 from the previously lost E's. When Dylan objected, Cagey told him that he would have to stand the cost of the heroin because the Bradford people were his contacts.

'They'd fucked on the transport,' Cagey told Dylan. 'I got the gear to them, it was in their possession, it was their fault that they got nicked.'

Dylan became suspicious. Not only was it a coincidence that the two deals that had gone down recently were both Cagey's, but there were other irregularities too. Later Dylan found out that the heroin that had been seized at the M62 services was not the same quality as the heroin that Cagey had given him a sample of a day or so earlier. The seized heroin had a lower purity of 32 per cent. Had Cagey switched the gear to a cheaper alternative, knowing that it was going to get caught by the police, leaving him free to sell the higher-quality stuff to a third party later on? It was a common ploy by grasses. In addition, Dylan found out that the police had definitely received intelligence before the ambush. He couldn't say it was Cagey for sure, but the odds were stacking up. Dylan didn't want to jump to conclusions. Looking at it objectively, Dylan's bad luck could have just been related to police surveillance and had nothing to do with Cagey. But if that was the case, why hadn't the police taken out any of his other consignments, not just those linked to Cagey? The plot thickened when he found out from other Cartel sources that Cagey was already under suspicion of being a police nark. A Cartel insider said that Cagey was a common denominator in several other unrelated cases, where tip-offs had been given to the police and fellow Cartel bosses had been nicked. For instance, Cagey had been involved in the deal with fellow Cartel Boss Spencer Benjamin.

Benjamin, along with his partner in crime, had resisted going to Amsterdam to buy drugs after deciding that it was too hot for the Liverpool mafia to be seen in the 'Flat Place'. Instead, they had persuaded a senior Cali Cartel member to come to the UK and they had started to buy drugs from him in London.

Cagey had soon learned of Benjamin's link. Had Cagey got jealous? Was Benjamin a threat to his own status within the Cartel? Did the London connection threaten to undermine his own theatre of operations in Holland? Was he being secretly tasked by the police? Cagey had been a pioneer of Cartel operations in Amsterdam. Once Scarface and Kaiser had got established over there, he had gone over with Curtis Warren and both of them had done very well. When Warren had got nicked in Sassenheim in 1996, Cagey had come back to Liverpool, but he still had a 'team' over there in Holland that made him lots of money and secured his position within the hierarchy.

By now, the Cali Cartel were thinking along the same lines as Scarface and Kaiser. The Amsterdam *politie* were cracking down, and maybe it was better to simply relocate to London, where they could do much better business with the Cartel. In 1999, the Cali dealers and the Liverpool mafia began an experiment. Venezuelan Ivan Mendoza di Giorgio, a 39-year-old who was later described in court as a 'very major player' in the British cocaine network, was given instructions by his bosses to link up with Spencer Benjamin, the rep from the Liverpool Cartel.

Benjamin was a rising star. He had recently moved out from the Toxteth ghetto to a new £120,000 home in Halewood. However, he had retained a shop on his manor with a flat above so that this could become the hub of his drugs operation.

In the spring of 1999, after receiving a tip-off, the Major Crime Unit placed a two-month watch on Benjamin and his 26-year-old associate Edward Serrano, following a lead that they were doing deals with di Giorgio. This was known as Operation Warren. The National Crime Squad put a coordinated watch on the Venezuelan, which was known as Operation Waterloo. The police quickly found out that the drugs were being smuggled from Colombia to Holland and from the Dam to the UK, proving that the Cartel were trying to run things out of Holland remotely from the UK.

In May 1999, police watched as Benjamin and Serrano handed over a plastic bag to Mendoza in a pizza restaurant in London. Benjamin returned to Liverpool, but Serrano stayed in London and met Mendoza again the next day. The plastic bag was passed back to him. Serrano then caught a train back to Liverpool, where police detained him. The bag contained four kilos of cocaine worth around £310,000.

The rumour was that Cagey had been lined up to buy the gear from Benjamin when it arrived in Liverpool with Serrano. But was it just a ruse to rat them out? Was Cagey the latest

Cartel boss to be turned by intelligence-led policing? Or, if he wasn't an informant, had he just wandered onto the MCU's radar, which then led them to Dylan and his boss Paul Lowe? Cagey bought and sold gear to both gangs. Things were getting complicated and dangerous.

At the London end of the operation, police followed Mendoza as he met another contact. The man was intercepted carrying two kilos of cocaine, and police then swooped on Mendoza's home in south-east London.

Bingo! Inside they found 46 kilos of cocaine worth £3 million, £140,000 in cash and documentation pointing to more than £10 million paid through bank accounts into companies in Europe.

Benjamin was then arrested and charged. All of them were given very long sentences in jail. Police, of course, never revealed if Cagey was an informant, but intriguingly they did admit that intelligence gathered during the Merseyside's MCU Operation Warren investigation was to lead later on to the larger-scale operation against Paul Lowe and Dylan. The missing pieces were falling into place. Either Cagey was an informant or at the very least he had led police to Dylan by accident.

CHAPTER 40

WARREN SELKIRK

1999

IN GLASGOW, CARTEL linkman and contract killer Ian McAteer was on top of the world. Over the past 20 years he had forged strong links with the city's main drugs lords. To wash his money, he traded in second-hand cars, which he had built up into a profitable business in its own right.

But his business with the Liverpool mafia was even more profitable. McAteer was buying heroin and coke from several Cartel distributors simultaneously, proving that he had preferred status as a distributor in Scotland. John Haase sold him heroin and also contracted other jobs out to him, such as underworld debt collection and protection. Paul Bennett got him cannabis and tablets. McAteer was a gun runner for Haase and Bennett. A steady stream of illegal guns travelled between Liverpool and Glasgow, and many of them were sold on to gangs in Northern Ireland. However, Dylan Porter's gang was McAteer's main supplier. They also sold McAteer heroin; they had a mutual acquaintance called Warren Selkirk who acted as a freelance money courier for both firms. In fact, the police who were watching Dylan and his gang had magically watched McAteer and Selkirk drift onto the radar as well. The whole of the police's theatre of operations involving drugs was rapidly becoming very good at locking onto villains. A whole network of simultaneous rolling operations were underway. They were confident they could link them to Dylan's heroin. The intelligence-led system was paying off. The system proved that its overarching, globalised way of looking at operations was dragging more and more suspects into the net.

The Analyst said, 'We were learning how to integrate our operations not only between different targets but also between different forces and national bodies. By standing back and not simply concentrating on one crime and one man, we were able to cast the net wide.'

Selkirk was not long out of prison. He didn't mind moving dirty money around, but he refused to touch drugs in case he got another long stretch inside. His only other vice was gambling.

Warren Selkirk was on the dole and had no visible means of income. However, he regularly spent thousands of pounds at the bookies. The police were convinced that he was a compulsive gambler. His weekly job was to ferry £30,000 in cash from Glasgow to Liverpool, which bought four kilos of heroin for McAteer. But instead of passing the cash straight on, Selkirk often skimmed fifties and twenties off the wads of tattered notes. He went to the bookies and gambled. Sometimes he won. Most of the time he did not.

Couriering for a drugs firm was a time-consuming job, with lots of waiting around. Contacts were notoriously flakey, and Selkirk often found himself stranded for hours in car parks and pubs waiting for his opposite number to turn up. He got used to the last-minute calls, the latest excuses: they were still in bed, they had lost their mobile or had been nicked for drink driving the night before – the multifarious explanations that petty villains dreamt up to cover their chaotic lifestyles. To kill time, Selkirk kept dipping into McAteer's cash and standing in front of the whiteboard and the SIS TV monitors in the nearest bookies, a better's mini pen hanging gormlessly from his mouth, a dead man's stare in his eyes.

For a while, McAteer ignored the fiddle. After all, what was a few hundred quid compared to the few hundred grand that he was making every year from his Cartel connection? In addition, Selkirk was good at his job: he could keep a secret and had never been taxed by rival robbers or nicked by the police. McAteer held his tongue until the debts reached nearly £40,000. It wasn't so much about the money: Selkirk was now becoming an embarrassment, a stain on McAteer's ferocious image. If Selkirk could take liberties without punishment, then McAteer was leaving himself wide open. McAteer began pressing him for the money. At first, Selkirk asked for time, then he started ignoring his calls and messing him around: all the usual stuff. He'd have to be taught a lesson.

In the last three weeks of October 1999, McAteer spent much of his time trying to lean on Selkirk to come up with the money. Like most drug dealers then, McAteer was never off the phone. He made 1,155 calls in 20 days, many of them to Selkirk and the people around him, checking on his movements and asking questions. At midday on 29 October, McAteer decided to travel down from Glasgow himself to smoke Selkirk out of semi-hiding, to pin him down. On the motorway journey down, he chatted to associates and girlfriends. He made 95 calls, some to Selkirk, on the 250-mile journey south.

McAteer told Selkirk to meet him in the car park of the Merton pub in Bootle at 11.30 p.m. Selkirk was cute. He knew McAteer wouldn't attack him in front of a witness, so he turned up with his girlfriend Lynne. It was a good move. McAteer was surprised by the unexpected guest, placatory, even going as far as proffering the possibility of giving Selkirk more time to pay the debt. Effectively, Selkirk had given himself a 24-hour stay of execution.

The next day, McAteer got hold of Selkirk once again, keeping up the pressure. Mobile-phone records show that Selkirk picked up the call at 7.42 p.m. He was driving along the M57 motorway, heading home to Bootle from Huyton after a Chinese meal with his two sons. McAteer told him to divert to Crosby marina, where they'd have a chat: no big deal, no dramas, just a chat about the next bit of graft. Again, McAteer wasn't threatening. In fact, he sounded as though he needed Selkirk to do some more work, sooner rather than later. Maybe he'd let the £40,000 go? thought Selkirk, according to pals later. Maybe McAteer would allow him to work the debt off? Selkirk was scared and cautious, of course, but he agreed to meet McAteer all the same. Once again he'd take along an insurance policy. He had the chance to drop his kids off at home on the way, but instead he decided to take the kids along. Surely McAteer wouldn't kill him in the presence of his own children? They would be his human shield.

Selkirk parked by the marina. He told his sons to be good in the car and got out. 'I'll only be five minutes, Joseph,' he told one of them. Their dad walked along a path and into the grass, heading to an isolated spot where he usually met McAteer for secret briefings.

'He got out of the car and it was dark,' one of the lads later recalled to the police. 'I watched him walk down the path until I couldn't see him any more.'

When he arrived at the spot, Selkirk was unnerved. McAteer had an accomplice with him. This time it was Selkirk's time to be surprised at the mystery guest – fearful even. According to sources close to the gang, McAteer told Selkirk that he wanted him to take another parcel to Glasgow. Inside, Selkirk was buzzing. He'd read it right: McAteer was going to give him a walkover on the debt. McAteer then handed him a plastic bag. But instead of the usual £40,000 cash inside, it was full of dog faeces. The message was: 'You're full of shit, Selkirk, and we've had enough of you talking shit to us.' Unfortunately, he didn't even have time for the insult to register.

Shortly after 8 p.m., five bullets were pumped into him from a small, palm-sized gun fired from less than a few feet away: one in the chest, four in the head as he lay on the ground. By 8.05 p.m., he was dead.

Meanwhile, his sons were still waiting in the car for their dad to come back.

'After about 25 minutes, I was getting worried. I said to my brother, "There's something wrong here, James,"' his son Joseph recalled. 'I shouted out of the window "Dad" and I was honking the car horn.'

Eventually, Joseph got so scared that he jumped into the driver's seat. Luckily, his dad had left the keys in the ignition. He drove the car 200 yards, out of the grass and scrubland and onto a road. Passers-by saw and helped, before calling the police.

A police patrol was quickly on the scene. The officers searched the area, but it was dark and there were no street lamps on the wasteground, so they couldn't find anything. Warren Selkirk's body was found the next morning by a dog walker. Selkirk was lying on his back near undergrowth. His fingers were still clutching a plastic bag containing dog dirt, handed to him as a sick joke a second before his death.

Dylan Porter said, 'I knew Warren. I'd done some graft with

him. When he was shot, I got blamed, but it wasn't me.'

McAteer was arrested and put on remand. McAteer was furious and blamed the police for stitching him up. He was convinced that he hadn't left any clues. Too clever, he thought. He'd beaten a string of cases already and had never been caught for 99 per cent of his crimes, so he thought it was an injustice from the start, just to be pulled in for it. McAteer was convinced that he'd carried out a near-perfect crime, right down to the gun: he'd used a miniature weapon, so that the discharges wouldn't be heard. Not even Selkirk's sons had heard their father being executed, from a few metres away. No one would testify against McAteer. Phone calls and links to the victim were all circumstantial – all easily explained away by a born criminal like himself. McAteer felt that the Scottish police were trying to frame him. He was confident and cocky, even boasting to Scottish detectives about wanting to kill a police officer. According to Detective Superintendent Julieanne Wallace-Jones, 'He openly bragged about his hatred of police, including wanting to shoot an officer. He was believed capable of using guns to resist arrest.'

1999 was shaping up to be a good year for the police. Earlier in the year they had managed to pin a conviction on yet another Curtis Warren associate and Cartel senior, Stan Carnall, known as 'the Big Fella'. Carnall was jailed for six years for passing over five kilos of heroin at a service station.

Warren wasn't faring much better. In a Dutch prison, he killed a Turkish inmate in an exercise-yard fight.

CHAPTER 41

A NEW AGE

2000

MEANWHILE, THE GANG war between Shaun Smith and the new generation of superscallies was hotting up. Shaun was not a member of the Cartel, but the new bucks identified him as a prestige target anyway. He didn't deal drugs, but the Cartel often used his small army of doormen to solve problems. If the upstarts could take down such a powerful figure, it would make their bones in the underworld. A clear message would be heard by the drug lords: that there was a new generation of gangsters in town – and they must be taken seriously.

One night, Terry cruised past Shaun's Halfway House pub in the Kirkdale area of Walton. Tuesday night was pool night. The pub was busy. Terry was driving a Lexus LS 400. Shaun was sitting outside, taking a breather with one of his crew, known as Big Pim.

Suddenly, one of the hoodies sitting in Terry's car's back seat shouted over to Shaun, 'Youse are getting it.'

Action stations.

Shaun said, 'I threw me top off and walked over to the car. But before I got there, a mixed-race kid popped out of the window, just as I was about to front them. He pulled out a gun. Without warning, he let off seven shots at us. I was exposed. I ran behind the back of a parked van to take cover. Big Pim, who was with me, ran back into the pub to get away. He locked the doors behind him, to stop the shooter running in, but this locked me out as well.

'I wasn't running anywhere. I stood my ground and decided instead to run after the car: attack was the best form of defence, in my opinion. When there was a gap in the firing, I took my chances and ran towards the car again, where the shooter was. As I ran, I threw a bottle at him, aiming at his head. But it missed him and he started firing again, so I had to take cover again.

'This time I ran towards the pub, but, as I said, the door had been locked by Big Pim to stop the shooters running inside. Big Pim was inside, but no one would open the door, even though I was stood there. Even so, the shooter started firing at the pub. The bullets missed me, but one bullet went through the bar.'

The shooter wriggled back inside the window and the car sped off. Shaun didn't want to ring the police: it was against the code of silence. Instead, members of Shaun's gang decided to hit back immediately. Terry, the kid who had originally started the feud and was in the shooter's car, had gone to ground. But Shaun's gang decided to mount a second attack on Terry's family's house instead, in the hope of flushing him out once and for all. The gang traced the family to a new address. Terry had recently moved his family to a leafy part of Liverpool popular with students.

Shaun said, 'The attack on Terry's home was nothing to do with me and I wasn't part of the attack. But I was told what exactly happened. The assailants who carried it out didn't have guns, just hatchets, knives and wood choppers. They went through the door and found the family screaming. Someone was crying with fear.

'One of the lads always carried a squirty bottle full of petrol in the car, because you can squirt it from up to ten to fifteen feet away and just light the victim up from a safe distance. He was shouting at the family: "I'll burn you. I'll burn this house with you in it."

'Of course, he didn't burn the family, but he would have, if required – it was just a warning to Terry to back off.'

Shaun went to stay in Manchester while things cooled down. A meeting was called with the heads of the family that Shaun worked with. The takeaway decision from the meeting was ominous: someone was going to have to be 'taken care of here', as one of the people there said. It was a euphemism meaning that someone would have to be murdered in order to bring the gang war to a close.

'This is getting silly,' Shaun told his associates and the family. 'And the worst thing is, it's not even my war.'

Shaun told the family he blamed for dragging him unnecessarily into the dispute that 'this is not my war, it's yours'. He wasn't happy that the family hadn't had the straightener when all of this could have been put to bed. However, a decision was made by Shaun and the family to either put Terry in hospital, cripple one of his cronies or wipe out his back-up. Shaun hadn't started the war, but he wanted to finish it.

In spring 2000, the Operation Pirate court cases got underway. The trials related to the Cartel's amphetamine factories set up by Frank Smith. On 3 March 2000, the mysterious Mr Big behind the £36 million plot, a Cartel veteran called Frederick Cook, was jailed for 12 and a half years. Frank Smith had never even met him. For the first time, he understood the enormity of the operation that he'd been involved in. The Cartel was like an iceberg, he told one of his mates on the wing. Most of it was hidden beneath the surface, and even when you're working for it, you never know who exactly you are working for. He wished he'd known the truth about the Cartel from the off, for he would never have got involved, he told his confidantes.

The judge in court knew the structure of the Cartel exactly. The details had been mapped out in evidence by the Crown Prosecution Service and the police. The judge described how Mr Big Frederick Cook had farmed out the manufacturing of the drug to 'a ragtag band of petty criminals', such as the hapless Frank Smith.

Unfortunately, Frank Smith never made it into the dock with his co-defendants to defend himself or give evidence. He died of natural causes while in custody: a sad end to a sad life. His life was a cautionary tale of what happened when a relatively ordinary person got sucked into Britain's most ruthless drugs operation.

The court heard how the gang had been caught red-handed while 'attempting to deluge the region's streets with poison' from their four illegal laboratories.

As the case against the speed makers had evolved, the Cartel members knew they were doomed. The prosecution's case was overwhelming. The Cartel members became more desperate to save their own skins and the case descended into a cut-throat defence, with everyone blaming everyone else. Deepening conspiracy theories heightened the tension, pitching the Scousers against the woolyback workers they had employed to carry out the donkey work at the factories.

It was claimed in court that Frank Smith had made £7.5 million worth of drugs at his most recent and most successful cook in Durham, the facility he had set up at the behest of David Parsons, a known police informant. The money had disappeared. Frank didn't seem to have it. If he didn't have the money, who did? Now the Cartel was claiming that Frank Smith had turned secret informant as well. They claimed that he had fled abroad with his alleged millions, to start a new life under police protection. Others wrongly claimed that David Parsons had shared the profits with the corrupt coppers he had in his pocket, the same ones who had allegedly allowed him to sell drugs. The police rubbished the gossip, saying it was a case of dirty tricks to weaken the prosecution. But the conspiracy was given legs when Frank's own son claimed that his dad was still alive. A photograph of Frank Smith's corpse that had been taken in the hospital where he died was produced as evidence of his passing, along with a death certificate. However, the Cartel boss Frederick Cook dismissed both as fakes in a bid to cause as much trouble in the case as possible. On the outside, the Cartel got up to its old tricks, trying to stir up some controversy in the press.

Then came yet another astonishing twist. Some of the co-defendants claimed that there had been a murder of someone connected to the case. The victim, they said, was the father of another one of the lower-rung members of the gang. Tony Johnson had been a close confidant of Frank Smith and had been the assistant who had roped in David Parsons and retrieved the hidden apparatus to set up the Durham factory. It was claimed that Johnson's dad had been murdered as a warning to his son. By exactly whom, they weren't saying, but the thrust of the allegation was clear: the accusers were trying to pin it on Parsons. The allegation was taken seriously enough by the police. An investigation was launched. The father's body was exhumed for a post-mortem. However, the police concluded quickly that all was not what it seemed. They said that it was a malicious allegation and that the victim had not been killed but had died of unrelated causes.

More rumours dogged the case. The National Crime Squad was hailing the convictions as a victory in the war on drugs, but more experienced officers in Merseyside Police had doubts, particularly concerning the use of heroin dealer David Parsons as an informant. A rumour surfaced that Parsons was later arrested for crack cocaine- and speed-making chemicals by a local bobby who was by this time chasing David Parsons's errant son. The bobby didn't know that Parsons was on the books of the NCS and arrested him anyway. This was embarrassing.

The back story seemed to drag the case further into disrepute. Parsons was allowed to deal drugs, the Cartel spin doctors claimed, as part of a tacit arrangement with his police handlers. While this absurd and unproven deal was in place, one of the heroin addicts that Parsons had sold to had committed a burglary on a pensioner's house. The addict had bought his heroin on Parsons's patch. The victim turned out to be the widow of the former Chief Constable of Merseyside Police, Sir Kenneth Oxford. She died three months after the burglary. The irony was not lost on some officers within Merseyside Police. Though they didn't believe that Parsons had been allowed to deal drugs on such a scale, they privately disagreed with the NCS's gung-ho methods of managing informants. Claims were made that Parsons had been allowed to peddle £250,000 worth of heroin in eight months while he was a police informant.

Whatever the truth, and none of it was proved definitively, the smears did not seem to affect the case. Cartel linkman John Byrne got six years in jail for the speed-making factories and a £101,000 confiscation order. As part of disclosure in his trial, in police statements it was revealed that David Parsons had been working for the NCS under Operation Lotus. As an informant, Parsons had clocked up a whopping strike rate: 41 arrests, including 39 convictions. His codename had been Bob Latchford, after the legendary Everton goal scorer. Even so, the trial judge said that the police were wrong to allow the informer to peddle heroin. It was claimed but not proven that the police had given him £4,000, knowing the money was going to be used for heroin dealing. In another statement, Parsons said that he had given £30,000 back to his NCS handlers. The memo was based on a sworn statement that

Parsons had made to his solicitors and was later used in court as part of his defence.

In a bid to cover his own back, David Parsons began turning on his handlers and spilling the beans. In a memo from his solicitors, Parsons claimed he and the police officers had made illegal purchases of chemicals and glassware to make the speed, thus inciting crimes. What's more, his solicitors claimed that Parsons had been secretly taping his NCS handlers. The memo was based on a sworn statement that Parsons had made to his solicitors and was later used in court as part of his defence.

The memo said: 'The tape recordings clearly show that he had the ability to call off surveillance at will and was actively engaged in moving chemicals and glassware from storage to Frank Smith.' Parsons said he had been paid £17,500 by police in the period that he had set up the case. However, all of the police officers involved denied any form of improper behaviour and collusion with Parsons in his criminal activities and were never charged or convicted of corruption.

More grief attached itself to the case when it was revealed that one of the original targets of the operation had gone on the run. Mark Lilley had been on the NCS's original hit list and David Parsons had promised to serve him up. He was sentenced to 23 years in his absence after going on the run during his trial. Unconfirmed sightings of him were reported in southern Spain and the Netherlands. Rumours abounded that he was being protected by the Cartel, that he was being held back until he could give evidence that would undermine the convictions of the others. Mark Lilley further attacked the National Crime Squad, saying that they asked him to set up Frank Smith. The National Crime Squad denied corruption and abuse of office and said their officers had behaved properly.

Through his solicitors and family, Mark Lilley began to confirm a lot of what David Parsons was saying. He said that the rumours going around were true. David Parsons then began to reveal more details about his involvement with the police. He said that the police allowed the gang to take possession and recycle 15 to 20 kilos of police-tested amphetamine and Ecstasy tablets and use them to 'set up' Frank Smith with lab materials that they had. He claimed that as part of his contract with the police, the gang was allowed to carry lab-restricted glassware. He also said that the police unknowingly tested BMK for another big drug dealer. He made an allegation that also said that an NCS officer tried to procure BMK. He said that the policeman wanted him to make amphetamine paste to cover their expenses – but this was never done. The police denied the allegations and said that they were not corrupt. The officer closest to David Parsons denied any form of corruption and the NCS believed they were being made into scapegoats.

Twenty people were charged in relation to the conspiracy. Frank Smith died in custody. Eventually 19 men went on trial charged with a variety of drug offences. Seven were allowed to have charges lie on file. The remaining men either admitted their part or were convicted by a jury. But the experience of using informants as the key resource in intelligence-led policing left a bad taste in some people's mouths. Intelligence-led policing was given a thumbs up for the amount of suspects that it could churn up, but badly behaved supergrasses were given the thumbs down.

Meanwhile, in a different case, the authorities were trying to attack the Cartel from a different angle: by confiscating their assets. In 2000, while drugs baron Eddie Gray was serving his sentence as a Category A prisoner at Full Sutton prison in York, the authorities set in motion a cash-grab case against him. But Gray refused to cooperate, telling the police that his Ferrari and luxury home with heated indoor swimming pool were the fruits of a modest taxi business he'd once owned. Investigators hoped to seize a fine collection of designer jewels for the Crown, but the case was to drag on for years.

Meanwhile, heroin dealer Dylan Porter still hadn't been nicked, despite his suspicions that the police were on him, after ten kilos of his heroin had been seized over Christmas, not to mention the £11,000 worth of E's before that. Dylan tried to rationalise the busts, concluding that they were isolated incidents. By the law of averages, this happened now and again, he told himself. But something else kept niggling him. Occasionally, a courier's drugs supply was seized, but the men at the top had no idea that they, too, were under the police spotlight. Was this the case with him? He was confused, but he had to crack on and take care of business. Everyone was relying on him. After New Year, he resumed his day-to-day job of organising imports and distribution for his boss Paul Lowe.

But it was only a matter of time. The net was closing fast. In fact, by the end of February 2000, the police had nearly everything they wanted to build a case against the gang – and they were poised for the final take-down. The timing couldn't have been worse for Dylan. A big consignment had just been picked up by the gang's disabled bagman Carl Frederick in France. He returned to the UK on 27 February. Mr Big Paul Lowe and his lieutenant Martin Neary were in the middle of making last-minute preparations for the arrival of this latest batch of Frederick's heroin. Neary made separate visits to the gang's heroin safehouse in Upper Parliament Street, Toxteth, to make sure that the right equipment was there to cut up the raw opium, bulk it out and then re-bag it before nationwide distribution. Before leaving the premises, he checked to see if anyone was watching the property. There was no one that he could see anyway. The adrenalin was flowing in expectation of the next payday just around the corner. Everything was going just as usual. They were buzzing in anticipation of the latest parcel 'getting home'. Neary contacted Lowe to let him know 'that he'd got all his ducks in a row'.

At the same time, Frederick sailed through Customs and headed north. He finally arrived in Liverpool with the smuggled heroin cargo in his specially adapted mobility car. Lowe and Neary were relieved. Frederick went straight back to his own home, where he planned to hand over the gear to his bosses. Neary arrived shortly afterwards to collect. He picked up the bags of heroin and took them to the safehouse. A few minutes later, the MCU team swooped on the property. Bingo! They found the newly arrived 26 kilos of heroin untouched without much of a fuss. It was worth £1.89 million, stashed in black bin bags.

As a more detailed police search got underway, Lowe turned up unawares. He didn't realise that the police were there and was arrested immediately. At his house around the corner, police found £24,270 in cash.

Now it was time for the detectives to move on to the next target in the gang: Dylan Porter. They began planning the swoop. The police laid off a fourth member called Jason Smith for the time being, because they didn't have enough evidence on him yet. They watched him for a further two months and eventually recovered 46 kilos of heroin, worth £3.25 million, and £36,000 in cash from his house. During their surveillance, police had also observed Ian McAteer buying heroin from the gang. They'd also watched Warren Selkirk ferry money around (obviously, this was before McAteer had killed Selkirk). At first, McAteer and Selkirk were also named on the drug-smuggling indictment but after the murder it was decided to try the Scot on the murder charge alone.

Dylan said, 'Everyone around me was getting done, and it didn't take them long to get round to me. I got nicked in February 2000, shortly after the others. I couldn't believe it, how quickly things had gone from bad to worse. Six weeks before I got nicked, I'd been doing great: no problems. I'd had £237,000 in cash in my kitty, and I was owed £120,000 in back payments from previous deals. In other words, I had a healthy cash flow. But in the space of those six weeks, in the run-up to me getting nicked, I'd lost £180,000. That included the money I had to give Cagey for E's and the heroin that'd gone down. And the money that the busies found when they came through the door. In my business, you're not insured, are you?

'I was interrogated, of course, but as usual I said fuck all. But I knew they'd got me with surveillance and whatever. Even so, the busies wanted me to do a deal. They wanted me to give evidence against Ian McAteer, who'd been accused of murdering Warren Selkirk.

'The officers said to me: "We will get you off the heroin charges. You will never see the inside of a prison cell. We will relocate your family to a safehouse and arrange for a financial package to be put in place.

'"In the meantime, we'll keep you in a police cell in one of our stations rather than sending you to a prison on remand, so that it will be easier for your wife to come and visit."

'In other words, I was being offered an easy time right away and some rewards in the future, in return for becoming a grass.'

Dylan sat back on his plastic chair.

CHAPTER 42

THE EMPIRE STRIKES BACK

2000

ON THE LAW-ENFORCEMENT side, the police were learning from the initial mistakes that had arisen from intelligence-led policing. Controversy over the use of participating informants, such as David Parsons in the amphetamine-busting Operation Pirate, and fabrication of evidence, in the case of John Haase, had led to a Home Office review. A new philosophy was born. The National Intelligence Model was introduced in 2000. It was to be a business plan for the management of hierarchical crime (i.e. the Cartel). Crimes were classified into three categories. For each category, a police structure was put in place to deal with exactly those activities. That part of the police would be geared up specifically to deal with crimes of that nature, with complementary resources and backed up by a flow of intelligence that was relevant. Gone was the one-size-fits-all approach. The Cartel had a hierarchy, so a rationalised police hierarchy was needed to fight it.

The crimes were classified into broad levels:

1. Level 1: Tackled by a Basic Command Unit that investigated crime that affected the police and community at local level, such as burglary.
2. Level 2: Serious and organised crime that affected the whole force on a regional level, encompassing cross-boundary issues into neighbouring forces. The crime group that attracted Level 2 heat

had to have greater organisation. Therefore the police needed to bring together resources from across the board and organise them to fight crime head on.

3. Level 3: Described international and national criminality, such as the Cartel. Merseyside Police were only the force outside of London that had Level 3 capability.

The Analyst said, 'What we did, as a force, made us unique outside of London. We were prepared to look at Level 3 at a time when other forces weren't prepared to take on the responsibility. It's a big commitment. But we knew we had to, because the Liverpool criminals were far ahead in the drugs business. We believed that we could take out our crime families and our crime groups by not setting ourselves boundaries, both geographical and otherwise. For the first time, we said: "We will go after the criminals no matter where they go in the world."

'As a force, we then built up relationships with national and international law enforcement, to take out the crime groups that were specifically affecting communities by distributing drugs in Liverpool. Previous to that, if you hadn't seen the drug dealers in Liverpool for three months at a time, because they were in Amsterdam, then there was nothing we could do; we had to wait for them to come back on our radar. The old-style operations simply hadn't worked in this respect, because we never had the resources to follow the criminals into other countries, the permissions and the protocols from those foreign forces and contacts over there. However, after we moved into Level 3, it was no longer a case of waiting until they returned. You had to actively chase them.

'So that's the style of the way we started to work: we would chase the criminal. And we soon got the protocols set up and the contacts in place.'

Until now, the Cartel had thought they were safe in Amsterdam, Spain and Portugal, at least from UK police, if not the local force. They thought that being out of the country put them out of harm's way. But suddenly the policing barriers were gone. New laws were enacted to boost the police's surveillance capability – but to control it as well, in a bid not to make the same mistakes that had occurred with participating informants, or with the use of foreign evidence, such as had occurred with the Curtis Warren case in 1992. If the police could be empowered to use new technology to gather evidence objectively, they wouldn't be so dependent on human intelligence. RIPA controlled the powers of all public bodies to carry out surveillance and investigation. The interception of communications was particularly important. The law was introduced to take account of the Internet. Strong encryption of emails and phone calls was cheaply available and the Cartel was using satellite phones.

'RIPA allowed direct and intrusive surveillance of drug dealers,' said the Analyst, who is probably the UK police's number-one expert on the legal text of RIPA and its practical implications. The Analyst had a geeky side that had hoovered up this stuff long after other coppers had switched off. He was coming into his own. 'It still had to be legal and necessarily proportionate,' he added. 'For instance, section 27 deals with organising surveillance and section 27(3) deals with surveillance anywhere.' In an instant, the Analyst could quote the sections and subsections verbatim, and cross reference them to related precedents under earlier case law. Alongside the true-crime books and police-training manuals stacked upon his office shelves, there were rows of law textbooks. They were well-thumbed and not just for show.

RIPA went hand in hand with the new National Intelligence Model. Unlike the old guard, who seemed to categorise police resources haphazardly, the new buzzwords were 'strategic', 'tactical' and 'operational'. What was surprising was that the new system seemed to work well. It was what the new generation of officers, such as the Analyst, had been waiting for, and they welcomed it with open arms. Existing resources and procedures within the force could now be run at their optimum level to achieve the best possible results. The piecemeal approach was gone. Standardisation enabled the smooth flow of information throughout the system.

Almost immediately, the Cartel began feeling the heat once more. By the turn of the millennium, the good times were over for Poncho. External pressure from the police led to a dramatic rise in arrests. Internally, guns, politics and paranoia were tearing the Cartel apart. Scarface and Kaiser were still trading in huge amounts of cocaine, but they were staying low-key and flitting from country to country in a bid to cover their tracks. Their operating expenses quadrupled, dramatically pushing up the price of their cocaine. Poncho's brother Hector saw the bad moon rising and started making plans to get out of drug dealing.

He embarked on a degree course at Manchester University.

Hector said, 'These were the bad times. You could tell that the police were catching up; you could feel it. You could sense the change in the air. They were getting the breaks now, not us. All that hazy, crazy Wild West era was over. Suddenly, it was cold out there.

'Things like that cause stress. Drugs themselves make you paranoid enough, and a lot of the lads, including me, were breaking the first rule: don't get high on your own supply.

'One of our close associates, Stephen Cole, had been macheted to death. And that was a kind of turning point as well, a warning signal: this game is turning nasty.

'It was no longer just about bringing in hundreds of kilos and then selling them with a phone call. It wasn't just business: it was more of a guerrilla war. It was getting cut-throat and people were getting murdered all over the place. I went to Manchester Uni and started doing a bit of graft there.

'By that time, Scarface and Kaiser were also on a bad run. The police were on them. One of their transports got hit by the busies. They lost a few million quid on a big consignment that never made it. It was coming on top all over the show.'

The police were glad that they no longer had to rely so much on informants. The difficulty in getting villains to turn Queen's Evidence was highlighted in Dylan Porter's case. The officers offered him witness protection and a new ID abroad to shop Mr Big Paul Lowe and everyone else in the Cartel he had dirt on.

Dylan said, 'They sat me down and went through a big list of things they could do for me if I ratted on my other co-defendants: freedom, money, new ID, emigrate abroad, security, new house. You name it. And, of course, not going to jail for a very long time for the heroin.

'"Have you finished?" I said to the copper.

'"Yes," he said, smiling. Thinking that I was gonna sign up.

'"Well, suck my fucking dick," I said to him and I laughed. "Fuck you – I'm not grassing anyone up."

'Later one of the busies tried to talk me around again. He tried to convince me that I wasn't the only one: that there were loads of top gangsters on their side.

'He said: "You'll be amazed who's on our books," meaning that loads of big names were turning grasses.

'But again, I said: "I'm not a snitch." How could I be sitting on a beach, with my kids, out of jail and living in Florida or somewhere, knowing that I've sent another man away to prison – and he won't see his kids for ten years. It just wasn't me.'

Meanwhile the war between Shaun Smith and the young Turks escalated. A female closely linked to Shaun was slapped by one of the gang. Shaun blamed the up-and-coming cocaine dealer Sidious. Without his knowledge, members of Shaun's gang sought retaliation for the incident – and revenge for the shooting outside Shaun's pub, which was still unresolved.

Sidious had been arrested in connection with the shooting incident outside the pub. He was remanded for four months until the case was dismissed due to lack of evidence. Now that he was back on the street, it was a perfect opportunity for him to be wiped out.

In May 2000, 15 doormen were 'called out' and told to prepare for an attack on Sidious. He'd been sighted in a pub called the Sefton Arms. The doormen armed themselves with clubs, machetes and knives.

The men burst into the pub and doused drinkers with tear gas. They couldn't find Sidious at first but instead cornered one of his known associates, Carlos Escoffery, in the bar. The order was given to cut up Escoffery. Anyone associated with the slapping incident was to be annihilated. Escoffery was left close to death, bashed and beaten. Sidious escaped the attack, but police were ordered to find the men who'd left Escoffery fighting for his life.

Shaun and two men close to him, called Michael Brown and Gary Hampton, were arrested and charged with attempted murder. During interviews for this book, Shaun Smith refused to name Brown and Hampton as his associates, or Escoffery and the others as his enemies.

'I'm not a grass,' he said, 'and I won't even name names under any circumstances, not to the police, writers, friends or enemies – no one.'

But the individuals concerned were named in court reports and newspaper articles from the period. Brown and Hampton were tough, but they were young and impressionable. They had come under the spell of older villains and were prepared to carry out their dirty work for them. They were facing a long time in jail if convicted for Escoffery's attack. According to police reports,

Hampton had previously been convicted twice for assault and also for carrying a flick knife in a public place. He wouldn't be getting an easy time from the judge. Brown had a previous conviction for incitement to inflict grievous bodily harm. But, astonishingly, the case collapsed in August 2000, when Escoffery withdrew his statement at the last minute. Once again, from the outside, it looked as though someone had got to the victim. For the police, the case was totemic, revealing a wider weakness in the justice system. The force might have got their act together, in as much as they were now catching big players as a matter of routine, but criminals were simply going around them, by waiting until the files were passed over to the Crown Prosecution Service before 'solving' the problem. The new generation had none of the respect for the courts that the older ones had. They just saw opportunities to pay off witnesses or intimidate them quite openly.

Terrified that Shaun's gang might finally find him, Sidious went into hiding, then fled Liverpool altogether. Later, he allegedly gave the names of six of the attackers to the police. Shaun's gang seized on the rumour and used it to decimate Sidious's reputation in the underworld. Word that he was a grass soon spread around Liverpool. Six-foot-high graffiti declaring 'Sidious – grass' appeared on the walls of a gym frequented by club doormen. Leaflets and posters were printed with stories on them, declaring that Sidious was a police informant. The *News of the World* even ran an article claiming that Sidious had switched sides. With Sidious on the run, there was room for another young gangster to take his place.

CHAPTER 43

GUERRILLA WAR

2001

IF A CASE got to court and, against the odds, there was a conviction, then the judges wasted no time in giving drug dealers a hard time. New Home Office guidelines, designed to tie in with more sophisticated policing, demanded longer sentences for drug dealers. The new era of tough justice did not bode well for Dylan Porter. If he was found guilty, not only could he expect a big sentence but also he'd be left with nothing: the police had vowed to strip his assets. Dylan had refused to turn informer. He was told to expect no quarter from the Crown Prosecution Service and the judge. The trial did not go well.

Dylan said, 'In court, as evidence, the police attributed a phone to me, which linked me to all kinds of deals. The phone records made me look like a number-one organiser. Then they had an eyewitness, saying that I'd been at the handover of the ten kilos of Cagey's heroin to the Bradford people at Chelwood Avenue. My argument was that even though I was bang at it, these two bits of evidence were wrong. I denied that the phone was mine, and I said that I wasn't anywhere near the handover. But at the end of the day, that's what convinced the jury – the phone and eyewitness – no matter how much I denied it. That evidence was a stitch.'

On 5 February 2001, the jury found Dylan guilty by a majority of ten to two. Dylan Porter got a weighty 21 years – the full force of the law – handed down by Judge Maddison.

Dylan said, '"Dis-honour Maddison" I called him. The Lockerbie bomber, whether he did it or not, only got 20 years. But what could I do? I took it on the chin; I didn't blame anyone but myself. I gave the thumbs up to the judge and said thanks very much. I put on a front, as much for my family as for me, but also a bit for the lads, to show that I hadn't crumbled.

'But inside I was devastated. I was gutted, but I didn't moan about it. I'd done the crime, now I'd do the time. I bit my lip and just cracked on.

'All my neighbours in the court were devastated also. But when I went to jail, my wife and kids got left on their own. I expected the lads to look after her, but no one came.

'Then I landed in Whitemoor Prison. I saw John Haase, but I wouldn't speak to him because he was a grass. I was Cat. A for six years after that.'

During the interviews for this book Dylan refused to name the members of his gang or those criminals he sold drugs to. However, their names were revealed on court documents. Ten people from the gang were jailed, including Paul Lowe, who got twenty-four years. Martin Neary got sixteen. Even disabled Carl Frederick, the supposedly disabled courier, got fourteen years. Jason Smith and safehouse keeper Anthony Ellis got sixteen years each. Bradford boss Mark Davey also got sixteen years. Five other runners got sentences ranging from six to twelve years. The message from the authorities was clear: drugs were now a big, bad offence, and if they reeled you in, you were staying until you were an old man. Sentencing was catching up with the police's capabilities. The political will in Whitehall was stiffening.

Inside their mansions and foreign boltholes, the Cartel bigwigs sat up and took notice. No one wanted to suffer the same fate as Dylan. But on the street, the younger generation wasn't listening. Caught up in the heat of battle, the up-and-coming gangs weren't concerned with consequences. None of them had been inside for long sentences, so they didn't understand the full, life-sucking horror of being a Category A prisoner for ten, fifteen years. They were high on life. By 2001, the conflict between Shaun Smith and the next generation of dealers had settled into a kind of asymmetric warfare. Shaun put a conventional force of doormen on the streets, to flush out the young scallies. Like a standing army, Shaun's troops were a constant presence, harassing and interdicting all known associates of his enemies. The other side, meanwhile, exploited their own strengths. They were more like a militia, an irregular force relying less on brute force and more on their flexibility and the element of surprise. They threw pipe bombs and hand grenades into pubs and nightclubs linked to Shaun. They paid 'creatures' to shoot at doormen in random drive-by attacks. 'Creatures' was the street name for heroin and crack users who would perform acts of violence for very little money. Crazed by addiction and desperate for gear, they would shoot someone for £500, stab someone for £200 or throw a grenade through someone's window for a bit more. In retaliation, Shaun's gang put money on the heads of the foot soldiers. The addicts were often kidnapped off the street and thrown into the back of a specially adapted van. It was no more than a mobile torture chamber, in which they were gassed, beaten and penetrated with broomsticks, their arms and legs smashed and slashed. Flames from cigarette lighters were held under their noses, burning deeply into the septum until they gave in. Their legs were broken until they confessed whom they were working for and gave their addresses.

Shaun said, 'We were driving around of a night in cars. The opposition were as well, so we were trying to find them. We used to go to the auctions and buy old Volvos and Granadas for £500. Of course, the cars weren't insured or nothing like that. It wasn't that bad then, for things like that. As long as it was taxed, it was OK. They were just our battleships, full of four or five doormen that we paid to put on the streets. If we saw them, then we'd just ram them off the road. We didn't have to pay all of the lads: the average doormen didn't want to get involved because it was personal family business. So there was a hard core of just our close associates who were prepared to fight against them.'

By 2001, Colin Smith (no relation to Shaun) was the undisputed king of the Cartel. He had taken up Curtis Warren's mantle. By now, he had brought in a well-known gangster called Stephen Lawlor to beef up his security. It was a risk. Though Lawlor had risen through the ranks, he still had one foot back on the street. He was involved in a long-running gang war over nightclub doors. His sworn enemy was a doorman called Stephen Clarke.

In time, Colin Smith delegated some responsibility for dealing directly with the Colombians to Lawlor. It was a decision that would come back to haunt him. The Cartel was already under strain from increased police scrutiny and internal strife. The Colombians were losing faith. A bad deal set up by Lawlor only added to the growing friction between the Colombian cartels and the Merseyside mafia. During the spring of 2001, Lawlor arranged for a cocaine shipment to be smuggled from South America to Amsterdam and then to Britain, according to senior underworld sources. Lawlor never saw a penny of the £72 million deal. In May 2001, he was shot as he left a party in Liverpool. Initially, the murder was blamed on a long-running feud between door boss Stephen Clarke and the Lawlor family. At first, Stephen Clarke's younger brother Peter was accused. But Peter Clarke was later acquitted of the murder. Even so, Stephen and Peter Clarke's older brother, Ian, was shot dead in what police believed was a revenge attack four months later. Ian Clarke's funeral cortège included 32 black stretch Mercedes and Daimler limousines. Weeks after that, Lawlor's brother, Tony, was murdered. During the dispute, a Scottish hit-man had been drafted in by the Cartel to kill the leader of the other side. During one attempt, he dressed up as an old woman and waited at a bus stop to catch his prey. But the target was carrying a child, so he let him go. Amid the ensuing chaos, the coke that Stephen Lawlor had allegedly ordered from the Colombians had vanished. Following Lawlor's untimely death, his boss Colin Smith was left to pick up the pieces. He told the Colombians that the Liverpool mafia had never received the missing drugs, even though underworld sources said it had arrived in Amsterdam safely and had been stored in containers that were lined up on the docks 'like a row of new cars'. The events led to a misunderstanding and the Colombians lost a bit of trust in Smith, some claiming that over time it grew into a grudge: one that would later play a crucial part in Smith's career as king of the Cartel.

The big-time deals were just telephone numbers to the rank and file 'soljas'. The street dealers never got close to the deals that made their bosses very rich. But it was from the lower rungs, the street kids, that the next generation of Cartel bosses was already coming up. A young scally known on the street as Kallas was busy making his bones. He was a friend of Terry, Kaim and Sidious: members of the young gang that had declared war on Shaun Smith.

At first, Kallas had been reluctant to get dragged into their troubles. He was too interested in making money. But one day

Shaun's gang came close to making a full-time enemy of the rising star. One of Shaun's younger relatives had beaten him up for selling drugs, not realising it was a bad move.

Shaun Smith said, 'Kallas was around 19, 20 years of age at the time. It was around a year before things kicked off really intensely. One of my relatives knocked Kallas out. Kallas had been selling weed outside the shop on his bike in Kirkdale, and trouble broke out.

'This kid who was part of our family done him in, then ran over his bike. He kept reversing over the bike four or five times while Kallas was watching. Kallas was saying: "You've fucked my graft up. That bike earns me my money."

'My person, known as the Young One, was just trying to teach him a lesson, that's all. This happened about a year before it all kicked off. But during that year, Kallas didn't go away. It didn't teach him a lesson and neither did losing his bike stop him from selling gear. Instead, he started getting a bit stronger by getting more into selling drugs.'

In the course of that year, Kallas had gone from selling weed to coke to heroin. In addition, he had a load of 'creatures' around him. They sold heroin and cocaine for Kallas on a shift system. Kallas paid his lads £200 a day to sell gear. The top salesmen got a free car thrown in. Shaun's forces were set on a collision course with the new kid on the block. Shaun wouldn't name them, but his two top enforcers were still Michael Brown and Gary Hampton.

Shaun: 'I had a couple of lads with me, who are now in jail doing 17 years each. They were best, best mates. There was also a member of the family called the Young One, who'd done in Kallas and run over his bike. Kallas wasn't really involved at that stage, but he was still holding a grudge from getting a pasting. We were ramming their cars off the road every night, but they always got away, the rats.

'Then one night we saw them in this little white Peugeot. I jumped out. I always carried bricks in the car: they were pebbles from Crosby beach. I painted them and put colours on them, so if I got stopped by the busies, I could just say they were the kids'. The lads used to call me "the Caveman" because I always had these big fuck-off rocks around me in the car. The reason I carried them was that they were fucking lethal. If you got hit in the head with one, you were going down. If I threw one at the car, the window would shatter, and then if it hit the driver, he was going to hospital.

'So I saw this white car and I smashed the window of the white car with one of these stones. One of my lads who was with me tried to get through the other window and get the person who was sitting on that side with a blade. But somehow they got free of us. The car drove off and we chased it. The lad I was with threw a hatchet and it hit this kid.

'It turns out to be this Kallas kid, who was already angry at being done in by one of us. So now he's got reason to be doubly upset. After that incident, he decided to go against us full-time and put his hand in with Kaim, Sidious and Terry. That's how his firm got involved.

'Soon after, they let off two shots down at the nightclub. Kallas rang me up and said: "You have got me involved now: now you are getting it."'

Kallas was on his feet with drug money and now took it upon himself to make repeated gun attacks on Shaun Smith. Using his resources, he was able to recruit more mercenaries. Smith found it difficult to retaliate. The new generation didn't own assets. They moved from one safehouse to another in speeding, blacked-out 4 x 4s, lying down in the back seat, or hidden in the boot, armed to the teeth with state-of-the-art sub-machine guns.

Shaun tracked the gang down to a grubby house on a run-down estate. Kallas and Sidious wouldn't use the front door in case they were seen. They entered the house through the back garden, climbing over a door that held down the wire fence, so that they were never seen going into the house.

Shaun Smith said, 'I couldn't find Kallas personally. We had men on the street just waiting for him to surface, but he refused to come out and fight. Even though I knew where their safehouses were, I could never get them. They were rats. So finally, in a last-ditch attempt, I went down to see his ma.

'I said to her: "Tell your son to give us a ring: he's getting involved in something and he might get himself hurt."

'But she didn't seem to care. She just said he got blamed for everything and she'd heard it all before. She just seemed to have given up on him.'

The attacks continued, each one more random and senseless than the last. Smith's gang were becoming frustrated that they couldn't pin Kallas down. He was becoming an embarrassment to them: a flea irritating an elephant. A few weeks later, hyped-up and angry, Shaun's main lieutenants Gary Hampton and Michael Brown were driving around the Bootle area of Merseyside looking for Kallas. Shaun refused to talk about the incident; however, the story was later revealed in court reports. Hampton and Brown thought they saw Kallas and jumped out of their car, along with two associates. In the confusion, they attacked the man they thought was Kallas. The victim suffered fifteen separate stab wounds, including four which would have been fatal on their own. The man tried desperately to run for his life but was caught as he attempted to clamber over a school wall. It wasn't Kallas: he was a completely innocent man, a 21-year-old joiner called Colin McGinty, from Crosby, who was doing nothing more than going out on the town with his mates. He had no connection with Kallas or the underworld or drugs and had never been in trouble with the police. It was a case of total mistaken identity.

Hampton and Brown fled the scene but were quickly identified by police and picked up. It was their young age and relative inexperience that had got them caught. There was evidence all over the crime scene. An underworld source described them as 'hotheads' who'd been brainwashed by unscrupulous bosses.

'It was as though they were in a cult,' the source said. 'They were in their early 20s, just kids really, and they'd been wound up by these older fellers and just been told to go out and kill.'

Hampton and Brown were jailed for life a few months later. The pointless murder should have given both sides pause to reflect. Instead, both sides rearmed with bombs and guns, ready for the next round.

Shaun said, 'I believe Gary and Michael were basically brainwashed by this family that I worked with. They sucked their youth away from them. They went to jail at 21 years of age and won't get out until they're 42. This is all down to one person not having a straightener at the beginning, and all this would have been forgotten about on the first night. If it had been settled on night one, none of this would have happened. I find it sad that these two are in jail over a fight that had nothing to do with any of us, that we were just dragged into unwittingly.'

CHAPTER 44

POTTED OFF

2002

BY 2002, INCREASED police integration, resulting from the National Intelligence Model, was paying off. Merseyside Police were getting good at tracking down the hidden assets of drug dealers because better intelligence was flowing into the hands of officers who could act on it. Cartel stalwart 'Fast Eddie' Gray was convinced that the police would never get their hands on his money. He'd been careful to put his property in other people's names, or to claim that it was bought using wages from his small businesses, such as a taxi firm that he was involved in. But the police didn't care: Gray was ordered by a judge to pay £417,343 to the Treasury. The Flash Harry gangster was warned that he faced an extra three years on top of his twenty-four-year sentence for drug dealing if he failed to pay up. The asset orders had much more of a demoralising effect on drug lords than anyone thought. Many Cartel bosses got comfort from the fact that if they went to jail they'd always come out to a nest egg. But assets recovery was rapidly eating into this insurance policy. Another drug trafficker, jailed for seven years, had his dreams of rich retirement banished by the judge. The police financial investigation unit confiscated £30,300 worth of assets, together with two cars and £50,000 in cash found at his home.

Dylan Porter's gang had been well and truly smashed. Glasgow boss Ian McAteer got 16 years for the heroin he used to buy from Dylan's gang, along with a life sentence for murdering

Warren Selkirk, who'd gambled away his life. The court heard that McAteer's final call to Selkirk had lasted just a few seconds and cost 35p – as well as his life.

McAteer was also dragged into an unrelated case, although at the time it was so sensitive that the police dared not make it public. In April 1999, BBC TV star Jill Dando had been mysteriously shot dead outside her Fulham home. A few months later, Cartel boss John Haase had been arrested for gun running. A secret police report claimed that some of the bullets that Haase had been trading in matched those that killed Dando. Haase had used McAteer as an enforcer and used to sell him heroin. McAteer was now being linked to the Dando killing as a possible suspect. The mystery deepened when a former associate of Haase's, a jailed Turkish heroin smuggler called Suleyman Ergun, claimed to have heard Haase's gang boasting about being involved in the Dando killing. Ergun claimed to have heard Haase's partner in crime, Paul Bennett, confessing that they had been part of a contract team that had killed the *Crimewatch* presenter. Bennett, according to Ergun, had claimed that the principal had been a Scottish crime lord languishing in a Spanish jail. The triggerman had been none other than Ian McAteer.

For the police, the cases against Dylan, Paul Lowe and the rest had been a turning point, the first proof that the National Intelligence Model did what it said on the tin. It was the first big blow struck against the Cartel. Between them, Operation Kingsway and Operation Warren seized a total of £12 million worth of drugs and £306,000 in cash. The cases signalled the end of the wishy-washy 1990s, during which the Cartel had set the agenda and the police had followed behind. The dance era was dead, and police vowed never to allow drugs to take a grip on popular culture again. Around 93 kilos of heroin and 52 kilos of cocaine had been taken off the streets, all of it of extremely high purity. The loss of 10,000 Ecstasy tablets had caused a drought in local nightclubs.

To add insult to injury, and to the glee of police officers, the trial judge in Dylan's case authorised the seizure of more than £5 million worth of assets from the gang. More than £500,000 in cash, houses, cars and jewellery were recovered straight away. For the new generation of officers like the Analyst, the case was evidence that the Major Crime Unit was the way forward. Detective Superintendent John Kerruish, who led the operation, said it had required a tremendous amount of Major Crime Unit manpower and resources, together with assistance from other forces and agencies. He said, 'One syndicate of the MCU was dedicated to this inquiry for the best part of two years. You need to invest all these resources over a long period if you are to make any impact at all on organised crime groups.'

For many in law enforcement, it was a watershed moment. Rather than denying the existence of the Cartel, like the FBI had done with the Mafia in 1950s America, the officers spoke openly about its insidious effect. For the first time, the main target was being identified in public.

Kerruish added, 'They are so sophisticated and they have their own organisation throughout the UK and abroad. They use all modern methods of communication.'

Almost immediately, the police decided to capitalise on their success and press on with their attack in the hope that a quick-fire succession of multiple blows would mortally wound the Cartel. This time, their target would be the next generation of rising stars. Danny Wall was only 21, but already he was a feared gangster whose violence had secured a wall of silence around him. Wall had fought his way upwards through Liverpool's tough boxing network. Boxing was still a platform for organised crime, and Wall had been canny enough to make some powerful contacts in the Cartel.

By now, Wall was selling massive amounts of crack cocaine and heroin in an area called Speke, in the shadow of Liverpool's John Lennon airport. Wall was in charge of a street-level distribution network. He bought in multiple-kilo amounts from Colin Smith. The power dynamic was simple. Within the hierarchy, Smith was the senior because he was a trafficker and Wall was a street seller. Smith made more money and accrued more status within the Cartel. Wall didn't see why this status quo had to exist. After all, most of the hard work in the chain was done by the 50 or so dealers he employed and managed on the streets. Without their point-of-sale deliveries to the end user, Smith wouldn't be able to realise his profits and power. Smith could bring in as many kilos as he liked, but he needed guys like Wall to shift them for him. Wall was determined to wrestle power from the likes of Smith and the other Cartel warlords.

He wanted to topple the vertical structure, making it more horizontal. In that way, he'd get his just desserts.

Wall was a contemporary of Kallas, Sidious, Terry and Kaim. Though they weren't close mates, they had the same contempt for the reputations of the Cartel bosses. Power grew out of the barrel of a gun. All big-time gangsters could be cut down to size, no matter how many millions they had.

On New Year's Eve 2002, a violent dispute in Speke gave the police a long-awaited entry to Danny Wall's world. As officers investigated the fight, they realised they'd walked into a crack and heroin business that had set up its base in the middle of a close-knit community. Speke was a traditional working-class community that had been ravaged by job cuts at the local docks. Though the Halewood Ford plant was still a big employer, the people on the estates now felt weakened. Residents were too scared to complain about the recent crime wave. Wall had started out as a small dealer, but his wares had turned the estate into a huge problem. The old-guard Cartel had tried not to involve 'civilians', but for the new generation of super hoodies, everyone was a potential victim.

Wall had handpicked several key players to sell on their own piece of turf. The cell system meant that each underboss was able to micromanage a few streets each. Nosey neighbours were terrorised into submission. Dealers were forbidden to fight with each other. The new generation had learned from the killing of David Ungi that violence only brought heat on them. The net result was that dealers were able to keep their activities quiet. From the outside, the area looked normal. The police said Wall's operation was 'relatively peaceful'. One resident said that Wall had 'camouflaged' his business to look like normal life.

Soon Danny Wall began to think that his network of 50 dealers was untouchable. He aimed to take over the region's crack cocaine and heroin trade without handling the drugs himself. Again, detectives were reluctant to rely on informants. It was a good tactic. Most were too frightened to come forward. So they had to start gathering evidence on dozens of suspects across south Liverpool.

In May 2002, a team of police launched dawn raids on the homes of suspected crack and heroin dealers. Wall and 41 other dealers were put behind bars for a total of 122 years. Wall got seven years after detectives infiltrated his inner circle. It was two–nil to the police.

CHAPTER 45

URBAN TERRORISM

2003

RICHARD CASWELL WAS an unusual 21-year-old. Solemn. Soulless. Angry. He was a loner in the classic Lee Harvey Oswald mould, showing little or no empathy for his friends, never mind strangers. He had only threats and hatred for his enemies. He was consumed by his own warped beliefs and the petty disputes that they had fuelled.

But on the street corners and in the drug dens in Liverpool, Caswell's personality was not unusual. Among the third generation of underclass urchins, he was typical. In fact, his type of outlook was seen as a means of survival.

As Caswell drove into Liverpool city centre on one Saturday night, on 20 September 2003, he stood out. His black K-reg Peugeot 103 was tatty, bought from a car auction for £500 cash a few days earlier. Among the black cabs and the Saturday night show-offs in their Porsche Cayennes, Benzies and Beamers, Caswell's car looked out of place. The city centre was buzzing. Caswell weaved his way carefully through the throngs of wannabe WAGs and tourists enjoying the tail end of the summer. The weather wasn't great: it was blustery, but the odd shower failed to dampen spirits. Thousands of Liverpool football fans had just got back from a victorious game at Leicester, and were streaming out of Lime Street station intent on enjoying a couple of pints before last orders.

But there was another reason Caswell slowed as he neared

Lime Street station on the way to his final destination. Caswell's car was a mobile bomb, packed with enough gunpowder and accelerants to cause the biggest explosion on mainland Britain since the fall of the IRA.

As usual, most of the clubbers were dressed for a night out. The girls were in their over-the-top trademark style, the look that would propel the WAG culture of Coleen Rooney, Alex Curran and Abbey Clancy into the tabloids and into the mainstream. Girls in bright colours and skimpy tops were queuing up to get into clubs before the prices went up after 11 o'clock. The lads were mostly in shirts. If the weather had been better, then hundreds more would have been queuing up. But the doormen were herding them in fast to get them out of the rain. Caswell stood out: he was dressed in his 'all blacks' – black jacket, black trackie top and black waterproof bottoms – topped off with a rolled-up balaclava.

Around 10 p.m., Caswell parked the car at the bottom of a hill called Mount Pleasant, near the nightclub where Shaun Smith ran the door. The club was owned by Jamie, the head of Shaun Smith's family. Up until recently, Caswell had been employed as a bouncer there, serving loyally under Shaun. But like many of the third generation, Caswell couldn't control his temper and was prone to fierce bouts of uncontrollable rage, which many put down to the fact that as kids they hadn't been properly socialised. Jamie had sacked him in line with the stricter rules that were now coming in to clean up the security industry. Caswell was furious. How could they be so hypocritical, he seethed. On the one hand, they were fighting a vicious war with Kallas and Sidious and on the other sacking him for getting a bit uppity with one of the punters.

Over the days that followed, a black mindset overtook him. There was only one thing for it. He'd switch sides and line himself up with Kallas and Sidious. The young pretenders had recently formed an alliance with a hard core crime family that had gained entry into the Cartel. Kallas and Sidious saw the alliance as a gateway into the Cartel. And, once inside, they were going to turn it on its head.

The crime family had agreed that Caswell could come on board for the big win – as long as he proved his loyalty by carrying out a massive bomb attack on the nightclub. Their strategy was simple: to defeat Shaun Smith by deploying overwhelming firepower. Anyone else who stood in their way would get the same treatment, whether they were Cartel warlords, firms from Manchester or London – or even the police.

The police should have seen it coming. Over the past few months there had been a huge number of mysterious explosions across the city. At the last count, thirty-one telephone kiosks and eight postboxes had been blown up. A homemade nail bomb, known as a 'pineapple', had been thrown into the Dickie Lewis pub in Walton, a premises linked to Shaun Smith. In most cases, the key component was made up of super-strength industrial fireworks, imported from China, which had not long been available in the UK. The tubes contained high volumes of explosive-purity gunpowder. Sometimes the fireworks were wrapped in sheet metal or silver foil to create a compact improvised explosive device that could be lit by a thick protruding fuse. At other times, the mini bombs were packed into petrol containers and strapped to other cans containing fuel and shrapnel.

Some of the recent explosions had been no more than acts of vandalism. Others had been tests, the gang experimenting with what worked and what didn't. The choice of targets – phone boxes – gave an insight into the people carrying out the test: they were only kids, who were usually smashing them up and writing graffiti on them, the next generation of creatures and urban terrorists.

Caswell claimed that he didn't build the bombs. His job was simply to guide them to their target.

Shortly after 11 p.m. on 20 September, Caswell lit the fuse on the car bomb and fled into the night. A huge bang was followed by a fireball as the full tank of petrol went up. The blast shattered windows in nearby shops and offices. Hotel guests spilled out onto the street after being evacuated from nearby buildings. At the Mount Royal Hotel, glass from several windows was sent flying into rooms and onto the street. At the Regent Hotel, opposite the nightclub, the first police on the scene escorted stunned residents to safety. Miraculously, no one was hurt by the blast, mainly because the queues to get into the nightclubs had been unusually short. Police cordoned off the whole area. The investigation quickly revealed that the car had been bought from a vehicle auction at Newsham Park, an area near Anfield. Patrols were stepped up in the city centre. CCTV footage was carefully examined.

Shaun Smith said, 'I went to see Jamie, the head of the family kind of thing. I said, "They've let a car bomb go off outside the club. I told you they were all dogs." My take on it was simple: to wipe them all out, right here, right now.

'But we still had the same old problem: we simply couldn't find them. Once again, they melted into air, like ghosts. They went to ground.

'One of the family, called Tyler, went and had a meeting with one of their dads. He told them: "One of them kids is going to end up in a body bag or in a wheelchair."

'That was that. That was all we could do until we could cop for one of them.'

But the hit-and-run attacks continued. Less than a month later, on 18 October, the gang mounted a second strike. A home-made bomb was hurled through a bedroom window and eight homes were damaged. At first, police didn't think it was linked to the feud, until a pattern began to emerge. A few days later, a car was blown up by a high-explosive firework in nearby Litherland Park.

The barrage continued the following month, shortly after Bonfire Night. Richard Caswell had been lying low since his car-bomb attack at the nightclub. But now he surfaced for the next phase of his terror campaign. However, this time the target would not only be Shaun Smith and his inner circle: he would also take the fight into the heart of the Cartel – into the millionaires' row at the exclusive Sandfield Park estate, home to the Banker, one of his lieutenants, and one of the masterminds behind the Operation Pirate speed factories, and several other Cartel bigwigs and hangers-on. The younger generation were taking a liberty and they knew it. The car bomb was a big warning to the old guard that their reign was coming to an end.

Caswell parked the car outside the home of Jamie's younger brother. Between midnight and 1 a.m., three explosions rocked the wealthy residents in their beds. Wayne Rooney's house at the time was just around the corner. Witnesses described the first bomb as going off with a 'massive bang'. The second and third were even louder. Six homes were extensively damaged and debris strewn all over the street. One house sustained £12,500 worth of structural damage. Most of the front windows were broken, and pieces of the car were embedded in the ceilings. Alongside the previous explosion at the nightclub, once again police described the bomb as 'the most powerful on the UK mainland since the ceasefire in Northern Ireland'. The mantra was becoming normal now, boring even, for the local reporters that had to cover the story. But there was no other comparison worth making, as it was true. Luckily, no one was injured, although the fire service said a woman suffered shock. The scene was sealed off for 48 hours.

Almost immediately, the police realised that they were dealing with a new phenomenon. The leading officer, Detective Superintendent Russ Walsh, acknowledged that 'This type of attack is taking criminality to a new, ridiculous level. What are they hoping to achieve, by planting bombs in a main street or in residential areas, where there is a high risk of injuring innocent people?' A Force Major Incident, codenamed Operation Thornapple, was set up the next day. Once again, the forensic experts concluded that the device was constructed from the contents of display fireworks, packed together with a number of petrol containers. The main bomb had been placed directly above the petrol tank of the car: a move that detectives believed was designed to cause massive devastation.

In the old days, the Cartel godfathers would have put a contract out on the men behind the bomb and anyone they suspected who knew them, such as Sidious and Kallas. After all, the bomb had put their own families at risk. But most of the Cartel bosses stood by paralysed, not knowing quite what to do, worrying that if they spoke out, they would get more of the same. If Shaun Smith and his army of street warriors couldn't defeat a ragtag bunch of scallies, who could? The old guard locked themselves in their mansions or fled to their boltholes in Amsterdam and Spain. But that was the problem. Their assets, the fruits of their criminal empires, had now become gilded cages, chains around their necks. The godfathers were tied to them and it made them easy targets. The new generation weren't tied to anything. Several key figures got messages to Shaun that they were backing him. They had little choice: he was now effectively a firewall between the young Turks and themselves.

The barrage continued. The next day, at about 12.30 a.m., there was another explosion in the nearby Fazakerley area, outside the home of a former partner of a member of the family and her 14-year-old daughter. Chief Constable Norman Bettison launched a national campaign to control the sale and import of fireworks.

To some in the underworld, it looked like Shaun Smith was on the run. Although this was far from the truth, that was the perception. Though he had nothing to do with the bombs, Sidious now felt confident enough to resurface, and he did so in some style. By now he was dating a very well-known celebrity, a former soap-star babe turned singer and pin-up. Though she was high profile, her lifestyle suited Sidious. For most of the time, she was on the road or working in London. Sidious stayed close to her side, making him a difficult target to pin down.

In a bid to draw him out, elements loyal to Smith sprayed up the celebrity's house with an AK-47 assault rifle. The star was not at home; she was away promoting her new pop record. But three shots were fired. One bullet went through the wooden front door and another shattered the frame. A police guard was mounted outside the house. The couple moved to a new home in Chiswick, London. But a fortnight later, a firebomb was thrown through a glass window in the front door. A second hit a neighbour's car. The terrified celebrity, who risked damaging her career by associating with the gangsters, splashed out on £20,000 worth of hi-tech security equipment.

But it offered little protection. In Liverpool, she was left screaming in terror after three masked men trashed her car and wounded her boyfriend Sidious with a machete. The couple fled for their lives after their Range Rover was surrounded by the gang, who ordered Sidious to get out of the vehicle. He was stabbed in the stomach.

The latest attacks had come at a time when police were convinced they were winning the battle against the Cartel. But at the same time, the savagery and scale of the new gang wars had taken the police by surprise. Even the National Intelligence Model seemed to creak under the strain of having to tackle a new generation of gangsters who had more in common with insurgents in a war zone than drug dealers. Old-school officers began to call for action instead of flow charts. What happened next looked like an outright victory for the dark side.

The police had made a breakthrough in Operation Thornapple, the investigation into the wave of firebomb detonations. Caswell's DNA had been linked to the car bombs. In addition, the police were making hundreds of arrests in a bid to destroy his backer's gang. But none of this seemed to bother the leaders. Richard Caswell's response to the police was unprecedented. He and his bosses decided to take on the police in much the same way as they took on their underworld enemies. First, they wrongly blamed the police for taking sides, as though investigating the bombs was equivalent to lining themselves up with Shaun Smith. Second, they decided to attack the police in the same way as they had attacked Shaun Smith. Caswell blew up a car outside Tuebrook police station in a bid to make the police back down. He and his leaders felt so powerful that they decided to confront the authorities head on. The blast left a permanent bomb crater in the road outside, which would have looked more at home in Sarajevo or Baghdad than in a built-up area of Liverpool. Bomb-disposal experts said more than 20 shock rockets were used, enough to kill.

As the gangland feud continued, the force urged all residents living near police stations to be on guard. In anticipation of a shoot-out, Caswell began stockpiling weapons in safehouses. For his own personal protection, he bought three firearms and ammunition.

A few months later, a similar bomb was targeted at Walton police station. A Ford Fiesta was parked underneath a nearby railway bridge and detonated at 10 p.m. Had the police lost control? No private criminal organisation had ever tried to bomb the police. To some, it looked like the police were no longer an effective deterrent to the gangs.

EPILOGUE

2003

BY 2003, THE Cartel was 30 years old. It had started out as a one-man band, the brainchild of a manipulative ex-petty criminal called Fred the Rat. Now it had grown into an international business with hubs in Amsterdam, Spain, Turkey, North Africa and South America. Thousands of people worked directly for the Cartel in multifarious roles. Thousands more were employed indirectly, or benefited from its economic activity in some other way: for instance, as part-time workers and sub-contractors. The Cartel's structure was sophisticated: a rolling, rigid hierarchy that resembled a group of trading partners. In some ways, the Cartel looked like an emerging international business with a basic command structure. Economists call the model an 'international area network'. Over the next decade, the shape of the organisation would change again, solidifying into a pattern normally found in modern global corporations, according to the police. In 2003, the Analyst began keeping a detailed database on the Cartel. Within five years, by around 2008, the Analyst would be able to map out the structure of a single division in great detail, identifying scores of managers and hundreds of employees meshed together in an extremely complex network of revenue flows and capital assets. Economists would describe the Cartel of having matured into something akin to a 'global matrix structure', a shape that made it possible to optimise the strength of participating units, distributing the pressure of business more evenly, avoiding duplication of functions.

EPILOGUE

Like a growing global business, the Cartel had gone through a familiar growth trajectory: formation, development, stabilisation and crisis. 2003 was a pivotal year. The crisis was two-fold, involving a combination of more effective policing and usual internal struggles that were threatening to rip the business apart. If the Cartel could work through its problems, it could expect to go through the same cycle again. But this time, the business would undergo the changes at twice the pace. The next decade, between 2003 and 2013, would see as much change as the Cartel had undergone in the previous 30 years.

But the big words and fancy structures didn't mean much to the likes of Dylan Porter. Dylan was one of the increasing number of Cartel members to end up in jail. By 2003, there were as many in prison as there were outside. This was the hidden cost of success, the one that the new recruits were never shown. On a personal level, Dylan Porter had to come to terms with life as a long-term prisoner. He soon became pals with some of Britain's longest-serving and most dangerous villains. Ironically, one of his new friends turned out to be Paul Dye, the heroin baron who'd claimed that the Cartel's influx of heroin in the early 1980s (and which Dylan had sold) had been part of a government conspiracy. But no matter how interesting the company was, when the conversation stopped and the lights went out, Dylan was alone.

'Anyone reading this might think prison sounds easy,' he said. 'Don't be fooled. You have to walk around every day carrying a knife and be careful not to look at somebody the wrong way, in case you upset them. It's not a normal way to live, is it? Because in dispersal prisons, people get stabbed because they haven't let on to somebody; they haven't said "all right" or "how's it going" in the morning.

'Crime definitely does not pay.

'I have missed my children growing up, and no matter what I can do, I can never get that time back. Education is the best route in life, not crime.'

In jail, Dylan kept a diary, which he turned into a 158-page unpublished manuscript called *The Belly of the Beast*. He wrote it to show his friends and family the reality of prison life. 'When my kids are old enough, I will let them read it,' he said.

For eight years out of his twenty-one-year sentence, Dylan remained a Category A prisoner, considered to be the highest danger to the public. He served time in four out of five of Britain's maximum security prisons: Whitemoor, Long Lartin, Full Sutton and Frankland.

Others went the same way. In 1996, John Haase and Paul Bennett had been pardoned by then Home Secretary Michael Howard. Three years later, in 1999, Haase was back behind bars after being arrested on guns and drug charges. In February 2001, inside a courtroom locked down by armed police, he was jailed for thirteen years: seven years for gun running and six years for drugs-related money laundering, after striking a deal with the prosecution to plead guilty to lesser charges.

Haase had been running guns to Ian McAteer among others. Paul Bennett went on the run after being wanted in connection with a cannabis conspiracy involving gangs from London and Spain. Many of the Cartel bosses would soon learn that Haase and Bennett had been informing on them since the early 1990s. One of Haase's fall guys remained behind bars, a garage owner from Stockport called Thomas Bourke, who'd been jailed for murder and falsely blamed for smuggling a gun into Strangeways Prison. Bourke has always maintained that he is innocent of the murders, and he and his family, led by his sister Jo Holt, maintain that the gun story influenced the jury into regarding him as a dangerous person and hence contributing to his guilty verdict. They have been campaigning for justice ever since.

For the time being, Shaun Smith was one of the lucky ones. He was still free. But he felt that he was far from enjoying his luck. The gang war that he was locked into felt like torture at times: misery, bloodshed, looking over his shoulder. On a personal level, he felt trapped in a loveless marriage, wedded to the daughter of the family for whom he acted as enforcer. At times, he said, it felt more like a marriage of convenience, to ally common business interests, than a proper relationship. Later, he would describe the family he worked for as 'like living in a cult'.

'One day,' he said, 'in the very near future, people will get to hear the facts about this family that I was so close to. Watch this space . . .'

Meanwhile, the gang war would rumble on for years and eventually cost Shaun dearly. It cost him his freedom. Shaun was sent to jail for possession of a firearm that he had got to protect himself against Kallas and his gang. Once inside, then and only then did the real fight begin. Surrounded by enemies and battling for survival, he would have to resort to extreme measures. For the first time in his life, he would be tempted to deal drugs.

'I'd resisted selling cocaine and heroin for 20 years. But now I was faced with a dilemma. My life had fallen apart, and the business that I had worked so hard to build was at risk of collapsing into ruins.

'On the outside, I'd had this big reputation. Now I was contemplating having to do some drastic things to maintain that status while I was in jail. One of the most terrible things was that drugs were being dangled in front of me. By that time drugs had become a very rich and powerful commodity in jail. What people don't understand is that drugs are far more valuable inside jail than they are outside and that if you can control the supply in jail, then you can become a very powerful figure.

'I'd never been part of the Cartel on the outside, but now I was being put in a position to do it on the inside. The temptation was strong. The big question was – would I give into it? Would I go against the code that I had believed in all my life? That's another story.'

With Shaun out of the way, the young pretenders, led by Kallas, saw their chance. They wanted into the Cartel badly and with it access to instant riches beyond their wildest dreams. For someone who had started off by selling drugs on a BMX bike, Kallas had done well. He'd had no backing. He hadn't come from a big gangster family, nor did he have contacts. But he quickly realised what Kaiser and Scarface had realised 20 years before: most of it was an act anyway. And it was possible to strip away the illusion of wealth and power from the leaders, if you were prepared to challenge them. The likes of Kallas and Kaim had nothing, but they saw this an advantage: the nothingness was powerful. They had no beliefs, no codes, no assets, no organisations, no memberships. That made them nimble and hard to destroy. Kallas began to leap up the rungs in the hierarchy and he ended up in Spain and Amsterdam, where he and his small gang began to deal drugs on a big scale. In a quiet Spanish urban area popular with Brit expats, they rented a large villa and turned it into an HQ from which they became responsible for selling coke in Marbella and tablets in Ibiza.

The godfathers were in a quandary. Was it better to let them inside the tent and effectively bribe them to stay onside, to placate them by giving up some of their own wealth and power? Or was it better to pick up the baton where Shaun left off and continue the struggle? The situation was further complicated by the entry into the Cartel of a whole new class of entrants who would all have a vote on the subject, including names such as Mikey Wright and David Hibbs-Turner.

Then there was the bigger picture. Inspired by the success of Kallas and Co., and fuelled by dramatic changes in society and policing, Britain was experiencing a growth in US-style street gangs. Over the next five years, these gangs would try to emulate what Kallas had done on a wider scale: cut the top off the pyramid, redistribute power and money from the traffickers at the top to themselves, the sellers at the bottom. It was a dangerous game. No one knew whether they would succeed. But one thing was certain: it would be a very violent fight.

The old guard Paul Burly had succeeded in eliminating his direct enemies. But now he risked being overrun by the new threat of street gangs. He'd bought a huge inner-city warehouse with the ambition of converting it into a community centre to help children. But it was surrounded by armed teenage thugs who believed that if they could shoot Paul, they could win his hard-won reputation. To survive, he would have to take them on. One day he hoped to escape his past by emigrating to Australia. But would his past eventually catch up with him?

Colin 'King Cocaine' Smith was sitting pretty at the top of the tree. Curtis Warren was in jail and Smith was now the top dog. But his rise to the top had made him a lot of enemies, not only within the Cartel, but also with contacts in Amsterdam, Spain and South America. Some of them started plotting his downfall. Soon the treason became so strong that it wasn't a case of 'if' but how long would it take and with what weapon.

By this time, Curtis Warren had served seven years since being busted in Holland in 1996. For killing a fellow prisoner – in self-defence, he claimed – he was jailed for a further four years. To make matters worse, he lost an appeal against his conviction, and Dutch police started to make formal appeals to recover £18 million in assets. One of his main oppos on the outside, a Middlesbrough-based car salesman called Brian Charrington, was deported from Spain to Germany to face drugs charges. He was jailed in 2003 in Frankfurt for seven years. Despite the setbacks, things weren't quite over for Britain's richest criminal yet. He had a few aces up his sleeve and he was determined to get out of prison. For the next seven years he plotted relentlessly to this end. Finally, he achieved it. The big question was for how long?

Warren's pal Phillip Glennon was jailed for six and a half years after pleading guilty to twenty-five counts of tax evasion and money laundering. Three million was ordered to be confiscated from offshore accounts.

Fred the Rat was still lying on a sunbed in Spain. Everything was going well. It looked like the man who had founded it all was going to see out the rest of his life in peace. Paul Burly believed that Fred was one of the luckiest criminals alive.

Paul Burly said, 'Fred was responsible for starting a drugs ring in Liverpool, which in turn became responsible for 60 per cent or more of the drugs that landed in this country. A man so like, and yet unlike, Curtis Warren, because this man has never been caught, but we in our fair city all know that he is as guilty as sin. Just as the police did but who never did anything about it.

'Even to this present day, the Rat lives on his ill-gotten gains with impunity, in Spain . . . and is not even on the wanted list. So he has no fear of getting his collar felt.

'The only thing he looks back on with distaste is not the misery that he is responsible for, but all of the many, many smacks and hidings that he has had at the hands of people he has sent to jail, or cheated. He got so fed up being floored by people that he once spread the word that he was suffering from the same thing that had killed his brother: cancer! Not that he really cared for his brother, because it is common knowledge that he set the poor man up during a drug-importing operation.'

But as if to prove that Paul had spoken too soon, fate stepped in to redress what seemed to many like an injustice. Fred's comeuppance came in the form of the accountant he had employed to manage his vast fortune. One day Fred told the accountant that he wanted all of his assets back, starting with those businesses that were in the accountant's name. Also, those in the names of third parties and nominee solicitors were to be transferred back to him with immediate effect. He saw no reason, now that he had escaped justice for 30 years, why everything shouldn't be put under his control. After all, he was a free man with no serious convictions.

To all intents and purposes, he was an upstanding member of society. Some of the legit holdings that he owned by proxy had grown into big businesses worth millions of pounds. Liverpool was now a boom city and property was at a premium. Fred had lots of it. Paul Burly told me that for several years, the accountant had been very busy instructing solicitors to ensure that almost all of Fred's money was tied up, legally. When the time came, the accountant told Fred that he couldn't have his money. First he threatened to have the accountant killed. Then he threatened to sue. The accountant told Fred that if he didn't behave, he'd be grassed up. Not to the police: as a de facto criminal, the accountant couldn't do that. But the accountant threatened to hand over a secret dossier of paperwork that they had compiled for over 20 years to the Inland Revenue.

'They might not be able to prove that you're one of Britain's biggest drug traffickers,' the accountant told him. 'But they will take every penny you own. You're going to have to do what I say or I'm handing over every piece of paper I've got to the taxman.' Fred went white. Like always, he decided to suck it up and negotiate the best deal he could get. The deal hurt. The accountant walked away with a substantial proportion of his net worth. They still remain friends.

Life went on for Scarface and Kaiser. Kaiser emigrated to South America full-time, where he continues to organise drug shipments to Europe. Scarface bought a house 'somewhere down south' in England, where he lives a double life, pretending to be a prosperous businessman while at the same time 'keeping his hand in' on the drugs game.

Poncho said, 'You wouldn't know he's been this big drugs-baron person. He lives in a quiet village with a family and no one knows his true identity.'

As for Poncho and Hector, they returned to Liverpool. As the drugs scene became increasingly violent and they settled down to have families, they gradually moved out of drug dealing. Today they run a couple of small businesses, enjoy a pint in the local pub and worry about their kids' education.

Poncho said, 'I've hardly got any mates from that time because most of them are dead or in jail. I am lucky. I don't do anything like that now. If the truth be known, some of the stuff that I did – the darker stuff that is, the real bad stuff which I can't even speak about – is still on my conscience. Some of that haunts me. It had made me think about life. It's made me humbler and more peaceful.'

Meanwhile, the Analyst carried on as usual. As the number of killings within the Cartel rocketed, he was transferred to the murder squad. Little did he know that within a few years he'd be investigating the gangland slaughter of the Cartel's new boss.

'It was good experience,' he said. 'I was able to develop my ability to investigate murder. I learned the elements required to investigate a complex murder, from arriving at the scene and having to make the decision that the person had been unlawfully killed through the whole detailed process of the murder inquiry. It provided great satisfaction, to support the victim's family throughout the investigation and eventually sit with them in court, seeing the person responsible for the murder of their loved one being found guilty and sentenced to life imprisonment. It felt like I could make a difference. It felt as though I could solve a set of manageable problems rather than be faced with an edifice so big that sometimes it felt overwhelming – even though, of course, it wasn't.

'As time moved on I'd kept my eye on the sophistication of organised crime and drug distribution. It was only a matter of time before I moved back into investigating that world. I knew who the main players were and it was inevitable that I would be involved in investigating their criminality. What I didn't know was under what circumstances, how and when. When it did happen it wasn't what I had expected!'

Between 2003 and 2012, the Cartel suffered several major setbacks, including the murder of a number of key bosses and, thanks to the success of the Analyst and his colleagues, the capture and incarceration of many of its members. Of those who survived, many of the founding members, who were reaching pensionable age, retired to their estates in Spain, the US, South Africa and elsewhere. A couple of the middle-aged powerhouses, who had accumulated hundreds of million in assets and complex international businesses, spent a lot of time and effort legitimising their holdings and distancing themselves from day-to-day criminal activity. In short, the Cartel was rapidly losing its management. But despite these problems, the Cartel defied convention and continued to grow. In fact, the last decade arguably became its most successful one.

One reason is that the Cartel seemed to change shape quickly to adapt to new threats and new markets. The natural shedding of the higher echelons made the Cartel flatter and less hierarchical. Power passed downwards onto the street. And instead of dissipating, the new underclass embraced it and made it their own, concentrating the power and using it to get rich and grow. As Dylan Porter said, 'We all thought it would die off. We thought that once we went to jail or got older or just got off cos we couldn't handle it that it'd all calm down.

'Of course, we knew that drugs would never go away completely. People like taking drugs – and anyway, what would the police and the judges and the solicitors do if tomorrow people like I used to be stopped dealing drugs? The jails would be empty. The whole justice system would come to a halt.

'It's not only criminals who benefit from organised crime. Let's face, it the so-called War on Drugs has been good for a lot of people over the years. A lot of bad things have been done in its name; a lot of lies have been told.

'But, putting that aside, today the drugs thing is worse than ever. Twelve- and thirteen-year-olds have got more power than the people who are supposed to be at the top, and they are more dangerous than we were.

'I just can't understand how that's happened.'